INTRODUCTION TO COMPARATIVE AND INTERNATIONAL EDUCATION

Education at SAGE

SAGE is a leading international publisher of journals, books, and electronic media for academic, educational, and professional markets.

Our education publishing includes:

- accessible and comprehensive texts for aspiring education professionals and practitioners looking to further their careers through continuing professional development

- inspirational advice and guidance for the classroom

- authoritative state of the art reference from the leading authors in the field.

Find out more at: **www.sagepub.co.uk/education**

INTRODUCTION TO COMPARATIVE AND INTERNATIONAL EDUCATION

JENNIFER MARSHALL

Los Angeles | London | New Delhi
Singapore | Washington DC

Los Angeles | London | New Delhi
Singapore | Washington DC

SAGE Publications Ltd
1 Oliver's Yard
55 City Road
London EC1Y 1SP

SAGE Publications Inc.
2455 Teller Road
Thousand Oaks, California 91320

SAGE Publications India Pvt Ltd
B 1/I 1 Mohan Cooperative Industrial Area
Mathura Road
New Delhi 110 044

SAGE Publications Asia-Pacific Pte Ltd
3 Church Street
#10-04 Samsung Hub
Singapore 049483

Editor: James Clark
Assistant editor: Rachael Plant
Production editor: Nicola Marshall
Copyeditor: Sarah Bury
Proofreader: Caroline Stock
Marketing manager: Catherine Slinn
Cover design: Jennifer Crisp
Typeset by: C&M Digitals (P) Ltd, Chennai, India
Printed in Great Britain by
CPI Group (UK) Ltd, Croydon, CR0 4YY

© Jennifer Marshall 2014

First published 2014

Apart from any fair dealing for the purposes of research or
private study, or criticism or review, as permitted under the
Copyright, Designs and Patents Act, 1988, this publication
may be reproduced, stored or transmitted in any form, or by
any means, only with the prior permission in writing of the
publishers, or in the case of reprographic reproduction,
in accordance with the terms of licences issued by the
Copyright Licensing Agency. Enquiries concerning
reproduction outside those terms should be sent to
the publishers.

Library of Congress Control Number: 2014933218

British Library Cataloguing in Publication data

A catalogue record for this book is available from
the British Library

ISBN 978-1-4462-7319-7
ISBN 978-1-4462-7320-3 (pbk)

MIX
Paper from
responsible sources
FSC® C013604

At SAGE we take sustainability seriously. Most of our products are printed in the UK using FSC papers and boards.
When we print overseas we ensure sustainable papers are used as measured by the Egmont grading system.
We undertake an annual audit to monitor our sustainability.

CONTENTS

LIST OF TABLES AND FIGURES

Tables

Figures

ABOUT THE AUTHOR

Jennifer Marshall is a senior lecturer at the University of Derby and has worked in a variety of educational contexts for over 20 years. She has taught in secondary schools in the USA and Japan as well as teaching English as a foreign language to children and adults in Poland. She worked for a number of years as an English for Speakers of Other Languages (ESOL) teacher, lecturer and Cambridge examiner in the UK. Working with international students over the years has led to research interests in higher education internationalisation policy and how institutions can meet the needs of international students. Jennifer currently teaches undergraduate modules in Comparative Education, Education and Globalisation and Education and Global Inequality as well as leading the ESOL pathway on the MA in Education at the University.

ACKNOWLEDGEMENTS

I would like to thank Jane Knight for granting me permission to reproduce her table entitled 'Approaches at the Institutional Level' (Knight, 2004). I need to offer a special thanks to my colleague James Chandler, at the University of Derby, who reviewed every single chapter in great detail. His thorough feedback and advice has been invaluable. Also, thanks go to James Clark, commissioning editor at Sage, not only for providing insightful comments on draft chapters but also for believing in this project from the very start. To my friend, Joss Stewart, who without fail always asked about the progress I was making on the book and, as a consequence, endured endless 'lectures' on educational topics. Lastly, to my wonderful family: Andy, Ellie, Shelby and mom Jane, for giving me the space to write and unwavering love and support to see me through the book's completion.

SAGE and the author would also like to thank the following reviewers whose comments helped to shape this book:

John Howlett, Keele University

Paul Miller, Brunel University

Lynne Parmenter, Manchester Metropolitan University

Robin Shields, Bath Spa University

David Thompson, University of Wolverhampton

PREFACE

This book was conceived out of a need to provide my students with an accessible, introductory text on comparative and international education. The aim of the book is to give students a clear overview of what comparative and international education is and to provide them with an accessible framework so that they are able to undertake their own comparative education research using secondary sources. The book is divided into two parts.

The first part explores how to make comparisons in education with particular attention to social, economic, cultural, political and historical contexts. It also evaluates the use of educational statistics, discussing important international surveys such as PISA and looking at databases such as Eurydice. Lastly, it explores education in developing countries, and the relationship between gender and education from a comparative perspective.

The second part of the book focuses on international education and the effects of globalisation on education. Chapters therefore centre on current debates in the field pertaining to global citizenship education, multicultural education, international schooling and the internationalisation of higher education.

A number of activities have been incorporated throughout the text. These have been designed to help extend students' knowledge on particular topics as well as challenging them to think critically. The book aims to be global in scope, drawing from a range of examples and case studies from around the world at the end of each chapter. This book has also tried to incorporate non-Western views in an attempt to see things from another perspective. Undergraduates, postgraduates and practitioners alike, looking to explore key themes in education studies will find this text useful.

Academics do not always agree on how to define key concepts. For years, scholars have debated about what comparative education is, how comparative education research should be undertaken, and so forth. When scholars disagree, it can be very challenging for students (and academics) to understand the meaning of key concepts and ideas in their field of study. An example is the contested term 'global citizen' – what does it mean to be one? Another example can be found in the globalisation debate. By and large, the debate has moved on from questioning whether globalisation exists to examining the effects of it. Again, scholars disagree – is the world becoming a much more unequal place as a result? Where is the evidence? Is globalisation a good or bad thing? Drawing from the literature, the book aims to present you with key arguments from top scholars in the field on fundamental topics pertaining to comparative and international education. By critically discussing a variety of topics, students are invited to join the debate.

Jennifer Marshall, Derby, 2014

PART 1

COMPARATIVE EDUCATION

CHAPTER 1

AN INTRODUCTION TO COMPARATIVE EDUCATION

This chapter explores:

- What comparative education is;
- How the field has developed over the years;
- The purpose of comparative education;
- Who compares;
- The challenges of undertaking comparative research.

 ## Activity 1.1 Defining terms

Before beginning this chapter, write down a definition of comparative education. At the end of the chapter, reflect on your definition. Is comparative education what you thought? How might this be similar to and different from international education?

Comparative education is often used interchangeably with international education. While these two fields certainly overlap, it can be argued that they are two distinct areas of study. There has been a long history of debate pertaining to the identity of comparative and international education, often called 'twin' fields (Bray, 2010), but what exactly is comparative education and how is it different from international education? This chapter aims to explain the nature and purpose of comparative education.

Historical development of comparative education

In order to define what the field is today, an understanding of the history shaping it is important. Many contemporary academics argue of the importance in understanding the historical development of comparative education in order to appreciate just how far the field has come from its earliest roots. Not only is there disagreement as to the definition of the twin fields, but disparity also exists in identifying their historical roots. How far back does comparative education go? When did it emerge as a distinct field of study?

Noah and Eckstein (1969) claim that the historical development of comparative education can be identified by five distinct stages, each with its own aims. The first stage is often referred to as 'travellers' tales'; stories were brought back from foreign travel and were generally descriptive in nature. When this first stage begins is less clear but for Noah and Eckstein it pre-dates the nineteenth century. Some writers go back as far as ancient times, citing examples from the Greeks and Romans and in particular how they admired the 'discipline of Spartan education' (Crossley & Watson, 2003, p. 12).

According to Phillips (2000), there was a large group of British travellers who fell into Noah and Eckstein's first stage. They visited countries such as Germany out of 'cultural and general curiosity' and they wrote with 'varying degrees of sophistication' (Phillips, 2000, p. 49). At this time, these tales did not systematically compare or analyse educational practice so have been dismissed by many scholars. However, others (see Rust, Johnstone & Allaf, 2009) have asserted that while these tales may have been descriptive they had much value and have been harshly judged by those who have a narrow view as to what counts as scholarly activity.

 Activity 1.2   Travellers' tales

Have you ever travelled to another country and come back with an education-related story to share? Or do you have friends who are from another country? Have they told you about education in their own country? Why would or wouldn't this be classified as research?

The second stage described by Noah and Eckstein (1969) begins from the nineteenth century. This phase coincides with the rise of national education systems in Europe. During the 1800s countries such as France, Germany and Great Britain were establishing national systems of schooling which eventually became free and universal by the end of the century. Many policy makers had great interest in the organisation and practice of education in other countries in order to help them devise their own. Noah and Eckstein (1969) argue that the work conducted in this stage was still very similar to the travellers' tales in previous years. Many of the writings during this time were 'encyclopedic descriptions of foreign school systems' (Noah & Eckstein, 1969, p. 5) and subjective in nature. 'These visitors came with a distinct purpose – to learn from a foreign example and through such learning to help improve the circumstances in their home countries' (Phillips, 2000, p. 49).

The third stage occurred around the middle of the nineteenth century and is still characterised by the accumulation of information in an encyclopaedic manner. However, Noah and Eckstein (1969) suggest that this exchange of scholars, students and publications was in the interest of promoting international understanding rather than in the interest of advancing one's own educational interests.

The fourth stage begins around the end of the nineteenth century. In this stage, a social science approach was beginning to develop as 'studies of foreign schooling became to a considerable extent studies of national character and the institutions that help form it' (Noah & Eckstein, 1969, p. 6). The recognition of the role of education in shaping society became important in this stage, as did the idea of cause and effect, and that national character determines education.

The fifth stage occurs after the First World War and coincides with the rise in statistical techniques in the social sciences. The adoption of quantitative methods after the Second World War and the empirical orientation of the social sciences began to reshape comparative education (Noah & Eckstein, 1969).

 Activity 1.3   Historic stages

Think about how comparative education has developed using Noah and Eckstein's five stages. Can you find any similarities between them and your own academic development? What criticisms can you think of regarding these five stages? Do you think the field developed in a linear fashion?

Similarly, in his classic book *Comparative Method in Education*, Bereday (1964) writes of phases in the history of comparative education. However, for Bereday the first phase begins in the nineteenth century and lasts for about 100 years. Like many other scholars (e.g. Green, 2003; Phillips & Schweisfurth, 2008; Acosta & Centeno, 2011), Bereday believes that the Frenchman Marc-Antoine Jullien, or Jullien de Paris, as he is also known, was 'the first scientifically minded comparative educator' (Bereday, 1964, p. 7). Jullien's aim was to improve French education by identifying the best schools in Europe and examining how they were organised, the teaching methods they used and what successful improvements they had implemented. Many writers in the field have called him the 'father' of comparative education as he was the first to use the term 'comparative education' (Crossley & Watson, 2003) and to use formal models of analysis (Gautherin, 1993). In Jullien's book, *The Esquisse d'un ouvrage sur l'éducation compare* or *Sketch and Preliminary Views on Comparative Education*, published in 1817, unlike his predecessors, he provided a 'systematic comparative classification of education systems, based on rudimentary questionnaire surveys' (Green, 2003, p. 84). According to Gautherin (1993), by using the comparative method successfully employed in anatomy, Jullien was trying to advance the science of education. Although his work was largely neglected throughout his lifetime, the first course on the science of education was officially introduced at the Sorbonne in Paris in 1883 (Masemann, 2006).

Bereday called this first phase in comparative education the period of 'borrowing' because 'comparison of the collected information was then undertaken in order to make available the best practices of one country for transplantation to others' (Bereday, 1964, p. 7).

Activity 1.4   Educational borrowing

What practices do you think early writers in the field reported on? Do you think borrowing these practices and transplanting them in your own country is effective? Why or why not?

For Bereday (1964), the second phase, called the period of 'prediction', occurred during the first half of the twentieth century and was led by the British educationalist Sir Michael Sadler. Like Jullien de Paris, Sadler was also interested in improving the English education system so looked to other systems, namely those in France, the USA and Germany, in order to draw comparisons. In his quest for reform, he became 'aware of the wider social implications any kind of educational innovation must have' (Mallinson, 1981, pp. 176–177). Scholars at this time paid attention to the relationship between education and society and the social causes underlying pedagogical practice. There was now a shift from cataloguing descriptive data to examining the social and cultural factors influencing education. In Kandel's classic text, *Studies in Comparative Education* (1933, p. xi), he writes: 'The problems and purposes of education have in general become somewhat similar in most countries; the solutions are influenced by differences of tradition and culture peculiar to each.' As a result, educators became much more careful when transferring ideas and practice from one country to another. Bereday (1964, p. 8) called this phase in comparative education as 'the period of prediction because the purpose of comparative study was now not primarily borrowing but predicting the likely success of a system of education in one country on the basis of the observation of precedents and similar experiences of other countries'.

At the time of writing his book, comparative education had only just embarked on the third phase, which Bereday called the period of 'analysis'. Bereday (1964, p. 9) believed 'that before prediction and eventual borrowing is attempted there must be a systematization of the field in order to expose the whole panorama of national practices in education'. Early scholars, such as Kandel (1933), even called for the development of better methods in the field. There was no universal agreement as to what kind of methods and systematisation that comparativists should follow. This disagreement was evident in much of the scholarly writing in the field after the Second World War.

However, critics such as Epstein (2008, p. 374) argue that the widespread view that comparative education 'evolved mainly in Darwinian-style stages of development' is misunderstood. Others believe that separating out the history of the field into phases is over-simplistic and that they 'are not necessarily linear or consistent across time, cultures or individuals' (Crossley & Watson, 2003, p. 21). William Brickman, another key figure in the field, asks us to challenge the role of Marc-Antoine Jullien as the 'father' of comparative education and asserts that there were, perhaps, others before him who used analytical approaches in their comparative studies (Brickman, 2010). Despite criticism, it is widely acknowledged that both Bereday and Noah and Eckstein's books have contributed greatly to the field (Bray et al., 2007).

What is the early history of comparative education in other parts of the world? Comparative education was developing in countries of Europe, North America and Asia between the latter parts of the nineteenth and the early twentieth century (Masemann, 2006). However, the historical development of comparative education in mainland China, for example, can arguably date back further than the 'traveller' tales of Western Europe. Due to its long history of civilisation, cases of 'borrowing' and 'lending' can be traced back to the Han Dynasty (206 BC–220 AD) and the Tang Dynasty (618–906 AD) where the influence of Indian Buddhism on Chinese education were evident (Bray & Qin, 2001).

In the Middle East between the twelfth and fourteenth centuries, scholars travelled extensively in the Arab region and their accounts represent the first comparative education documents in the region (Benhamida, 1990, in Halls, 1990). Like in the West, during the latter part of the nineteenth century, the establishment of public schooling required a more systemic way of studying foreign education. It was not until the 1940s and 1950s that comparative education, led by the prominent Syrian Sati al-Husari (1882–1968), began to develop into the field we understand as it is today (Benhamida, 1990, in Halls, 1990).

In Latin America during the nineteenth century, there are examples of 'traveller tales' from those such as José María Luis Mora from Mexico, Andrés Bello from Venezuela, Domingo Faustino Sarmiento from Argentina, and José Pedro Varela from Uruguay, who looked at education practices that they could borrow from Europe and the USA (Acosta & Centeno, 2011). For example, Sarmiento, an intellectual and social activist in Argentina, travelled to France, Prussia, Switzerland, Italy, Spain and England to learn new ideas in his quest to bring education to the masses and improve the social conditions of women and children in particular (Bravo, 1994).

In the twentieth century, the Second World War had a tremendous influence on the field of comparative and international education (international education will be discussed in Chapter 7). Many international organisations which undertake comparative research in education, such as the United Nations Educational, Scientific and Cultural Organisation (UNESCO) and the World Bank, were created to help rebuild a world shattered by war (Crossley & Watson, 2003).

Comparative education societies and journals

Over the years, other organisations have played a key role in shaping comparative education. The first Comparative Education Society (renamed in 1969 as the Comparative and International Education Society, or CIES) was formed in the USA in 1956. Other societies soon followed in Europe and elsewhere. The main purpose of the CIES is to foster cross-cultural understanding, scholarship, academic achievement and societal development through the international study of educational ideas, systems and practices. The Society's members include more than 2,000 academics, practitioners and students from around the world (CIES, 2012). The society consists of not only educators but also historians, sociologists, economists, psychologists and anthropologists. This multidisciplinary approach reflects the field at large, adding to the variety and richness of the research and activities that the society undertakes.

In 1970, the World Council of Comparative Education Societies (WCCES) was established to bring together these newly created comparative education societies (Masemann, Bray & Manzon, 2008) and currently meets every three years to discuss international issues in education. It is a non-government organisation (NGO) and works together with UNESCO. It was created to advance the field of comparative education and also promote research involving scholars in various countries. Research topics include theory and methods in comparative education, education of women and girls, teacher education and education for peace and justice (WCCES, 2012).

Now, there are now over 36 member societies: four Africa, six Americas, 16 Asia and Middle East, 16 Europe, and one in Oceania. The size and

Table 1.1   Comparative education societies 1950s–1960s

Comparative and International Societies (1950–1970)	Dates founded
Comparative and International Education Society (formerly Comparative Education Society) (CIES)	1956
Comparative Education Society in Europe (CESE)	1961
Japan Comparative Education Society (JCES)	1965
Comparative and International Education Society of Canada	1967
Korean Comparative Education Society (KCES)	1968

membership of these societies varies, as does the year in which they were formed; some have been established since the 1970s (e.g. the Dutch Speaking Society for Comparative Studies in Education or, in Dutch, *Nederlandstalig Genootschap voor Verglelijkende Studie van Opvoeding en Onderwijs*, (NGVO)); others later, such as the Gulf Comparative Education Society which was formed in 2008. The main goals of each of these societies are similar to and in line with the WCCES, which is primarily to promote research and scholarly exchange in the field of comparative education. In order to do that, many of these societies produce academic journals and host conferences to share research and ideas.

Activity 1.5   Comparative education societies

Have a look at the following comparative education society websites and their respective journals:

The Spanish comparative education society (SEEC) available at: www.sc.ehu.es/sfwseec/index_en.htm

The Australian and New Zealand Comparative and International Education Society (ANZCIES) available at: www.iejcomparative.org/

The Comparative and International Education Society of Canada (CIESC) available at: www.iejcomparative.org/

What are the stated objectives of these societies? What topics are published in their journals? To what extent do you feel they meet these objectives?

Since their inception in the late 1950s, these societies have contributed greatly to the advancement of the field through their research and promotion of it, and in the 1960s, comparative education embarked on a whole new era of scholarly activity. By this time, there were a number of prominent comparativists such as Nicolas Hans, Issac Kandel and Edmund King, in the USA, Europe and elsewhere.

As well as societies, a number of comparative education journals were established in the twentieth century, many being the official journals of the societies with which they were affiliated. The first comparative education journal was produced in Germany in 1931 under three titles (German, English and French): *Internationale Zeitschrift für Erziehungswissenschaft*, International Education Review and *Revue Internationale de Pédagogie*. The journal was interrupted briefly several times but started again permanently in 1955 with the English name changed to International Review of Education (Bray, 2003a). In 1957, the Comparative Education Society (now the CIES) launched their official journal entitled *Comparative Education Review*. The journal 'investigates education throughout the world and the social, economic, and political forces that shape it … [its aim is] to advance knowledge and teaching in comparative education studies' (CIES, 2012).

Methodological debates

In the 1960s and 1970s, the field was embroiled in debates about methodology. In other words, disagreement arose as to how research in the field should be carried out. These debates reflected what was happening in the wider social sciences where positivism had dominated academia since the nineteenth century. From a positivist perspective, the laws of science typically used to study and understand the physical world are applied to the social world. If we can find the laws of cause and effect that govern society, we might be able to predict and control it. Many such as Noah and Eckstein (1969) argued in their seminal text, *Toward a Science of Comparative Education*, that researchers in the field should adopt a positivist or scientific approach using quantitative methods. In fact, they applauded their predecessors, such as Sadler, Kandel and Hans, for their qualitative attempts to explain the relationship between society and education. However, they felt that in order for comparative education to fulfil its potential for education planning, it had to offer a means of reliable prediction and without a quantitative base; they felt that this could not be suitably achieved (Noah & Eckstein, 1969).

Much of the work carried out during the 'borrowing' phase of comparative education in the nineteenth and early twentieth century was criticised by post-war educationalists (Crossley & Watson, 2003). The criticism stemmed from the fact that previous research had been mostly historical, descriptive and explanatory. Many thought this 'approach lacked scientific rigour because it failed to draw causative links between schools and society' (Crossley & Watson, 2003, p. 26). Therefore, through the scientific approach, researchers such as Bereday (1964) and Noah and Eckstein (1969) were trying to see if it were possible to identify laws governing the relationship between education and society (Crossley & Watson, 2003). Indeed, Bereday (1964) writes: 'As in all social sciences, this final stage of the discipline is concerned with the formulation of "laws" or "typologies" that permit an international understanding and a definition of the complex interrelation between the schools and the people they serve' (Bereday, 1964, p. 25).

 Activity 1.6   Scientific laws and comparative education

How can you apply the scientific approach to the study of education systems and the societies that they are a part of? What are the benefits and limitations of this approach?

However, as stated previously, not everyone in the field agreed with the 'scientific' approach being proposed. In fact, Edmund King, a professor of Comparative Education in King's College, University of London, and editor of the journal *Comparative Education* from 1978 to 1992 was one such critic. King (1965) believed that comparative education is really about the study of human behaviour and is therefore complex.

> Let us take a single example from several dangerous fantasies in our field. We are sometimes invited to simplify our research work and make it more 'scientific' by inventing some formula or 'theoretical construct' of a near-mathematical type that will enable us to 'identify', to 'classify', and to 'predict'. Some misguided people seem to resemble unmathematical schoolboys, hoping to find a routine formula for the magic solution of equations, or for working out percentages and dividends. Perhaps it works in mathematics. It will not work with behaviour.
>
> (Edmund King, 1965, p. 151)

King (1965) also criticised the problem approach as proposed by Bereday (1964). Bereday believed that this was an essential part of the research process. 'It involves a selection of one theme, one topic, and the examination of its persistence and variability throughout the representative educational systems' (Bereday, 1964, p. 23). For Bereday, solutions to these problems can be found by examining how others in the world have solved similar ones. In fact, Kandel (1933) listed a number of problems which he felt were universal among nations. Some of the problems posed by Kandel over 80 years ago (see below) may seem fairly relevant today, even in the ever-changing educational landscape. However, looking at them critically, were these problems really universal and are they still today? Furthermore, King (1965) argued that without careful attention to sociological, psychological or economic perspectives, this approach could be seen as amateurish and even 'dangerous'.

Kandel's selected 'problems of education' (1933, p. xviii) were as follows:

- What is the place of private education and of private schools?
- What is the scope of post-elementary or secondary education?
- What should be the curriculum in each type of school?
- How are teachers prepared and what is their status?
- How can standards be maintained? What should be the place of examinations?
- Who shall formulate curricula and courses of study?
- What is the meaning of equality of educational opportunity?

Bray, Adamson and Mason (2007) point out that debates concerning methodology were not happening equally around the world and the work emanating from English-speaking countries came to dominate the literature. By the 1980s, attempts to exert one single method over another had subsided and the debate over methodology waned (Altbach & Kelly, 1986, cited in Bray et al., 2007). New concerns emerged in the field with the arrival of the concept of globalisation in the late 1980s. Current debates have centred on the relationship between globalisation and education and the challenges this poses for comparative education (see Dale, 2005). This relationship will be explored in Chapter 8.

Comparative education: A discipline?

Over the years, many have been concerned with whether comparative education is a discipline, a field of study, an approach or a method – a way of collecting data. Can comparative education really be considered a discipline? In order to consider this, the first question has to be 'what is a discipline?' Traditional disciplines such as history, economics, sociology and psychology have their own departments and offer degrees in the subject at colleges and universities. They have an accepted and established way of doing research and producing knowledge, often published in their own academic journals. There is no single method in comparative education nor is there any agreement as to which method is best. In fact, Bereday wrote that 'comparative education relies on the methods of a host of other fields, from philosophy to psychology, from literature to statistics...' (Bereday, 1964, p. x).

Some might ask, 'does it really matter?' While others see that it really does, Manzon (2011) believes that this lack of clarity concerning the nature and identity of comparative education is problematic. She writes: 'How can a field of study survive, develop and perpetuate itself if its scholarly community are unclear, much less unanimous, about their field's identity, aims and contents? (Manzon, 2011, p. 2) Much of the literature in the field focuses on this exact debate.

Can students acquire degrees in comparative education like they can in other disciplines, such as history or sociology? Comparative education was first taught as a course or module by James E. Russell at Teachers College, Columbia University, USA, in 1899 (Bereday, 1963). The title of the course was Comparative Study of Educational Systems. According to a university announcement, the course was 'designed to present a comprehensive view of a typical foreign school system and to aid students in making intelligent comparisons of the practical workings of this system with other systems at home and abroad' (Bereday, 1963, p. 189). Furthermore, during the academic year 1899–1900, special attention was given to the national education of Germany as compared with characteristic features of the systems of France, England and America.

Elsewhere, the first comparative education courses were taught by Isaac Kandel at Manchester University, England, in 1905; by Peter Sandiford in Canada at the University of Toronto in 1913; and in the 1920s at other universities in Bulgaria, Czechoslovakia, Poland and Uganda (Manzon, 2011). Furthermore, Manzon reports that in the 1930s, comparative education subjects were also taught in the Far East: at Tokyo University in Japan; in China at Beijing Normal University and at the University of Hong Kong. In the 1940s, similar trends were also seen in Brazil, Cuba and Australia, and by the end of the Second World War, comparative education had become an established academic subfield of education departments in universities around the world (Manzon, 2011).

From its inaugural course at Teachers College at Columbia University, comparative education has had strong links to teacher training (Planel, 2008), with many programmes around the world including it as an optional or elective component of their degrees. However, recent reports suggest that comparative education in initial teacher training has declined over the years in Western countries (O'Sullivan et al., 2008; Planel, 2008). In the UK, at undergraduate level, comparative education can be found in general education programmes such as the BA (Hons) Education Studies and may come under a variety of titles such as comparative pedagogy, educational systems abroad, Education in Europe, and so forth. Very often, elements of comparative education may be found in other courses on global citizenship, philosophy of education or in modules with titles incorporating the terms global or international. Most full degrees in Comparative Education are offered at Master's level rather than undergraduate level and the number of institutions offering this worldwide is small in comparison to other Master's degrees, such as those in Business Administration.

Most scholars would probably now agree that comparative education is a subfield of Education Studies. Even Bereday (1964, p. ix) writes: 'Comparative education is a young subfield in the very old discipline of pedagogy.' Others, such as Phillips and Schweisfurth (2008), have argued that comparative education is a 'quasi-discipline'. They believe that:

Comparativists cover a huge range of topics which demand expertise in many areas of academic inquiry. What brings them together in an identifiably coherent way is the common attempt at comparison, and comparison is a method used by various disciplines rather than an activity which can conceivably be described as a discipline in itself.
(Phillips & Schweisfurth, 2008, p. 11)

Colclough (2010) contends that it is largely because of the vast range of topics within the field that comparative education is not constrained by disciplinary boundaries. Nor is it likely or desirable to be so. In fact, Crossley and Watson (2003, p. 66) believe that a major advantage of the field is its multidisciplinary approach and 'engagement with a diversity of theoretical frameworks'.

What topics are covered in comparative education? Looking through various comparative education journals, one can easily see a variety of content. However, some topics have been popular for decades (Bray, 2003b). These include 'issues of power and control, education for national development, importation of educational ideas, and reform of education' (Bray, 2003b, p. 5). Theoretical themes have also dominated the literature: postmodernism, feminism, post-colonialism and, more recently, globalisation. It is precisely this variety which makes comparative education a hugely exciting field and therefore attractive to a great number of students and scholars alike.

How can we define what comparative education is?

Halls (1990, p. 21) states that '"comparative education" has always been conceptually awkward to define' and that '[t]he lack of a precise definition of the field of "comparative education" has continued to block its development' (p. 26). Epstein (1992, p. 409) supports this view: '"Comparative education" and "international education" are terms that are often confused...' and that '[t]he confusion is sustained by the literature, which is mute on the differences between the two domains'. Some of this confusion is bound to rest in the fact that many, if not most, comparative studies transcend national boundaries and are international or global in scope. If this is the case, how can we understand what it is? In an attempt to do this, we will look at several definitions. Manzon (2011) offers one of the most comprehensive definitions of the field.

Manzon (2011, p. 215) defines comparative education as:

An interdisciplinary subfield of education studies that systematically examines the similarities and differences between educational systems in two or more national or cultural contexts, and their interactions with intra- and extra-educational environments. Its specific object is educational systems examined from a cross-cultural (or cross-national, cross-regional) perspective through the systematic use of comparative method, for the advancement of theoretical understanding and theory building.

Epstein (1992, p. 409) defined comparative education as 'a field of study that applies social scientific theories and methods to international issues of education'. He also believed that although related to international education, comparative education was distinct from it. International education as a separate field will be discussed in Chapter 7, but for the purpose of understanding this distinction, it needs to be defined here as well. Hayden (2006), a distinguished scholar in the field of international education, asserts that there is no simple definition of international education either. Epstein (1992, p. 409) refers to international education as 'organised efforts to bring together students, teachers, and scholars from different nations to interact and learn about and from each other'. For the purpose of this book, Halls' (1990) definition below will be used. He, in fact, created a typology (system or classification) of comparative education that has been accepted by some academics (see Philips & Schweisfurth, 2008) in helping to make sense of such a vast field. In this model (see Figure 1.1), Halls acknowledges that it is flawed as the categories are not mutually exclusive and overlap.

What is more, there is no universal agreement among comparative educationalists as to the usage of these terms. For example, many scholars would argue whether international education is a subfield of comparative education. Nevertheless, Halls defined 'Comparative pedagogy as the

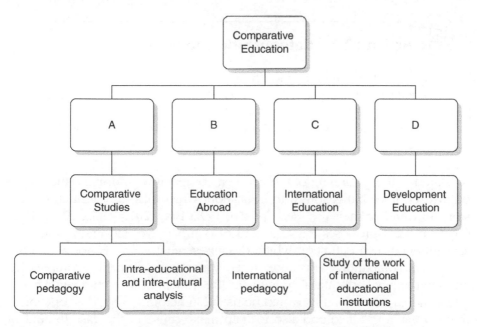

Figure 1.1   Halls' typology of comparative education (Halls, 1990, p. 23)

study of teaching and the classroom process in different countries'. 'Intra-educational and intra-cultural analysis investigates education by its various levels, and also systematically researches the historical, social, cultural, political, religious, economic and philosophical forces that partly determine and are partly determined by the character of the education systems, and compares the resultant outcomes in two or more systems, areas or even globally.' 'Education abroad is the study of aspects of an educational systems or systems other than one's own; this includes area studies'.

Halls subdivides international education into 'international pedagogy' and 'Study of the work of international educational institutions'. 'International pedagogy is the study of teaching multinational, multicultural and multiracial groups, for example in international schools, transnational schools (such as those of the European community), or the education of linguistic or ethnic minorities'. 'It is also the study of such subjects as education for international understanding, peace education, international population and ecological studies'. Within this area, Halls also includes the resolution of intra-national differences regarding the teaching of controversial subject-matter, efforts to 'objectivise' textbooks, the harmonisation of curricula and the establishment of international teaching norms. 'Study of the work of international education institutions is concerned with policy matters, such as the establishment of international acceptability of qualifications, the promotion of educational exchanges and the initiation of cultural agreements.' 'Development education is the production of information and plans to assist policymakers, particularly in "new nations", the development of appropriate educational methods and techniques, and the training of personnel to implement programmes.'

⊞ Activity 1.7   Categorising the field

Using Halls (1990) typology, look through various journals such as *Compare*, *Comparative Education Review* and *Comparative Education Research*. Scan the titles of the articles and abstracts. Can you classify the type of article according to Halls' model? Do studies fit neatly into the categories?

As stated at the beginning of the chapter, comparative and international are often used interchangeably with education, which has led to much discussion surrounding their use (see Epstein, 1992; Bray, 2010; Little, 2010). Bray (2010, p. 722) proposes that the field of comparative education would be strengthened by a definition which describes 'what is and is not within the bounds of comparative education, international education, and comparative and international education'. Indeed, for the student new to comparative and international education this would be useful in helping to build a conceptual framework of the field and also to help make sense of the vast amount of literature. Little (2010) concurs with Bray that the meanings of terms such as 'education', 'comparative', 'international' and 'development', for example, are used and combined differently by various scholars. Again, there is no agreement on their usage and for the student; this can be confusing. However, as no suitable alternatives exist, the terms as described by Halls will underpin this book and provide the basis for both its structure and format.

 Activity 1.8   Defining comparative education

Find other definitions in either books, journal articles or on the internet. Compare and contrast these to the definitions previously discussed. Can you then synthesise (combine) them to produce one that demonstrates your own understanding of what comparative education is? Be prepared to justify it.

What is the purpose of comparative education and who compares?

Comparative studies in education are undertaken for a variety of reasons and by a variety of people and organisations. Some of the reasons are listed below. However, the list is not exhaustive and there is overlap, as well as one reason possibly being the result of another.

- To learn about our own education system and that of others
- To enhance our knowledge of education in general
- To improve educational institutions; their content, processes and methods
- To understand the relationship between education and society
- To promote international understanding
- To find possible solutions to educational issues

 Activity 1.9   Purpose of comparative education

Using the same articles from Activity 1.7, can you identify the nature and purpose of the comparative studies being published? Who is conducting the study? Why?

The first and foremost purpose of comparative education is in the name – to compare education in one or more countries. Traditionally, this has involved examining national education systems as the focus of study. It is now widely accepted that comparative education can include intra-national comparisons or, in other words, comparing within countries, perhaps different states, provinces or regions. Bereday (1964, p. 5) believed that 'Comparative education seeks to make sense out of the similarities and differences among educational systems'. Looking at the reasons behind these enables us to learn about not only others but ourselves as well. Nevertheless, Bereday believed that the foremost justification for comparative education was intellectual. 'Knowledge for its own sake is the sole ground upon which comparative education needs to make a stand in order to merit inclusion among other academic fields' (Bereday, 1964, p. 5). Having said this, he was also a firm believer in the practical application of comparative education and its contribution to teaching and the social sciences in general.

There are a number of reasons why you as a student may wish to study comparative education. Perhaps you intend to teach abroad and therefore can benefit from the insights gleamed from exploring other educational systems. Comparisons enable us to view education from alternative perspectives, potentially leading to a greater understanding of the world, the people who live in it, and the issues they may face. This can also help prepare you for teaching in a multicultural context either at home or abroad. Planel (2008, p. 386) argues that comparative education and, in particular, comparative pedagogy, 'could give teachers a better understanding of how pupils' learning is affected by cultural understandings'. In an age of global migration, schools have become increasingly multicultural, so an understanding and appreciation of this diversity is crucial in the twenty-first-century classroom. Lastly, the subject itself is 'eye-opening' and interesting, particularly if you have grown up a monocultural environment.

 Activity 1.10   Benefits and challenges to studying comparative education

Can you think of any other benefits that students might gain from studying comparative education? Are there any limitations? Why or why not?

What are the challenges to making comparisons? How can you overcome these?

Much of the literature in the field has been written by academics for other academics and policy makers rather than for a student audience. 'Academics undertake comparisons in order to improve understanding both of the forces which shape education systems and processes in different settings, and of the impact of education systems and process on social and other development' (Bray, 2007, p. 16). There is also intrinsic value in knowing about education outside our own borders. For centuries, scholars have been internationally mobile in their academic pursuits (see Kim, 2009). Many have travelled abroad out of sheer intellectual curiosity, such as those in the early 'traveller tales'.

As previously stated, many international organisations undertake comparative studies in education (which is further discussed in Chapter 2). The main ones include UNESCO, the World Bank and the OECD. The aim of many of these organisations is to reduce educational inequalities by expanding access for all and improving the overall quality of education for the betterment of both individuals and society. These organisations often undertake education research and produce factual data through the use of quantitative methods. Statistics and other information are published on their websites, making data readily available for comparisons between two or more countries.

Policy makers and education planners are interested in comparative education for a number of reasons. 'Governments are paying increasing attention to international comparisons as they search for effective policies that enhance individuals' social and economic prospects, provide incentives for greater efficiency in schooling, and help to mobilise resources to meet rising demands' (OECD, 2007, p. 3). Market forces and the marketisation of education have demanded more cost-effective and efficient ways of delivering education provision. Governments are also under pressure to improve the quality of education provision, particularly in response to international league tables such as PISA (Programme for International Student Assessment) and TIMMS (Trends in International Mathematics and Science Study) (to be discussed in Chapter 2). In their quest for improvement, policy makers may attempt to 'borrow' educational models or learn important lessons from elsewhere (see Case Study 1). Bereday (1964, p. 6) believed a major goal of comparative education was 'first, to deduce from the achievements and the mistakes of school systems other than their own, lessons for their own schools (or to warn policy makers that such lessons cannot be light-heartedly sought where valid comparison is impossible); and second, to appraise educational issues from a global rather than an ethnocentric perspective, or in other words, to be aware always of other nations' points of view'.

In the aftermath of the Second World War, Bereday (1964, p. 5) also believed that 'knowing about other nations is now not only a matter of curiosity but of necessity'. This statement is as valid today as it was over 40 years ago. Rapid advances in technology, communication, travel and so forth have led to the increased interconnectedness of the world. This interconnectedness has resulted in the 'globalisation' of nearly all aspects of society. While Bereday was perhaps referring to peace in the wake of two world wars, it can be argued that knowing about other nations has now become necessary as a result of globalisation (the relationship between globalisation and education will be further explored in Chapter 8). In fact, many scholars believe that comparative and international research in education is being 'revitalised' as a result of globalisation (Crossley & Watson, 2003).

What are the challenges of studying comparative education?

Challenges of methodology aside, perhaps, potentially one of the greatest barriers for comparativists is that we all hold values and beliefs about the nature of purpose of education which are inextricably linked to our own experiences. As Bereday previously pointed out, there is a danger of adopting an 'ethnocentric' approach when making comparisons. Schultz and Lavenda (2011) define ethnocentrism as 'The opinion that one's own way of life is natural or correct and, indeed, the only true way of being fully human'. When making comparisons, we have to be aware that we do not impose our own values and beliefs on others, particularly if we think our own way of doing something is 'best'. This can lead to bias and even prejudice if we are not careful.

Another challenge stems from the data used in comparative education (discussed in Chapter 2) and the need to critically appraise not only how it was arrived at, but the source of it as well. We need to check our sources carefully to make sure they are reliable, accurate and that there is no hidden agenda. For example, newspapers may over-exaggerate international league table results and report on them inaccurately, so there is a 'story' to sell. Sometimes, statistics are presented by governments in such a way so that they are seen in the best possible light (Clarkson, 2009). This may be particularly true around election time when governments try to demonstrate that improvements to education have been made.

And, more importantly, are we comparing the same things? When we talk about courses, for instance, do we mean modules or programmes? Is the first grade (USA) the same thing as year one in the UK? In other words, are we comparing like for like? We also need to carefully consider the 'thing' we are analysing – education. Education does not mean the same thing to everyone. As Grant (2000, p. 310) points out, '[i]t may have quite different aims, operate under different conditions, and be assessed by different criteria'. Are comparisons fair if we are not looking at the same thing?

As previously mentioned, 'borrowing' educational best practice from other countries is common in comparative education. Many examples of borrowing can be found in the UK and elsewhere. In the UK, one such example was the abolition of the tripartite system of education, where children were segregated by ability into grammar, secondary modern or technical schools in the 1960s, which was replaced with a comprehensive system of schooling based on the American High School model (Clarkson, 2009). However, the transference of ideas from one context to another is a highly complex affair (Phillips & Schweisfurth, 2008). Education planners cannot simply transpose one set of ideas on another without taking into consideration the social, cultural, historical, and even economic factors involved. Historically, there are many examples worldwide (both successful and unsuccessful) where comparative studies in education have played a significant role in influencing policy (see Case Study 1).

Conclusion

Comparative education has successfully emerged in the twenty-first century as a multidisciplinary field of study with a strong scholarly base. There have been a number of individuals and organisations throughout history (too many to name in such a short chapter), which have contributed greatly to its establishment and academic advancement. The interest in, and indeed the importance of, comparative education can be seen in the worldwide growth of societies, organisations, academic journals, specialist courses and even postgraduate degrees in the subject.

There are many students, academics, policy makers and practitioners engaged with comparative education for a variety of reasons worldwide. Whatever the purpose, the field has contributed, and will continue to contribute, greatly to our understanding of education – both of others and that of our own.

 Case Study 1   Educational 'borrowing' in China, 1949–1966

Throughout the centuries, and at different points in time, China, like many nations, has looked elsewhere for answers to educational dilemmas. The search for Western knowledge can be traced back to the sixteenth century and the Italian Jesuit missionary Matteo Ricci (Lee & Mak, 2010). Although Ricci went to China with the aim of spreading Christianity, he also played a key role in spreading European scientific knowledge, particularly in mathematics and astronomy. In later years, China looked to the former Soviet Union for educational reforms. From 1949 to the mid-1950s, the dominant slogan in China was 'learn from the Soviet Union', and over 10,000 Soviet experts went to China to help set up a Soviet model of education (Pepper, 1996, p. 158). The Soviet model was incorporated at all levels from primary schooling through to higher education, and Soviet thinking continued to directly influence policy until the early 1960s (see Tsang, 2000). During this time universal primary schooling was introduced as well as efforts to reduce illiteracy rates. As a result, over 100 million Chinese between the ages of 14 and 45 became literate from 1949 to 1966 (Arnove,

(Continued)

(Continued)

1984). Furthermore, massive expansion in schooling lead to increased enrolment rates. In 1949, only about 20% of young people were attending school, but by 1980 90% of school-age children were enrolled (Arnove, 1984).

Changes in higher education 'Soviet style' were also made as the Chinese government looked to reform it. Soviet academic material was translated and used as the primary source of the curriculum. Central planning was a key component of Soviet-style management, which led to an emphasis on uniformity, standardisation and the adoption of the exact same course syllabus and teaching plans in institutions across China. By mid-1954, curriculum revision for over 170 academic specialisms was complete and their use enforced (Pepper, 1996). In the 'Great Leap Forward', the number of higher education institutions increased from 229 in 1957 to 1,289 in 1960, and within this same three-year period, total enrolment also increased from 441,181 to 961,623 (Yu et al., 2012). The increase in the number of students along with the mechanical copying of Soviet-style education is attributed to the decrease in the quality of higher education during this time.

Key questions:

- Why did China look to the Soviet Union for ideas?

- Why do you think there was a push to educate the masses during this time?

- Were there any benefits to copying Soviet-style education?

- What challenges do you think the Chinese government faced?

- What role does comparative education play in helping governments to reform educational policy?

- Can you find other examples of educational 'borrowing', successful or otherwise? Why are they successful or not?

Suggested reading

Bereday, G. (1964) *Comparative Method in Education*. New York: Holt, Rinehart and Winston
A classic text which has been hugely important in the methodological debates of comparative education.

Kandel, I. (1933) *Studies in Comparative Education*. London: George Harrap & Co
A seminal text in the field of comparative education and a must read, particularly for those studying at Master's level.

References

Acosta, F. & Centeno, C. (2011) Re-bordering comparative education in Latin America: Between global limits and local characteristics. *International Review of Education*, 57, 477–496

Arnove, R. (1984) A comparison of the Chinese and Indian education systems. *Comparative Education Review*, 28(3), 378–401

Bereday, G. (1963) James Russell's syllabus of the first academic course in Comparative Education. *Comparative Education Review*, 7(2), 189–196

Bereday, G. (1964) *Comparative Method in Education.* New York: Holt, Rinehart and Winston

Bignold, W. & Gayton, L. (eds) (2009) *Global Issues and Comparative Education.* Exeter: Learning Matters

Bravo, H.F. (1994) Domingo Faustino Sarmiento, *Prospects: The Quarterly Review of Comparative Education*, 24(3/4), 487–500

Bray, M. (2003a) Comparative education in the era of globalisation: Evolution, missions and roles. *Policy Futures in Education*, 1(2), 209–224

Bray, M. (ed.) (2003b) *Comparative Education: Continuing Traditions, New Challenges, and New Paradigms.* The Hague: Kluwer Academic Publishers

Bray, M. (2007) Actors and purposes in comparative education, in M. Bray, B. Adamson & M. Mason (eds), *Comparative Education Research: Approaches and Methods.* Hong Kong: Comparative Education Research Centre

Bray, M. (2010) Comparative education and international education in the history of *Compare*: Boundaries, overlaps and ambiguities. *Compare: A Journal of Comparative and International Education*, 40(6), 711–725

Bray, M. & Qin, G. (2001) Comparative education in Greater China. *Comparative Education*, 37(4), 451–473

Bray, M., Adamson, B. & Mason, M. (eds) (2007) *Comparative Education Research: Approaches and Methods.* Hong Kong: Springer

Brickman, W. (2010) Comparative education in the nineteenth century. *European Education*, 42(2), 46–56

Clarkson, J. (2009) What is comparative education? in W. Bignold & L. Gayton (eds), *Global Issues and Comparative Education.* Exeter: Learning Matters

Colclough, C. (2010) Reflective pieces: Development studies and comparative education: Where do they find common cause? *Compare*, 40(6), 821–826

Comparative & International Education Society (CIES) (2012), www.cies.us

Crossley, M. & Watson, K. (2003) *Comparative and International Research in Education: Globalisation, Context and Difference.* Oxford: Routledge

Dale, R. (2005) Globalisation, knowledge economy and comparative education. *Comparative Education*, 41(2), 117–149

Epstein, E.H. (1992) Editorial. *Comparative Education Review*, 36(4), 409–416

Epstein, E.H. (2008) Setting the normative boundaries: Crucial epistemological benchmarks in comparative education. *Comparative Education*, 44(4), 373–386

Gautherin, J. (1993) Marc-Antoine Jullien ('Jullien de Paris'). *Prospects: The Quarterly Review of Comparative Education*, 23(3/4), 757–773

Grant, N. (2000) Tasks for comparative education in the new millennium. *Comparative Education*, 36(3), 309–317

Green, A. (2003) Education, globalisation and the role of comparative research. *London Review of Education*, 1(2), 84–97

Halls, W.D. (ed.) (1990) *Comparative Education: Contemporary Issues and Trends*. London: Jessica Kingsley/UNESCO

Hans, N. (1949) *Comparative Education*. London: Routledge & Kegan Paul

Hayden, M. (2006) *Introduction to International Education*. London: Sage

Kandel, I. (1933) *Studies in Comparative Education*. London: George Harrap & Co

Kim, T. (2009) Shifting patterns of transnational academic mobility: A comparative and historical approach. *Comparative Education*, 45(3), 387–403

King, E. (1965) The purpose of comparative education. *Comparative Education*, 1(3), 147–159

Lee, W.O. & Mak, G.L.C. (2010) From knowledge transfer to knowledge interaction: The development of comparative education in China through the lens of comparative journals. *Compare: A Journal of Comparative and International Education*, 40(6), 761–780

Little, A. (2010) International and comparative education: What's in a name? *Compare: A Journal of Comparative and International Education*, 40(6), 845–852

Mallinson, V. (1981) In the wake of Sir Michael Sadler. *Compare: A Journal of Comparative and International Education*, 11(2), 175–183

Manzon, M. (2011) *Comparative Education: The Construction of a Field*. Hong Kong: CERC/Springer

Masemann, V. (2006) Afterword. *Current Issues in Comparative Education*, 8(2). Available online at: www.tc.edu/cice/Issues/08.02/82masemann.html

Masemann, V., Bray, M. & Manzon, M. (eds) (2008) *Common Interests, Uncommon Goals: Histories of the World Council of Comparative Education Societies and its Members*. Hong Kong: Comparative Education Research Centre

Noah, H. & Eckstein, M. (1969) *Toward a Science of Comparative Education*. New York: Macmillan

OECD (2007) *Education at a Glance 2007*. Paris: OECD

O'Sullivan, M., Maarman, R. & Wolhuter, C. (2008) Primary student teachers' perceptions of motivations for comparative education: Findings from a comparative study of an Irish and South African comparative education course. *Compare: A Journal of Comparative and International Education*, 38(4), 401–414

Pepper, S. (1996) *Radicalism and Education Reform in Twentieth-Century China*. Cambridge: Cambridge University Press

Phillips, D. (2000) Beyond travellers' tales: Some nineteenth-century British commentators on education in Germany. *Oxford Review of Education*, 26(1), 49–62

Phillips, D. & Schweisfurth, M. (2008) *Comparative and International Education: An Introduction to Theory, Method and Practice*. London: Continuum

Planel, C. (2008) The rise and fall of comparative education in teacher training: Should it rise again as comparative pedagogy? *Compare: A Journal of Comparative and International Education*, 38(4), 385–399

Rust, V., Johnstone, B. & Allaf, C. (2009) Reflections on the development of comparative education, in R. Cowen & A. Kazamias (eds), *International Handbook of Comparative Education*. London: Springer

Schultz, E. & Lavenda, R. (2011) *Cultural Anthropology: A Perspective on the Human Condition* (8th edition). Available online at: www.oup.com/us/companion.websites/9780199760060/book/?view=usa

Tsang, M.C. (2000) *Education and National Development in China since 1949: Oscillating Policies and Enduring Dilemmas*. Available online at: http://tc.columbia.edu/faculty/tsang/Files/7.pdf

World Council of Comparative Education Societies (WCCES) (2012), www.wcces.com

Yu, K., Stith, A.L., Liu, L. & Chen, H. (2012) *Tertiary Education at a Glance: China*. Boston, MA: Sense

CHAPTER 2

HOW ARE COMPARISONS MADE?

This chapter explores:

- Secondary sources in comparative education;
- The statistical use of data in educational comparisons;
- Databases on national systems of education;
- The use of international surveys on student achievement.

Many students studying comparative education will not have the opportunity to conduct primary research in another country. Primary research is original research where you collect raw data through a number of research methods, such as observation, experiment or interview. Collecting your own data, and especially in another country, is not only time-consuming but also very expensive. Therefore, in order to make comparisons, you may have to use a range of secondary sources. Secondary sources can include policy documents, curriculum frameworks and educational statistics. The internet has played a key role in making this kind of educational data widely available. Educational data is collected by a number of organisations and for a variety of purposes. Particularly in comparative education, the use of statistics has played a key role. Who collects data on national education systems and for what purpose? What kind of data is collected and are there limitations of using statistical sources?

 Activity 2.1   Primary versus secondary data analysis

What is primary data and how is it different from secondary data? Can you think of any advantages and disadvantages to collecting and analysing both forms of data?

Organisations and statistics

In Chapter 1, we saw how Marc-Antoine Jullien tried to make comparative education a science by systemically analysing data gathered from survey research. Years later, as the scientific approach came to dominate the social sciences, scholars such as Bereday (1964) and Noah and Eckstein (1969) believed that researchers in the field should adopt a positivist, or scientific, approach using quantitative methods. This positivist approach is evident in much of the statistical work of international organisations such as the United Nations Scientific Education Organisation (UNESCO) and the Organisation for Economic Cooperation and Development (OECD), and also in international surveys of student achievement such as the Programme for International Student Assessment (PISA), and the Trends in International Mathematics and Science Study (TIMMS) (Crossley, 2012). More importantly, 'governments are paying increasing attention to international comparisons as they search for effective policies that enhance individuals' social and economic prospects, provide greater efficiency in schooling, and help to mobilise resources to meet rising demands' (OECD, 2012).

UNESCO plays a vital role in both the production and sharing of information and knowledge in the field of education. It has had a statistical function since its inception in 1945 and in the 1950s and 1960s UNESCO was the 'premier education statistics institution' (Heyneman, 1999, p. 66). In 1999, the UNESCO Institute for Statistics (UIS) was established 'with functional autonomy to meet the growing need for reliable and policy-relevant data' (UNESCO, 2013). Today the UIS produces statistics on: educational programmes, access, progression, school completion and human and financial resources. They also cover public and private institutions at a range of levels from pre-primary to higher education. Additionally, the UIS publishes the *Global Education Digest*, which reports the latest education statistics from across the globe.

▦ Activity 2.2   UNESCO statistics

Have a look at UNESCO's UIS website at: www.uis.unesco.org/Education/Pages/default.aspx

What kind of data is being presented: qualitative or quantitative? What topics are featured?

The Organisation for Economic Cooperation and Development (OECD), formed in 1947, was created in the aftermath of the Second World War to help rebuild Europe. There are currently 34 member countries worldwide with its headquarters in Paris. The OECD's stated mission is 'to promote policies that will improve the economic and social well-being of people around the world' (OECD, 2013a). The OECD has an interest in education because it plays a central role in benefitting both a country's economy and society. A key way that children are socialised is through the process of schooling. Children learn about the society they live in; its values and norms or codes of behaviour (Wood, 2011). Education can lead to social cohesion and social mobility. Through education, social mobility (the ability to move between social classes) and improving your 'lot' in life can be made possible (Curtis & Pettigrew, 2010). In addition, education is often linked to economic growth by giving individuals the knowledge and skills to be productive workers (Allen, 2011). 'In today's globalised economy, education is a major driving force for growth and development' (OECD, 2011a). The aim of organisations such as the OECD is to help governments share information and analyse trends on a range of topics, including education, in order to bring about social and economic benefit.

Due to a demand for better ways of collecting and interpreting data on national education systems from member countries, the OECD developed a set of international indicators that display key features of their systems in statistical form. The first set of these indicators was published in 1992 in *Education at a Glance* (see OECD, 2004). *Education at a Glance* is an annual report which 'looks at who participates in education, what is spent on it, how education systems operate and the results achieved'.

▦ Activity 2.3   *Education at a Glance*

Look at previous issues of *Education at a Glance* on the internet at: www.oecd-ilibrary.org/education/education-at-a-glance_19991487 Choose two countries to compare. Look at the indicator 'Educational expenditure per student'. How much is spent on each student? Look at the OECD average. Who spends more per student? What do or don't these statistics tell us?

Another key source of education statistics is Eurostat. Situated in Luxembourg, it is the statistical office of the European Union and provides statistics at a European level that enables comparisons between countries and regions. They publish statistics on a range of topics from the economy to education and vocational training. Eurostat believe that 'democratic societies do not function properly without a solid basis of reliable and objective statistics' and furthermore '...the public and media need statistics for an accurate picture of contemporary society and to evaluate the performance of politicians and others' (European Commission, 2013).

 ## Activity 2.4   Eurostat and statistics

Evaluate the previous statements by Eurostat. How important are statistics in our everyday life? How important are they in providing evidence in order to make decisions? Can they ever be purely reliable and objective?

Educational databases

A good starting point for conducting research on other countries is a database that provides information on national education systems. Eurydice, administered by the EU Education, Audiovisual and Culture Executive Agency (EACEA), is a database that contains information on and analyses of European education systems and policies. It can be accessed openly and online (http://eacea.ec.europa.eu/education/ eurydice/index_en.php). As from 2013 it consists of 40 national education systems in Europe (EACEA, 2009). The stated mission of Eurydice is 'to provide those responsible for education systems and policies in Europe with European-level analyses and information which will assist them in their decision making' (EACEA, 2013a).

The Eurydice network also provides comparative thematic reports to do with policy, practice and research on topics such as mathematics and science education, citizenship education and the teaching of reading in a European context (EACEA, 2013b). In addition, it produces information on 34 countries in its Key Data Series, the aim of which is to combine statistical data and qualitative information on European education systems (EACEA, 2012). You can also find facts and figures related to education, such as national education structures, school calendars, comparison of salaries and of required taught time per countries and education levels (EACEA, 2013a).

> ### ⊞ Activity 2.5   Eurydice
>
> Choose a country from Eurypedia, which is part of the Eurydice network. You can find it at: ehttps://webgate.ec.europa.eu/fpfis/mwikis/eurydice/index.php?title=Hom
>
> Focus on a particular structure within the system, for example, primary schooling. Compare features of that structure to your own country. Features could include the starting age, curriculum or assessment.

Another good source of comparative data on education policy can be found at the former INCA (International Review of Curriculum and Assessment Frameworks Internet Archive) website (www.nfer.ac.uk/what-we-do/information-and-reviews/inca.cfm). Although the last and final update was in March 2013, it still provides fairly recent and up-to-date information on educational policy in Australia, Canada, England, France, Germany, Hungary, Ireland, Italy, Japan, Korea, the Netherlands, New Zealand, Northern Ireland, Scotland, Singapore, South Africa, Spain, Sweden, Switzerland, the USA and Wales. The focus is on curriculum, assessment and initial teacher training frameworks for pre-school, primary, lower secondary and upper secondary education in schools (3–19 age range) (NFER, 2013).

The INCA website was managed by the National Foundation for Educational Research (NFER) in conjunction with the Department for Education (DfE) in England. The INCA project began in 1996 in order to monitor the English curriculum. The stated aims of the INCA project were to:

- Build, maintain, update and develop an accurately researched and ready-to-use resource of 'country archives', comprising descriptions of government policy on the aims, organisation and control, and structure of the education system, on the curriculum and assessment frameworks, and on the initial teacher training systems in mainstream and special education across all countries of the international review.

- Provide comparative tables, thematic probes and thematic studies in specific areas of interest.

- Provide detailed information on specific areas to enable the DfE to evaluate the English National Curriculum and assessment frameworks.

- Help the DfE and policy colleagues analyse the outcomes of international comparisons.

(Sargent et al., 2012, p. 3)

If you are looking for information outside the European Union, the International Bureau of Education or IBE (www.ibe.unesco.org/en.html), which is part of UNESCO, has a number of databases that are useful in comparative education research. There are five databases in total which include: the World Data on Education (WDE), which gives access to profiles of national education systems worldwide, particularly to information on curricula and curriculum development processes; Country Dossiers, which include official reports and links to curricular resources as well as national education agencies; and the IBE Digital Library of National Reports 1932–2008, which is a unique collection of over 3,000 reports on education covering several decades (IBE, 2013).

International student surveys

There are a number of international surveys of student achievement whose findings have greatly influenced educational policy and practice across the globe (Crossley, 2012). There is great interest in these studies as the findings can help us to understand how well our own education systems are doing compared to other nations and systems. They can also tell us if our education systems are efficient, productive and cost-effective (Leimu, 2004). Perhaps the most well-known survey is the Programme for International Student Assessment (PISA). PISA, launched in 1997, is administered by the OECD in over 70 countries and 'evaluates education systems worldwide by testing the skills and knowledge of 15-year-old students' (OECD, 2013b). PISA is conducted every three years in reading, mathematics and science with a primary focus on one of those subjects in each cycle. 'The tests are designed to assess to what extent students at the end of compulsory education, can apply their knowledge to real-life situations and be equipped for full participation in society'; furthermore, PISA is not linked to any particular school curriculum (OECD, 2013b). In the 2012 round of assessments, approximately 510,000 students completed the two-hour long, paper test from 65 participating countries and economies (OECD, 2013d).

The 2012 PISA assessment results show wide variations in educational outcomes both within and between countries. At the top of the table on the overall mathematics scale was China (Shanghai), Korea, Japan and Liechtenstein, and at the bottom Peru, Indonesia and Qatar (OECD, 2013d). PISA also looks at whether systems are equitable by examining links between a student's socio-economic background and their achievement. Based on the 2009 PISA results, it was found that, '[o]n average across OECD countries, disadvantaged students are twice as likely to be among the poorest performers in reading compared to advantaged students'. The UK is below average in terms of fair opportunities for pupils, while Shanghai in China, South Korea and Finland are top (OECD, 2013c).

In the UK, this has been attributed to the fact that there have been long-standing social divisions between rich and poor students and there is also the suggestion of widespread acceptance of underachievement among poorer pupils (Coughlan, 2013).

 Activity 2.6   Are countries moving towards a more equitable system?

Have a look at the *PISA In Focus* number 25 report, available at: www.oecd.org/pisa/pisainfocus/

Which education systems are more equitable? How can we explain these differences? What role do policy and culture play in narrowing the gaps between advantaged and disadvantaged students?

The influence of PISA on educational policy is now well documented (see Ertl, 2006; Grek, 2009; Takayama, 2009; Bulle, 2011). PISA has had a tremendous impact on educational reforms in Germany (Grek, 2009). The 2000 results caused widespread debate and calls for major changes in secondary provision there. One of the reasons it caused such a shock was that Germany has always had one of the most highly regarded education systems in the world (OECD, 2011b). Germany has had a long-standing reputation for quality education and in the 1800s, many of the early educational 'travellers' (as discussed in Chapter 1) were drawn to Germany for its excellent reputation in schooling (Brickman, 2010).

In 2000, Germany scored an average of 484 points for reading, which was below the OECD average of 500 (OECD, 2001). It also showed high levels of inequality in the German educational system, especially for those from lower socio-economic backgrounds who were found to be particularly disadvantaged. Furthermore, '[i]n 2000, German students spent less time in the classroom than students in many other countries: only 796 hours per year in primary school and 903 hours in lower secondary school, against OECD averages of 841 hours and 936 hours' (Pearson Foundation, 2013). Some of the main reasons used to explain Germany's weak overall performance in the 2000 PISA were: the tripartite structure of secondary education; wide variations in standards and curricula across the country; lack of fluency in German; and the short school day. Subsequent reforms, such as the adoption of national educational standards, increased school hours and improvements in teacher quality have been implemented in order to address these issues (OECD, 2011b). As a result, Germany's lowest-achieving students did better in the 2009 PISA tests than in 2000 and the negative impact of students' socio-economic background lessened (Pearson Foundation, 2013). In the 2012 PISA results, Germany made further improvements with an overall mean score of 514 in mathematics, 508 in reading and 524 in science (OECD, 2013d).

Another key organisation involved in international student assessment is the International Association for the Evaluation of Educational Achievement (IEA), established in 1958 (IEA, 2011a). Since its inception, the IEA has conducted over 30 comparative studies in educational achievements in subjects such as mathematics, science, reading, citizenship (IEA, 2011b). The Trends in International Mathematics and Science Study (TIMSS) is perhaps one the biggest and most well-known of the IEA studies. The initial TIMSS assessment was carried out in 1995 and subsequently in 1999, 2003, 2007 and 2011 (IEA, 2011c). TIMSS assesses students enrolled in the fourth (ages 9–10) and eighth grades (ages 13–14) in mathematics and science.

The East Asian countries of Singapore, Korea, and Hong Kong SAR, followed by Chinese Taipei and Japan, were the top performers at the fourth grade level in the results from the TIMSS 2011 (Martin et al., 2012). Likewise, at the eighth grade level, Korea, Singapore and Chinese Taipei surpassed all other countries, followed by Hong Kong SAR and Japan (Martin et al., 2012). Trailing behind the five top performers, but still in the top ten at the fourth grade, were Northern Ireland, Belgium (Flemish), Finland, England and the Russian Federation, and at the eighth grade, the Russian Federation, Israel, Finland, the United States and England (Martin et al., 2012, p. 7).

Other IEA Studies include the Progress in International Reading and Literacy Study (PIRLS), the International Computer and Information Literacy Study (ICILS), the International Civic and Citizenship Education Study (ICCS) and the Teacher Education and Development Study in Mathematics (TEDS-M) (see IEA 2011d).

▦ Activity 2.7   IEA studies

Choose one of the IEA studies mentioned above. You can find more information at: www.iea.nl/. What is the aim of the study you have chosen? Which countries have participated and how do they compare to one another. Have a look at TIMSS and choose a country that has also participated in PISA. How do the results compare?

Why do countries participate in studies like PISA, TIMSS and PIRLS? The findings from international surveys can help inform policy makers where they might choose to focus their efforts. The impact of the PISA 2000 results on Germany is one such example. Other examples can be found in Canada, the USA and Japan. To illustrate this, the Canadian government announced that it would use data from PISA to improve its systems of education: 'PISA 2009 will be a valuable resource for education researchers and government policy makers who wish to study and propose improvements to Canada's systems of education' (CMEC, 2009).

Mullis, Martin and Foy (2005, p. 5) believe that the findings of TIMSS can point out relative strengths and weaknesses in the curriculum: 'TIMSS 1995, 1999, and 2003 have shown that, on average, eighth-grade students in the United States perform relatively poorly on geometry items and relatively well on data items'. They argue that this kind of information is vital to policy makers and educators when discussing the overall goals of learning and the aims of the curriculum across the country. Ultimately, it can be argued that governments want to know whether the money they are investing into their education systems is paying off. How successful is our system? One way of measuring this is by comparing yourself to other countries, but are international surveys the only way to measure success?

 Activity 2.8   Measuring success

Would you consider the education you received to be a 'success'? What about the country you live in? Would you say it has a successful education system? How would you define and measure 'success'?

Both TIMSS and PISA compare mathematics and science achievement so how then do these two surveys compare? Making direct comparisons between the two is problematic for a number of reasons. The most obvious issue is that individual test questions and content are different so are we comparing apples and oranges? According to Murat and Rocher (2004), PISA is much more concerned with students' ability to apply knowledge rather than possessing the knowledge itself while the TIMSS tasks are very close to those tasks that students are involved with at school. The aim is to examine the results in comparison with the curricula.

Furthermore, Mullis et al. (2005, p. 5) reported that 'The TIMSS content domains are fairly consistently found in the curricula of the participating countries and the results provide an indication of curriculum areas on which students perform relatively better of [sic] worse, both within and across countries'. Hutchinson and Schagen (2006, p. 25) sum up the differences by stating that 'TIMSS is inside the school wondering what makes it tick, while PISA is outside the street waiting to see what's coming out'.

In an analysis of PISA and TIMMS, Wu (2010, p. 3) found that 'at the country level, it appears that Western countries perform relatively better in PISA as compared to their performance in TIMSS. In contrast, Asian and Eastern European countries tend to do better in TIMSS than in PISA'. What are the possible reasons for these differences? One explanation is offered by Balazsi (2006, cited in Hutchinson & Schagen, 2006, p. 25), who says: 'TIMSS focuses on the curriculum-related tasks, while PISA is literacy-based. [The] Hungarian school system still highly relies on factual knowledge and traditional teaching strategies, so students are relatively good in tasks which are close to their usual classroom tasks, while they meet relatively few literacy-based tasks and they do not know what to do with these'. However, can student performance in PISA and TIMSS really be explained by whether students were taught in a 'traditional' manner? What other factors could really be at play?

Benefits of statistics

According to Keates (2012), international education statistics '... should be seen as a potentially helpful way in which education systems around the world can hold a mirror up to their own progress and achievements and take a closer look at what they might be able to learn from elsewhere'. Analysing data from secondary sources has a number of advantages for the student researcher. As previously mentioned, you can access high-quality data without the time and expense of collecting it. Many of the data sets offered by the OECD, UNESCO and the IEA can be considered of high quality. There are a number of reasons why they could be considered as such. To start, the data sets are collected in a fairly rigorous way (see OECD, 2004), cover a wide geographical spread, and the collection process is highly resourced and overseen by highly experienced researchers. The IEA, which administers TIMSS, has been established for over 50 years. During this time, they have been able to gain a considerable amount of experience and therefore expertise in the design and implementation of student achievement tests. Hutchinson and Schagen (2006, p. 2) believe that 'IEA and TIMSS are widely respected, rightly for competence, integrity, innovation and relevance to the needs of the countries involved'.

This gives data published by major international organisations significant advantages over that which is collected by students. They also offer the opportunity for longitudinal analysis (see Bryman, 2008), which enables you to monitor progress in a particular area over time. Longitudinal studies gather data on the same subjects over a period of time, years or even decades. Longitudinal research is beneficial when looking at changes or trends. Furthermore, Eurostat, the statistical arm of the EU, believe that statistics can answer many questions, such as the following:

- Is society heading in the direction promised by politicians?

- Is unemployment up or down?

- Are there more carbon dioxide emissions compared to ten years ago?

- How many women go to work?

- How is your country's economy performing compared to other EU member states?

Statistics can be a really useful tool in formulating background information on different countries. The European Commission believes 'they are an important, objective and down-to-earth way of measuring how we all live' (European Commission, 2013).

 Activity 2.9   Statistics

Before reading the next section, consider the limitations of using some of the statistics discussed in the chapter. What might these be?

Limitations and criticisms

Despite the ease in which student researchers can access internationally published data, statistics have their limitations, as captured in the quote: 'There are three kinds of lies: lies, damned lies, and statistics' (author unknown). Crossley and Watson (2003) point out a number of issues with statistics when conducting comparative research. 'First, raw statistics ignore the human and cultural dimensions of a society, which for many comparativists, are at the heart of what they are studying' (Crossley & Watson, 2003, p. 42). They go on to say that raw data do not reveal the underlying philosophy or rationale of an education system, which helps to explain anomalies and reasons for differences to other systems. Some have suggested that culture has played a huge role in Finland's success in international assessments, particularly in literacy, as reading has a high social value and is a large part of life (Buckingham, 2012, p. 6).

Another criticism is that statistics are open to multiple interpretations. 'Government statistics, publicity brochures and official publications often seek to portray a system, or a country, in the most favourable light. In doing this, figures may be officially massaged if it is perceived that this will be politically advantageous' (Crossley & Watson, 2003, p. 37). Keates (2012) reported that the publication of the OECDs annual *Education at a Glance* 'provoked a considerable amount of debate, some well-informed but much reflecting a deliberate misrepresentation of its findings and their implications'. Naumann (2005, p. 230) stated that much of the discussion in Germany surrounding the aftermath of the 2000 PISA assessments was 'shaped by alarmist interpretations about the "mediocrity" of Germany within the group of countries compared'. Naumann (2005, p. 230) believed the reasons for this were partly because the statistics do not look at medium and long-term development trends, '...nor the reasons for certain countries reaching the top positions ... nor why some have "dropped down" to their present position'. Moreover, can countries really 'drop down' in these 'international league tables'? The number of countries that take part in PISA, for example, has increased with every cycle up until 2009. The number of countries participating in 2000 was 43, in 2003 it was 41, in 2006 it was 56, in 2009 it was 65, and in 2012 it was 65 (OECD, 2001, 2004, 2007, 2010, and 2013d). This changes the total number of participants and therefore questions whether it is fair to judge performance between surveys.

One of the main issues with statistical data lies in the comparability of it, particularly as definitions and educational terms vary from country to country. Postlethwaite and Leung (2007, p. 223) also ask: 'So is it fair to compare the nine year olds in the Netherlands who have had five years of schooling with the nine year olds in South American countries who have just started school?'

There has been much criticism that statistics focus on the nation state as the primary unit of analysis (Crossley, 2012). There are many who argue that, as a result of globalisation, the power of national governments to influence educational policy and practice is in decline (see Spring, 2009). We live in an increasingly interconnected, borderless and multicultural world so should we be studying societies or groups of individuals within nations rather than nations themselves?

Nations vary in geographical size and population. How does this affect the sample? Does it accurately represent the entire nation, particularly those which are multicultural? Despite best efforts, surveys are only conducted on a sample of the population and can 'only represent an estimate of the performance of the target populations', added to which 'statistics cannot meaningfully take account of variations in different groups with complete accuracy and therefore errors can be included' (Edwards, 2009, p. 59). Then, should we only compare countries that are similar in size and ethnic composition? Buckingham (2012) points out that many of the top-performing countries in PISA and TIMSS are small nations or city-states. Countries like Australia, where the schools are spread over a large landmass (23 times the size of Finland, for example), have greater logistical challenges. Moreover, 'Australia is also much more culturally, ethnically and socioeconomically diverse than the top five PISA countries' (Buckingham, 2012, p. 5).

Linked to cultural and ethnic diversity is language. Some countries are more linguistically diverse than others. Edwards (2009, p. 49) asks the question: 'When measuring literacy levels is it fair to directly compare the performance of those nations which have speakers of many different first languages with those in which there is one mother tongue?' Other language issues can be found in the translation of tests into students' own language. While there are strict translation and adaptation guidelines, poorly translated test items challenge the validity of international studies in achievement (Hambleton, 2002). Furthermore, is the questionnaire design largely based on 'Western' models of learning and cognitive development (see Naumann, 2005)? Hambleton also points out that the test formats can be problematic; for example, multiple choice items may be less familiar to students in some parts of the world, such as China and Africa.

Another disadvantage of international surveys is that fees are charged to participate. For example, the fees for TIMSS 2011 were 22,500 euros or US dollars per year to test one year grade or 32,000 euros or US dollars to test two year grades for each of the four years of the project (2009–2012) (IEA, 2011c). Schneider (2009, p. 74) estimates that in the United States if all states participate, the total cost would be around $25 million per PISA assessment and $15 million per grade in TIMMs. Some question whether this is money well spent and others might ask who really benefits from such testing?

In other words, it is very expensive to participate in international surveys. Perhaps due to the huge costs involved, Kamens and McNeely (2010) report that only 35% of countries take part in international testing or, looking at it another way, 65% are not yet involved. In addition, about 43% of the poorest countries have not done international testing, although some have completed one or more national assessments (Kamens & McNeely, 2010). It could be argued that international surveys are largely the domain of industrialised or developed countries. For lower income countries who participate, is it fair to compare them with high-income countries as they are at different stages of their development?

Conclusion

Despite the criticisms surrounding international statistics and surveys, they are likely to remain an important source of comparative education data. They provide information on national education systems which help governments to decide on educational policy. They can show what our relative strengths and weaknesses are and point us in the direction of how we might improve. They tell us how well our schools are preparing our citizens to enter a world that is increasingly interconnected and fiercely competitive. For students, policy makers, academics and researchers, at the heart of comparative education lies the key question: what can we learn from others? Statistics and international surveys can help us do that. However, to fully understand, appreciate and utilise them to their fullest capacity, they need to be explored in the context of a country's culture and certainly with a healthy amount of caution. Kandel (1933, p. xxv) wrote in the early part of the twentieth century that 'In course of time it may be possible to secure some international standards in educational statistics or evolve methods for reducing the present statistics to common standards'. Eighty years on, has this now been achieved?

Case Study 2   The Finnish success story

In all the PISA assessments since 2000, Finland has consistently ranked at the top and also performs consistently across schools. In 2012, while it did not rank in the top five for maths, it came 12th out 65 and was above the OECD average of 494 with an overall mean score of 519.

Table 2.1   Top five highest PISA results

2000	2003	2006	2009	2012
Reading	Maths	Science	Reading	Maths
1. Finland 546	Finland 544	Finland 536	Shanghai China 556	Shanghai China 613
2. Canada 534	South Korea 542	Canada 534	South Korea 539	Singapore 573
3. New Zealand 529	Netherlands 538	Japan 531	Finland 536	Hong Kong China 561
4. Australia 528	Japan 534	New Zealand 530	Hong Kong China 533	Chinese Taipei 560
5. Ireland 527	Canada 532	Australia 527	Singapore 526	Korea 554

Source: OECD, 2001, 2004, 2007, 2010, 2013d

According to an OECD (2011b, p. 118) report, 'no other country has so little variation in outcomes between schools, and the gap within schools between the top and bottom-achieving students is extraordinarily modest as well'. Finnish schools are highly equitable and offer fair opportunities for all its students regardless of family background or socio-economic status (OECD, 2013c). According to the Finnish National Board of Education (2011), 'The main objective of Finnish education policy is to offer all citizens equal opportunities to receive education, regardless of age, domicile, financial situation, sex or mother tongue. Education is considered to be one of the fundamental rights of all citizens.'

Because of its remarkable success, Finland has become a destination for modern-day education 'travellers' who are looking to find the reasons behind the success of Finnish schooling.

Key questions:

• Conduct some research on Finland. How is the system organised? Who is responsible for education? Who are the teachers and how are they trained? What do students study? How do the answers to these questions (and any others you have thought of) contribute to the Finnish success?

(Continued)

(Continued)

- Do you think Finnish schools might be more equitable and if so why?

- What are the reasons behind Finland's success?

- Is it possible for other countries to copy the Finnish system?

- With strong performances from Asian countries in the 2012 PISA round, will China in particular become the next destination for education 'travellers'?

Suggested reading

Crossley, M. & Watson, K. (2003) *Comparative and International Research in Education: Globalisation, Context and Difference*. Abingdon: Routledge
Chapter 3, 'Difficulties in conducting comparative and international research in education', is of particular interest. For example, it offers subsections on the bias and accuracy of data and on the limitations of statistical data.

Explore any of the websites mentioned in this chapter or in the list of References. Start compiling your own database of useful statistics and country-specific information.

References

Allen, R. (2011) The economics of education, in B. Dufour & W. Curtis (eds), *Studying Education: An Introduction to the Key Disciplines in Education Studies*. Maidenhead: Open University Press

Bereday, G. (1964) *Comparative Method in Education*. New York: Holt, Rinehart and Winston

Brickman, W. (2010) Comparative education in the nineteenth century. *European Education*, 42(2), 46–56

Bryman, A. (2008) *Social Research Methods* (3rd edition). Oxford: Oxford University Press

Buckingham, J. (2012) Keeping PISA in perspective: Why Australian education policy should not be driven by international test results. Available online at: www.cis.org.au

Bulle, N. (2011) Comparing OECD educational models through the prism of PISA. *Comparative Education*, 47(4), 503–521

CMEC (Council of Ministers of Education, Canada) (2009) *PISA 2009 FAQ*. Available online at: www.cmec.ca/docs/pisa2009/PISA2009-FAQ-EN.pdf

Coughlan, S. (2013) *UK Weak in School Fairness Rankings*. BBC News: Education and Family. Available online at: www.bbc.co.uk/news/education-21411251

Crossley, M. (2012) Comparative education and research capacity building: Reflections on international transfer and the significance of context. *Journal of International and Comparative Education*, 1(1), 4–12

Crossley, M. & Watson, K. (2003) *Comparative and International Research in Education: Globalisation, Context and Difference*. Abingdon: Routledge

Curtis, W. & Pettigrew, A. (2010) *Education Studies: Reflective Reader*. Exeter: Learning Matters

EACEA (2009) *Eurydice*. Available online at: http://eacea.ec.europa.eu/education/eurydice/index_en.php

EACEA (2012) *Key Data on Teaching Languages at School in Europe*. Available online at: http://eacea.ec.europa.eu/education/eurydice/documents/key_data_series/143EN.pdf

EACEA (2013a) *About Eurydice*. Available online at: http://eacea.ec.europa.eu/education/eurydice/about_eurydice_en.php

EACEA (2013b) *Thematic Reports*. Available online at: http://eacea.ec.europa.eu/education/eurydice/thematic_reports_en.php

Edwards, A. (2009) High schools and high stakes assessments, in W. Bignold & L. Gayton (eds), *Global Issues and Comparative Education*. Exeter: Learning Matters

Ertl, H. (2006) Educational standards and the changing discourse on education: The reception and consequences of the PISA study in Germany. *Oxford Review of Education*, 32(5), 619–634

European Commission (2013) *About Eurostat*. Available online at: http://epp.eurostat.ec.europa.eu/portal/page/portal/about_eurostat/introduction

Finnish Board of Education (2011) *Education Structure*. Available online at: www.oph.fi/english/education/overview_of_the_education_system

Grek, S. (2009) Governing by numbers: The PISA 'effect' in Europe. *Journal of Education Policy*, 24(1), 23–37

Hambleton, R. (2002) Adapting achievement tests into multiple languages for international assessments, in National Research Council, *Methodological Advances in Cross-National Surveys of Educational Achievement*. Washington, DC: National Academy Press

Heyneman, S. (1999) The sad story of UNESCO's education statistics, *International Journal of Educational Development*, 19, 65–74

Hutchinson, D. & Schagen, I. (2006) Comparisons between PISA and TIMMS: Are we the man with two watches? National Foundation for Educational Research, presented at the IEA Second International Research Conference, Washington, DC, 9–11 November 2006. Available online at: www.brookings.edu/gs/brown/irc2006conference/HutchinsonSchagen_presentation.pdf

IBE (2013) *IBE Databases*. Available online at: www.ibe.unesco.org/en/services/online-materials/databases.html

IEA (2011a) *Brief History*. Available online at: www.iea.nl/brief_history.html

IEA (2011b) *IEA Studies*. Available online at: www.iea.nl/studies.html

IEA (2011c) *IEA TIMSS 2011*. Available online at: www.iea.nl/?id=290

IEA (2011d) *IEA Current Studies*. Available online at: www.iea.nl/current_studies.html

Kamens, D. & McNeely, C. (2010) Globalization and the growth of international educational testing and national assessment. *Comparative Education Review*, 54(1), 5–25

Kandel, I.L. (1933) *Studies in Comparative Education*. London: George Harrap & Co

Keates, C. (2012) Education at a glance: Looking at the evidence objectively. *The Guardian*, available online at: www.guardian.co.uk/teacher-network/2012/sep/12/oecd-education-at-a-glance-overview

Leimu, K. (2004) Comparing results from different countries, subjects and grade levels, in J. Moskowitz & M. Stephens (eds), *Comparing Learning Outcomes: International Assessment and Education Policy*. London: Routledge

Martin, M.O., Mullis, I.V.S., Foy, P. & Stanco, G.M. (2012) *TIMSS 2011 International Results in Science*. Boston, MA: TIMSS & PIRLS International Study Center

Mullis, I., Martin, M. & Foy, P. (2005) *TIMSS 2003 International Report on Achievement in the Mathematics Cognitive Domains: Findings from a Development Project*. Boston, MA: TIMSS & PIRLS International Study Center

Murat, F. & Rocher, T. (2004) The methods used for international assessments of educational competences, in J. Moskowitz & M. Stephens (eds), *Comparing Learning Outcomes: International Assessment and Education Policy*. London: Routledge

Naumann, J. (2005) TIMSS, PISA, PIRLS, and low educational achievement in world society. *Prospects*, 35(2), 231–248

NFER (2013) INCA International Review of Curriculum and Assessment Frameworks Internet Archive. Available online at: www.inca.org.uk/index.html

Noah, H. & Eckstein, M. (1969) *Toward a Science of Comparative Education*. New York: Macmillan

OECD (2001) *Knowledge and Skills: First Results from PISA 2000*. Available online at: www.keepeek.com/Digital-Asset-Management/oecd/education/knowledge-and-skills-for-life_9789264195905-en

OECD (2004) *OECD Handbook for Internationally Comparative Education Statistics: Concepts, Standards, Definitions and Classifications*. Paris: OECD

OECD (2007) *Science Competencies for Tomorrow's World*. Available online at: www.oecd.org/edu/school/programmeforinternationalstudentassessment pisa/pisa2006results.htm#Vol_1_and_2

OECD (2010) *PISA 2009 Results: What Students Know and Can Do – Student Performance in Reading, Mathematics and Science (Volume I)*. Available online at: http://dx.doi.org/10.1787/9789264091450-en

OECD (2011a) *CERI: Centre for Educational Research and Innovation*. Available online at: www.oecd.org/edu/ceri/38446790.pdf

OECD (2011b) *Lessons from PISA for the United States, Strong Performers and Successful Reformers in Education*. Available online at: www.oecd-ilibrary.org/education/lessons-from-pisa-for-the-united-states_9789264096660-en

OECD (2012) *Education at a Glance 2012: OECD Indicators*. Available online at: http//dx.doi.org/10.1787/eag-2012-en

OECD (2013a) *About the OECD*. Available online at: www.oecd.org/about/

OECD (2013b) *About the OECD Programme for International Student Assessment (PISA)*. Available online at: www.oecd.org/pisa/pisaproducts/#d.en.192289

OECD (2013c) *PISA: In Focus*. Number 25. Available online at: www.oecd.org/pisa/pisainfocus/

OECD (2013d) *PISA 2012 Results: What Students Know and Can Do – Student Performance in Mathematics, Reading and Science (Volume I)*. Available online at: www.keepeek.com/Digital-Asset-Management/oecd/education/pisa-2012-results-what-students-know-and-can-do-volume-i_9789264201118-en#page3

Pearson Foundation (2013) *Strong Performers and Successful Reformers in Education: A Video Series Profiling Policies and Practices of Education Systems that Demonstrate High or Improving Performance in the PISA Tests*. Available online at: www.pearsonfoundation.org/oecd/germany.html

Postlethwaite, N. & Leung, F. (2007) Comparing educational achievements, in M. Bray, B. Adamson & M. Mason (eds), *Comparative Education Research: Approaches and Methods*. Hong Kong: Springer

Sargent, C., Houghton, E. & O'Donnell, S. (2012) *INCA Comparative Tables*. Available online at: www.inca.org.uk/documents/INCAcomparativetables October2012final.pdf

Schneider, M. (2009) *The International PISA Test: A Risky Investment for States*. Available online at: http://educationnext.org/files/fall09-international-pisa.pdf

Spring, J. (2009) *Globalization of Education: An Introduction*. Abingdon: Routledge

Takayama, K. (2009) Politics of externalization in reflexive times: Reinventing Japanese education reform discourses through 'Finnish PISA Success'. *Comparative Education Review*, 54(1), 51–75

UNESCO (2013) *About the UIS*. Available online at: www.uis.unesco.org/ AboutUIS/Pages/default.aspx

Wood, K. (2011) *Education: The Basics*. London: Routledge

Wu, M. (2010) *Comparing the Similarities and Differences of PISA 2003 and TIMSS*. OECD Education Working Papers, No. 32. OECD Publishing. Available online at: http://dx.doi.org/10.1787/5km4psnm13nx-en

CHAPTER 3

CULTURE AND EDUCATION

This chapter explores:

- The meaning of culture, and national culture in particular;
- The relationship between national culture and education;
- The cultural context in which education takes place.

 Activity 3.1   What is culture?

How would you define culture? Can you give examples of what represents your national culture?

Why is it important to understand culture and education?

When we compare education systems, we inevitably find both similarities and differences. How do we account for these? Does the answer rest with cultural difference? In Chapter 2, we saw that a major criticism and limitation of statistics was that they fail to consider the cultural dimension of education: 'Culture is the context in which things happen; out of context, even legal matters lack significance' (Trompenaars & Hampden-Turner, 1988, p. 8). Can we fully understand PISA results, for example, without reflecting on the relationship between education and the wider society? Is there something about Finnish culture that promotes and encourages students to achieve? 'The degree to which culture – history, social norms, religion, and other factors – influences the philosophy, principles, and practices of schooling cannot be overstated' (Mazurek & Winzer, 2006, p. 15). There are many different layers of culture, where the top layer or the 'highest level is the culture of a national or regional society' (Trompenaars & Hampden-Turner, 1988, p. 7).

This chapter explores the relationship between culture – national culture in particular – and education as a means to explain both similarities and differences between systems. The focus of this chapter is on this top layer or national culture as national systems of education are the primary unit of analysis in comparative education. There is also a lot of data available on national systems of education, as shown in Chapter 2. When we examine education in different countries, it soon becomes clear that the subjects which are studied, the status and role of teachers and the organisation of the school day are some of the things that can be attributed to the culture in which they take place. Learning does not happen in isolation (Nieto, 2010) and is a cultural activity (Curtis & Pettigrew, 2009).

Many scholars in the field have argued the very same point. As discussed in Chapter 1, there was a shift in the first half of the twentieth century from cataloguing descriptive data to examining the social and cultural factors influencing education. At this time, it was recognised that educational ideas, policies, practices could not just be borrowed and transplanted from one country to another without considering context. Furthermore, Kandel (1933, p. xxii) wrote that '...educational systems are dominated by national ends'. This idea was not new as philosophers such as Jean Jacques Rousseau believed that education was an important tool for building nations (Wiborg, 2000). For Rousseau, education played a huge role in creating future citizens; it was something that could not be left as the sole responsibility of parents. Furthermore, one of the primary functions of all legitimate governments was to provide a system of public education. Rousseau's ideas, along with others (such as Condorcet, Fichte) '... have been powerful forces in the creation of national education systems within and outside Europe' (Wiborg, 2000, p. 235).

Kandel (1933, p. 8) felt it was important to understand how education contributed to nationalism, whereby 'Nationalism implies a common language, common customs, and a common culture'. Alexander (2001, p. 168) writes: 'So in France, what it is to be French is, and has long remained, an explicit focus for national educational goals and curricula (citizenship, general culture, the disciplined mind) and for structure (consistency and equality of provision at every level from primary school to university, and a competitive and meritocratic ethos from secondary level onwards).'

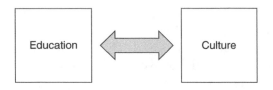

Figure 3.1   Education and culture: a two-way process

There are two important questions that need to be asked regarding these ideas. First, how does education contribute to a common culture and, secondly, in light of globalisation, does a common culture exist nationally? The answer to the second question will be explored in Chapter 8.

Kandel (1933, p. xxiv) further argued that 'Each national system of education is characteristic of the nation which has created it and expresses something peculiar to the group which constitutes that nation'. He also believed that, '[a]t the same time … educational systems are living things, compounded of traditions, culture, and ideals' (Kandel, 1933, p. xxiv). In other words, how is education shaped by culture?

What is culture?

Before we can delve into the relationship between national culture and education, we need to first think about what culture is. Raymond Williams, a key academic in the field of cultural studies, wrote that: 'Culture is one of the two or three most complicated words in the English language' (Williams, 1983, p. 87). Laugani (2007, p. 30) similarly states that: 'Like most abstract words such as intelligence, personality, goodness, virtue, the word "culture" is also difficult to define.' There is no agreed definition on the meaning of culture and numerous definitions abound (see Anderson-Levitt, 2012; Wren, 2012). However, there are a number of ways of looking at culture that can help us identify its relationship to education.

Culture is what many anthropologists are interested in studying and the term was first used by the British anthropologist Edward B. Tylor in his seminal work *Primitive Culture*. He defined culture as 'that complex whole which includes knowledge, belief, art, morals, law, custom, and any other capabilities and habits acquired by man as a member of society' (Tylor, 1871, in Wren, 2012, p. 28). Many scholars in comparative education apply definitions of culture from the field of anthropology to their work in education. For example, Masemann (2013, p. 114) cites a definition proposed by Keesing (1960) which says that culture is 'concerned with actions, ideas, and artifacts which individuals in the tradition concerned learn, share and value'. Sternberg (2007, p. 5) defines culture from the work of Barnouw (1985) as 'the set of attitudes, values, beliefs and behaviours shared by a group of people, communicated from one generation to the next via language or some other means of communication'. Lastly, Thaman (1993, p. 249), writing about culture and the curriculum in the South Pacific, put forward the following:

> For the purposes of this discussion, culture is taken to mean the way of life of a discrete group of people, including its body of accumulated knowledge and understandings, skills, beliefs and values. Following the tradition of cognitive anthropology, culture is seen as central to the understanding of human relationships and acknowledges the fact that members of different cultural groups have unique systems of perceiving and organising the world around them. This means that the ways in which we are socialised, to a very large extent, influence our behaviour and ways of thinking – in other words, the way we see the world around us.

For the purposes of this book, a definition of culture is taken from the research of Geert Hofstede, a professor of organisational anthropology. Hofstede, Hofstede and Minkov (2010) have referred to culture as mental software which guides peoples' patterns of thinking, feeling and acting. The programming for the software stems from the social environment – family, schooling, the community, friends, and the workplace – and '[m]ental programs vary as much as the social environments in which they were acquired' (Hofstede et al., 2010, p. 5). Because culture is shared or partly shared with the people who live in the same social environment, it is said to be a collective phenomenon. 'It is the collective programming of the mind that distinguishes the members of the group or category of people from others' (Hofstede et al., 2010, p. 6). The term culture can be applied to any human collective or group of individuals. This chapter is interested in how education and schooling in particular help to 'programme' individuals, societies and nations' 'software' of the mind.

Activity 3.2   Education and socialisation

What is meant by socialisation? How are we socialised through education? Why might this be culturally-specific? Can you give an example?

A set of core values and traditions is a primary feature of all cultures (Laungani, 2007) and can be defined as 'a broad tendency to prefer certain states of affairs over others' (Hofstede, 2001, p. 5). According to Hofstede, our values are programmed early in life and are concerned with things such as evil versus good; dirty versus clean; dangerous versus safe, and so forth. In other words, values determine what is 'good' or 'bad' and are closely related to the ideals shared by a group (Trompenaars & Hampden-Turner, 1988). Our values are invisible but can show themselves in our behaviour (norms) and form the basis for order in many aspects of society. Norms are how we should behave and can be both formal (law) or informal. Education plays a key role in promoting the shared values of a particular culture.

 Activity 3.3   Values and norms

Here is a list of values: Aggressiveness; Discipline; Equality; Fairness; Innovation; Punctuality; Silence; Youthfulness. Think about your region or country. Can you identify any of these values people may or may not hold? Can you add any values to the list? Can you think of any norms (how people should behave) that are based on these values?

How does culture shape education?

How does schooling in particular transmit culture? Many would agree that education plays a major role in teaching young people about the world in which they live. 'It is a way of passing on information from one generation to the next; but more than this, it is a way of preserving particular cultures and traditions. The young are inducted into the values and beliefs which an individual society holds dear. Aboriginal stories, Chinese revolutionary fables and English fairy tales, are all about teaching young children the ideas and values which are important to their society' (Wood, 2011, p. 35).

 Activity 3.4   Literature and values

Think of some of books or stories that were central to your learning in primary school or are part of the curriculum. What values or beliefs were proposed? Is this beneficial to society? Can you think of instances where there might be a clash of values?

Decisions about education (for example, what is taught and how it is taught) are based on beliefs and values or ideologies (Bartlett & Burton, 2012). Numerous educational ideologies have been offered over the years. According to Meighan and Harber (2007, p. 218), 'An ideology of education may be defined as the set of ideas and beliefs held by a group of people about the formal arrangements for education, specifically schooling, and often, by extension or by implication, also about informal aspects of education, e.g. learning at home'.

The educational ideology adopted by a society or country will depend on their cultural values and beliefs. Educational ideologies can emphasise the individual (the needs and interest of the learner being central), knowledge (the importance of formal knowledge arranged in subjects and where students start by learning basic facts and then progress through complex levels) or society (to develop, improve and modernise the economy) (Bartlett & Burton, 2012).

Curriculum and culture

Educational ideologies play an important role in shaping the curriculum, and nowhere is culture more evidently displayed than in a country's curriculum (Joseph, 2010). '[The] curriculum embodies distinct beliefs about the type of knowledge that should be taught in schools, the inherent nature of children, what school learning consists of, how teachers should instruct children, and how children should be assessed' (Schiro, 2013, p. 2). What is chosen for pupils to learn can have an immense influence on society and the economy.

 Activity 3.5   Curriculum and culture

What does your country value (for example, creativity, sport)? How is this shown in the curriculum?

Robin Alexander (2001), in his comparative research on primary education in England, France, Russia, India and the United States of America, looked at the cultural context in which education takes place, hence the title of his book *Culture and Pedagogy*. In terms of the curriculum, he found that the 'combination of similarity and difference extends to the curriculum as a whole' (Alexander, 2001, p. 156). This related to the subjects taught, how the curriculum was interpreted, and how it was ultimately implemented in schools. He reported distinct variations in the amount of attention given to science. In England, the core curriculum includes English, mathematics and science; in France, core subjects consist of French, history, geography and civic education. Beliefs and values in what is important for society and the economy are demonstrated by this finding. Referring to the above distinction in the English and French curriculum, Alexander writes: 'On the one hand we have imperatives of economy and employment; on the other those of civil society and citizenship' (2001, p. 157). What aspects of culture, then, influence education in this way?

Activity 3.6 Subjects studied and international surveys

Using the example above concerning the English and French curriculum, look again at TIMMS and PISA results. Which country performs better in science? Why is science an important part of the National Curriculum for England and Wales?

Dimensions of national culture

'Nowhere do cultures differ so much as inside Europe' (Trompenaars & Hampden-Turner, 1988, p. 8). There is much evidence for this when looking at dimensions of national culture. Hofstede (2001) conducted research on how cultural values influence the workplace with IBM employees between 1967 and 1973 in 72 countries. His work revealed four dimensions of national culture: power distance (the extent to which the less powerful members of organisations and institutions accept and expect the power is distributed unequally); uncertainty avoidance (the extent to which a culture programmes its members to feel either uncomfortable or comfortable in unstructured situations); individualism versus collectivism (the degree to which individuals are supposed to look after themselves or remain integrated into groups, usually around the family); and masculinity versus femininity (refers to the distribution of emotional roles between the genders). A fifth dimension, long-term versus short-term orientation (which refers to the extent to which a culture programmes its members to accept delayed gratification of their material, social, and emotional needs) was added independent of the IBM studies based on the research of Michael Bond (Hofstede, 2001). More recently, Hofstede et al. (2010) included a sixth dimension, indulgence versus restraint (indulgence stands for a society that allows relatively free gratification of basic and natural human drives related to enjoying life and having fun whereas restraint stands for a society that suppresses gratification of needs and regulates it by means of strict social norms). The sixth dimension is based on the work of Michael Minkov's anlaysis of the World Values Survey data for 93 countries.

 Activity 3.7 Dimensions of national culture

Go to the Hofstede website at: http://geert-hofstede.com/the-hofstede-centre.html. The information on the website can be found in the book entitled *Cultures and Organizations: Software of the Mind* (Hofstede et al., 2010). Look in the tabs entitled National Culture and then countries. Select two or more countries and compare their cultural dimensions. How might these relate to education?

How do dimensions of national culture relate to education? A good example can be seen when comparing power distance differences between countries. Power distance (PDI) basically measures how society deals with inequality. In societies with high PDI, such as Slovakia, Malaysia and Guatemala, inequality is seen as 'the basis of societal order' whereas in societies with low PDI, such as Denmark, Israel and Austria, inequality is seen as 'a necessary evil that should be minimized' (Hofstede, 2001, p. 97). In terms of education, mental programming is developed in schools whereby teachers and pupils instil the values upheld by their culture (Hofstede, 2001). Values concerning equality are therefore reinforced through education.

In societies with low or small PDI, where inequalities among people should be minimised, students treat teachers as equals and see them as experts who transmit knowledge objectively. Teachers expect students to take initiatives in class and the quality of learning depends on two-way communication and the excellence of the students. Those who are less educated hold more authoritarian values than those who are more educated. Lastly, in low PDI societies, education policy focuses on secondary schools (Hofstede et al., 2010).

In comparison, in societies with a high PDI, where inequalities among people are accepted and even sought after, students give teachers respect both in and outside the classroom. Teachers are expected to take the initiative and the quality of learning depends on their excellence rather than the students. They are considered 'gurus' who transfer personal wisdom rather than objective knowledge. Authoritarian values are demonstrable equally in those who are more educated and less educated. Finally, educational policy focuses on universities (Hofstede et al., 2010).

In cultures with a high PDI teachers are treated with respect and there is much formality in the student–teacher relationship. Van Oord (2005) recounts a conversation with a Peruvian student (Peru has a high power distance), from a non-expatriate background, who left her country for the first time to attend an international school in Norway. The student was asked about what she felt was the biggest difference between the two countries. She complained a little bit about Nordic food, but the biggest difference was the relationship between students and teachers. 'In Peru, she explained, teachers were close to almighty and would always be addressed by their last name. It took her at least two months, she said, to get used to the Nordic custom of using the teachers' first names' (Van Oord, 2005, p. 185). Then when she went back to Peru during Christmas break she visited her old school. There she addressed one of her former teachers by saying, '"Nice to see you, Enrico!" Enrico was shocked. How dare she address him by his first name!' (p. 185). In societies with a high PDI, like Peru, clearly calling a teacher by their first name is too informal and therefore very disrespectful.

Power distance and equality can be looked at in other ways. As mentioned in Chapter 2, PISA (Programme for International Student

Table 3.1   Selected countries with PDI scores and equity values. PDI scores range from 11 to 104; Equity scores range from 20 (high equity) to 140 (low equity)

Power Distance scores (PDI)	Equity levels
Slovakia 104	87
Panama 95	110
Russia 93	78
Romania 90	86
Serbia 86	65
Mexico 81	85
Slovenia 71	88
Bulgaria 70	130
Peru 64	131
Austria 11	105
Israel 13	104
Denmark 22	86
Ireland 28	86
Sweden 31	92

Source: Hofstede et al., 2010 and OECD, 2013

Assessment) looks at whether systems are equitable. 'Ideally, school systems provide high-quality educational opportunities for all students, irrespective of the student's backgrounds. Students from socio-economically advantaged families and those from disadvantaged families should be equally likely to succeed in school' (OECD, 2013). Indeed, this may be true for countries with low power distance, where inequalities among people should be minimised. One might expect, then, a correlation between equity levels found in PISA and PDI scores (see Table 3.1). The higher the PDI means the greater the power distance between individuals. However, high power distance does not always mean that educational systems are inequitable.

Some countries with a high power distance score, such as Panama, Bulgaria and Peru, also demonstrate high inequality in educational opportunities. However, other countries, such as Austria, Israel and Sweden, exhibit low power distance scores but higher levels of inequality in educational opportunities. The question remains, therefore, why are these educational systems not more equitable and fair if equality is an underpinning core value of their culture?

Individualism versus collectivism is another dimension of national culture. Hofstede (2001, p. 225) defines it as:

> Individualism stands for a society in which the ties between individuals are loose: Everyone is expected to look after him/herself and her/his immediate family only. Collectivism stands for a society in which people from birth onwards are integrated into strong,

cohesive groups, which throughout people's lifetime continue to protect them in exchange for unquestioning loyalty.

Essentially, individualistic societies are where the interests of the individual prevail over the group (Hofstede, 2001). In these types of society, '[t]he purpose of education is to enable children to stand on their own feet' (Hofstede et al., 2010, p. 91). Individualistic countries include, at the top of the list, the United States, Australia, Great Britain, Canada, Hungary and the Netherlands. Collectivist countries include Guatemala, Ecuador, Panama, Venezuela, Colombia and Pakistan (Hofstede et al., 2010).

There are several key differences between collectivist and individualist societies in school. In individualist societies, students are expected to speak up in class whereas in collectivist societies students mainly speak up in class when permitted by the group. The purpose of education is seen differently; in individualist societies the aim of education is learning how to learn. This means instilling in individuals a love for learning that will carry on throughout their life (lifelong learning). Education should enable people to be resilient and help them to develop strategies for dealing with the new and unexpected (Hofstede et al., 2010).

In collectivist societies, the purpose of education is on learning how to do. This means there is an emphasis on learning new skills and how to be an acceptable member of the group. 'Learning is more often seen as a onetime process, reserved for young people, who have to learn how to do things in order to participate in society' (Hofstede, 2010, p. 119). Additionally, educational qualifications provide entry to higher status-groups in collectivist societies whereas in individualist societies they increase one's own economic worth and self-respect, placing more emphasis on the self rather than the group.

 Activity 3.8 Individualism versus collectivism

Which type of society do you come from? Individualist or collectivist? How did your experience at school reflect this? Was there an emphasis on 'knowing how to learn'?

A good example of this can be found in Japan. Although Japan falls somewhere in the middle between individualism and collectivism according to Hofstede's (2001) research, it generally considers itself to be group-oriented and homogeneous. Jandt (2009, p. 173) writes: 'In such an extremely homogeneous society, you are not seen as an individual, nor do you regard individualism as a positive trait. It has been said that group life is to the Japanese what individualism is to the United States.

Homogeneity is the core value of society that substantially defines other values and permeates all areas of life.'

According to Hays (2009), '[t]he Japanese educational system lays emphasis on cooperative behaviour, group discipline, and conformity to standards. In school children are taught cooperative behaviour and functioning in groups. There is an emphasis on uniformity in Japanese schools.' Therefore, values of collectivism influence behaviour and play an important role in Japanese culture and society. Education serves to reinforce these values and socialise young Japanese children to behave according to them. 'In every aspect, teachers teach pupils how to behave in group life' (Numata, 2006, p. 39).

The final cultural dimension to be discussed in this chapter is that of masculinity versus femininity. Masculine societies have very clear, distinct and traditional gender roles. Hofstede (2001, p. 297) says: 'Men are supposed to be assertive, tough, and focused on material success; women are supposed to be more modest, tender, and concerned with the quality of life. Femininity stands for a society in which social gender roles overlap: Both men and women are supposed to be modest, tender, and concerned with the quality of life.' According to Hofstede (2001), masculine countries include Slovakia, Japan, Hungary, Austria, Venezuela, Italy, Great Britain and the United States. On the other hand, feminine countries include Sweden, Norway, Latvia, the Netherland, Denmark, Slovenia and Lithuania (Hofstede et al., 2010).

So how does being a 'masculine' or 'feminine' country influence education? In masculine countries, competition plays a major role in education. In class, students are encouraged to be competitive and students try to outdo each other. Competitive sports are part of the curriculum and aggression by children is accepted and sometimes even encouraged. In their quest to be the best, students will exaggerate their own abilities and failing in school is not an option. There is also a distinction between men and women in terms of what they study and more women teach young children than men. Lastly, more non-fiction is read in masculine societies and they engage in more report talk (impersonal and efficient information exchange) (Hofstede et al., 2010).

In feminine societies, competition plays more of a minor role in education as compared to masculine ones. In class, weaker students tend to receive all the praise and therefore there is less jealousy towards those who excel. Being the best student is not the norm, so students tend to underrate their own abilities and failing is only minor. Competitive sports are extracurricular rather than part of the curriculum and children are socialised to be non-aggressive. Teachers should be friendly and both men and women teach young children. Lastly, there is less distinction between the subjects men and women study, more fiction than non-fiction is read, and they engage in more rapport talk (building relationships) than report talk (Hofstede et al., 2010).

As stated above, women teach young children in masculine countries. Is this really the case? Looking at the United Kingdom (masculine), individuals working in early years education (birth to five years old) are 97% female (Fong & Phelps, 2008). Similarly, in Japan (masculine), approximately 94% of those working in early years (kindergarten) are female (Ministry of Internal Affairs and Communication, 2008). The gender ratio is very much the same in primary education as well. In the UK, 86% of teaching staff is female (Peeters, 2007). What about in feminine countries? Do more men work in early years and primary education? The most feminine countries, according to Hofstede et al. (2010), are Sweden, Norway, Latvia and the Netherlands. In a research report for the European Trade Union Confederation, it was stated that the percentage of male teachers in primary education is highest in Albania (45%)[masculine/feminine unknown], while in Cyprus [unknown], Denmark [feminine], Greece [middle], Serbia [feminine] and Sweden [feminine], male teachers make up between 20% and 40% (Galgóczi & Glassner, 2008). Even at secondary school level, the Netherlands [feminine], Malta [feminine] and Sweden [feminine] are the only countries that reported more male teachers (51%) than female teachers (Galgóczi & Glassner, 2008).

Limitations

When comparing education systems, there may be noticeable differences in attitudes, values and behaviours that are not easily understood. There is a danger that these may be explained away in terms of cultural differences and '[t]he term "culture" may then become the wastebasket into which unexplainable, unacceptable, social and moral behaviours are often dropped' (Laungani, 2007, p. 30). Aspects of culture may be hard to determine, particularly if we are an outsider looking in.

Also, as an outsider, one has to be careful of adopting an ethnocentric approach (Bereday, 1964), as mentioned in Chapter 1. 'An ethnocentric approach is when a person looks at, and evaluates, the experience of other countries against their own norms and values' (Kay-Flowers, 2009, p. 96). An ethnocentric approach usually involves us seeing our own culture as best and therefore we make judgements according to our own standards rather than those which are culturally appropriate. This can lead to bias and in some situations even prejudice.

In contrast, we should try to frame our understanding of cultural differences within the context of cultural relativism. 'Relativists claim that knowledge must be framed within cultural contexts. Knowledge is constructed, maintained and evaluated within culture. The truth or otherwise of a proposition is dependent on the cultural settings it exists in' (Curtis & Pettigrew, 2009, pp. 40–41). By adopting a relativist position rather than an ethnocentric one, you stand a greater chance of being objective in your research. 'Objectivity in social research is the principle drawn from positivism that, as far as is possible, researchers should remain distanced from what they study so findings depend on the nature of what was studied rather than on the personality, beliefs and values of the researcher' (Payne & Payne, 2004). As mentioned in Chapter 1, many comparative education scholars, such as Noah & Eckstein (1969), argued that the field should adopt a positivist approach. However, can this suitably be achieved when trying to understand another culture?

Nations consist of multi-ethnic, multicultural groups of individuals and are therefore not homogeneous. Can research on national culture really draw from a truly representative sample? In fact, Schwartz (1999) argues for caution when making inferences about national cultures, even when data is obtained from representative national samples. Nations consist of different demographic groups of people (for example, the elderly, single parents, low-income families, male/female, and so on). The values held by the different demographic groups need to be taken into consideration when comparing the values of representative national samples. Schwartz (1999, p. 34) states: 'Consequently, even when comparing the values of representative national samples, it would still be necessary to control for demographic differences between nations before we could confidently ascribe observed differences in value priorities to national cultural alone.' Lastly, as a result of multiculturalism (discussed in Chapter 10), is there a true national culture to which everybody subscribes?

Hofstede's model of culture is one of the most widely used frameworks for understanding cultural difference (Ghemawat & Reiche, 2011). However, it is not without its criticisms (see McSweeney, 2002; Williamson, 2002; Ghemawat & Reiche, 2011). Williamson (2002) points out that Hofstede's model is too simplistic. 'National culture is a complex social phenomenon. It can be argued that to capture it in just four or five quantified dimensions misses much of what is essential to, or claimed to be represented by, national culture' (Williamson, 2002, p. 1384). How many dimensions of national culture are there then? Trompenaars & Hampden-Turner (1998) have 'found' seven, while Hofstede et al. (2010) claim there are six. Is this really a complete picture?

McSweeney (2002) basically argued that Hofstede's methodology was flawed and therefore his data have led us to incorrect assumptions about national culture. Moreover, the data were collected from just one organisation, IBM, a multinational corporation. It must be questioned whether we can generalise from this small section of society national characteristics of culture (McSweeney, 2002). Ghemawat and Reiche (2011) also point out Hofstede's data are now relatively old and it may not capture recent changes in the political environment or the workplace. However, despite these limitations, Hofstede's research has provided us with a body of knowledge and literature enabling us to think about national culture and its relationship with society.

Conclusion

The relationship between education and culture is important if we are to understand both the similarities and the differences when comparing education across national boundaries. We cannot understand aspects of education without examining the cultural context in which it takes place. Societies all hold values and beliefs which influence education – from what is taught to how something is learned. Education plays a key role in transmitting these values to its members. Students across the world experience education differently as a result. This difference can only be explained, in part, when we look very closely at national culture.

Case Study 3 Classrooms and national values

Osborn et al. (2003) conducted a study comparing the experience of young learners in England, France and Denmark in order to examine the relationship between national educational cultures, individual biographies and classroom practices in creating the context for learning. As part of their study they looked specifically at the classroom context as a reflection of national values. One aspect of this was examining teacher–pupil relationships. Before discussing their findings, how are these three countries characterised according to Hofstede's cultural model? How might these dimensions of national culture shape the classroom environment and the teacher–pupil relationship in particular?

Denmark has a PDI score of 18, France 68, and the United Kingdom 35. In terms of individualism, the UK is the most individualistic with a score of 89. This is followed by Denmark with a score of 74 and then France with a score of 71. Finally, the most masculine of the three is the UK with a score of 66, followed by France with a score of 43 and then at the bottom is Denmark with a score of 16 (Hofstede et al., 2010).

Osborn et al. (2003, p. 115) found the following:

- The distance between teacher and pupils was at its greatest in France.

- There was more inequality between teacher and pupil status in France than in England or Denmark and more formality (pupils used the *vous* from to address teachers, teachers used *tu* to pupils).

- The non-involvement of teachers in France with the affective domain of children's learning led to a relationship which was mainly restricted to the intellectual development of pupils.

- Interactions between French teachers and pupils were mainly restricted to the classroom context.

- The role of the French teacher prioritises subject expertise and pedagogic skill at transferring knowledge to pupils. Knowledge equates with power in the French classroom.

(Continued)

(Continued)

Key questions:

- How can Hofstede's model of national cultural dimensions be used to help explain Osborn et al.'s findings? Which dimension is more relevant when looking at pupil–teacher relationships?

- How might Hofstede's model also be used to explain other differences, such as assessment practice, attitudes to learning, the organisation of schools and motivation to learn?

Suggested reading

Alexander, R. (2001) *Culture and Pedagogy*. Oxford: Blackwell
This book demonstrates comparative education research at its best. Alexander's book compares the education systems at the school and classroom level of five countries: England, France, India, Russia and the United States. He used documentary, interview, observational, video and photographic data between 1994 and 1998. A core theme of this book is how national culture shapes classroom practice and the teaching and learning inside it.

Hofstede, G., Hofstede, G.J. & Minkov, M. (2010) *Culture and Organisations* (3rd edition). London: McGraw Hill
A worthy book mainly aimed at those working in a cross-cultural management capacity but equally important and a must read for those interested in understanding dimensions of national cultural and how it might link to other societal institutions such as education.

Osborn, M., Broadfoot, P., McNess, E., Planel, C., Ravn, B. & Triggs, P. (2003) *A World of Difference? Comparing Learners across Europe*. Maidenhead: Open University Press
Another example of excellent comparative education research. The book is based on research conducted in England, France and Denmark in order to examine the relationship between national educational cultures and learning in order to improve secondary education.

References

Alexander, R. (2001) *Culture and Pedagogy*. Oxford: Blackwell
Anderson-Levitt, K.M. (2012) Complicating the concept of culture. *Comparative Education*, 48(4), 441–454
Bartlett, S. & Burton, D. (2012) *Introduction to Education Studies* (3rd edition). London: Sage
Bereday, G. (1964) *Comparative Method in Education*. New York: Holt, Rinehart and Winston
Curtis, W. & Pettigrew, A. (2009) *Learning in Contemporary Culture*. Exeter: Learning Matters

Fong, B. & Phelps, A. (2008) *Apprenticeship Pay: 2007 Survey of Earnings by Sector*. DIUS Research Report. London: Department for Innovation, Universities and Skills. Available online at: http://dera.ioe.ac.uk/8726/1/DIUS-RR-08-05.pdf

Galgóczi, B. & Glassner, V. (2008) *Comparative Study of Teachers' Pay in Europe*. Available online at: http://download.ei-ie.org/Docs/WebDepot/Teachers%20 Pay%202008%20Report.pdf

Ghemawat, P. & Reiche, S. (2011) *National Cultural Differences and Multinational Business*. Available online at: www.aacsb.edu/resources/ globalization/globecourse/contents/readings/national-cultural-differences-and-multinational-business.pdf

Hays, J. (2009) *Education System in Japan*. Available online at: http://factsand-details.com/japan.php?itemid=833

Hofstede, G. (2001) *Cultures Consequences* (2nd edition). London: Sage

Hofstede, G., Hofstede, G.J. & Minkov, M. (2010) *Culture and Organisations* (3rd edition). London: McGraw Hill

Jandt, F. (2009) *An Introduction to Intercultural Communication: Identities in a Global Community* (6th edition). London: Sage

Joseph, P. (ed.) (2010) *Understanding Curriculum as Culture* (2nd edition). New York: Routledge

Kandel, I. (1933) *Studies in Comparative Education*. London: George Harrap & Co

Kay-Flowers, S. (2009) Education and social care: Friends or foes? in W. Bignold & L. Gayton (eds), *Global Issues and Comparative Education* Exeter: Learning Matters

Laungani, P. (2007) *Understanding Cross-Cultural Psychology*. London: Sage

Masemann, V. (2013) Culture and education, in R. Arnove, C. Torres & S. Franz (eds), *Comparative Education: The Dialetic of the Global and the Local* (4th edition). Plymouth: Rowman & Littlefield

Mazurek, K. & Winzer, M. (eds) (2006) *Schooling around the World: Debates, Challenges and Practices*. Boston, MA: Pearson

McSweeney, B. (2002) Hofstede's model of national cultural differences and their consequences: A triumph of faith – a failure of analysis. *Human Relations*, 55(1), 89–118

Meighan, R. & Harber, C. (2007) *A Sociology of Educating*. London: Continuum

Ministry of Internal Affairs and Communication (2008) *Chapter 25: Education*. Available online at: www.stat.go.jp/english/data/chouki/25.htm

Nieto, S. (2010) *Language, Culture, and Teaching: Critical Perspectives* (2nd edition). London: Routledge

Noah, H. & Eckstein, M. (1969) *Toward a Science of Comparative Education*. New York: Macmillan

Numata, H. (2006) Japanese schooling: Tradition and modernization, in K. Mazurek & M. Winzer (eds), *Schooling around the World: Debates, Challenges and Practices*. Boston, MA: Pearson

OECD (2013) *PISA: In Focus*. Number 25, Available online at: www.oecd.org/pisa/ pisainfocus/

Osborn, M., Broadfoot, P., McNess, E., Planel, C., Ravn, B. & Triggs, P. (2003) *A World of Difference? Comparing Learners across Europe*. Maidenhead: Open University Press

Payne, G. & Payne, J. (2004) *Key Concepts in Social Research*. Available online at: http://srmo.sagepub.com/view/key-concepts-in-social-research/n32.xml

Peeters, J. (2007) Including men in early childhood education: Insights from the European experience. *NZ Research in Early Childhood Education*, 1. Available online at: http://stop4-7.be/files/janpeeters10.pdf

Schiro, M. (2013) *Curriculum Theory: Conflicting Visions and Enduring Concerns* (2nd edition). London: Sage

Schwartz, S. (1999) A theory of cultural values and some implications for work. *Applied Psychology: An International Review*, 48(1), 23–47

Sternberg, R. (2007) Culture, instruction, and assessment. *Comparative Education*, 43(1), 5–22

Thaman, K.H. (1993) Culture and the curriculum in the South Pacific. *Comparative Education*, 29(3), 249–260

Trompenaars, F. & Hampden-Turner, C. (1988/1998) *Riding the Waves of Culture: Understanding Culture Diversity in Business* (2nd edition). London: Nicholas Brealey

Van Oord, L. (2005) Culture as a configuration of learning: Hypothesis in the context of international education. *Journal of Research in International Education*, 4(2), 173–191

Wiborg, S. (2000) Political and cultural nationalism in education: The ideas of Rousseau and Herder concerning national education. *Comparative Education*, 36(2), 235–243

Williams, R. (1983) *Keywords: A Vocabulary of Culture and Society* (revised edition). London: Fontana Paperbacks

Williamson, D. (2002) Critique of Hofstede's Model of National Culture. *Human Relations*, 55(11), 1373–1395

Wood, K. (2011) *Education: The Basics*. London: Routledge

Wren, T.E. (2012) *Conceptions of Culture: What Multicultural Educators Need to Know*. Plymouth: Rowman & Littlefield

CHAPTER 4

ECONOMIC, POLITICAL, SOCIAL AND HISTORICAL CONTEXTS FOR COMPARISON

This chapter explores:

- The economic variables that affect education;
- The political forces that shape education;
- The relationship between society and education;
- The historical context for understanding comparisons.

All education systems have been shaped by many internal and external forces: economic, political, social and historical. However, this is a two-way process as education plays a significant role in moulding individuals to take their place in society, including their participation in economic and political activity. This chapter seeks to examine what those factors are and how they influence both structures and features. Kandel (1933, p. xix) believed that 'the factors and forces outside the school matter even more than what goes on inside it'. The last chapter looked at the relationship between culture and education and in particular how culture might influence, for example, who becomes teachers, what students learn and even how students learn. When you research education across national boundaries, not all similarities and differences can be attributed to national culture. Again, Kandel (1933, p. xix) reasoned that '[i]n order to

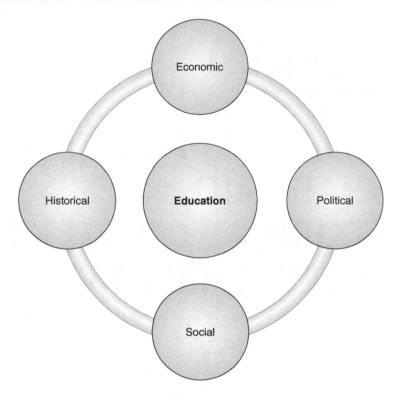

Figure 4.1   Factors that influence education

understand, appreciate, and evaluate the real meaning of the educational system of a nation, it is essential to know something of its history and traditions, of the forces and attitudes governing its social organisation, of the political and economic conditions that determine its development'.

 Activity 4.1   Factors influencing education

Before beginning this chapter, can you list some of the economic factors that affect education? What about political and social factors? Why is it important to look at the historical context of current education systems? How might these variables overlap?

Economic factors

To start, how much is spent on education? When comparing national education systems a key consideration is the amount of money available for governments to spend. This is determined by the overall wealth of a country and is usually measured by Gross Domestic Product (GDP).

According to the UK Treasury (HM Treasury, 2006), GDP is a measure of the total domestic economic activity, the sum of all incomes earned by the production of goods and services in a country's economic territory, wherever the earner of the income may reside.

The countries with the largest GDPs are the United States ($14.99 trillion); China ($7.32 trillion); Japan ($5.87 trillion); Germany ($3.60 trillion); France ($2.77 trillion); Brazil ($2.48 trillion) and the United Kingdom ($2.45 trillion) (World Bank, 2013a). So how much do these countries spend on their education? On average, OECD countries spend 6.2% of their GDP on education (OECD, 2012a). However, this varies from 8.1% in Iceland to 4.7% in the Slovak Republic (OECD, 2012a). Non-OECD countries listed in Table 4.1 range from 3.5% in India to 7.0% in Argentina.

Table 4.1   OECD and other G20 countries' percentage of GDP spent on all levels of education (M = missing data)

OECD countries	Percentage of GDP spent on education	OECD countries	Percentage of GDP spent on education
Australia	6.0	Austria	5.9
Belgium	6.7	Canada	6.1
Chile	6.8	Czech Republic	4.8
Denmark	7.9	Estonia	6.3
Finland	6.4	France	6.3
Germany	5.3	Greece	M
Hungary	4.8	Iceland	8.1
Ireland	6.3	Israel	7.2
Italy	4.9	Japan	5.2
Korea	8.0	Luxembourg	M
Mexico	6.2	Netherlands	6.2
New Zealand	7.4	Norway	6.2
Poland	5.8	Portugal	5.9
Slovak Republic	4.7	Slovenia	6.0
Spain	5.6	Sweden	6.7
Switzerland	6.0	Turkey	M
United Kingdom	6.0	United States	7.3
Other G20			
Argentina	7.0	Brazil	5.5
China	M	India	3.5
Indonesia	3.6	Russian Federation	5.5
Saudi Arabia	M	South Africa	4.8

Source: Based on data from OECD (2012), *Education at a Glance 2012: OECD Indicators,* OECD Publishing. http://dx.doi.org/10.1787/eag-2012-en

> ▦ **Activity 4.2 Spending on education**
>
> Look at the data available on educational expenditure at: www.oecd.org/edu/educationataglance2012oecdindicators-chapterbfinancialandhuman resourcesinvestedineducation-indicators.htm How much is spent on each sector (primary, secondary, tertiary) of education? Why do you think more money might be spent in the different sectors?

In conjunction with GDP, we need to also consider is how big a country is in terms of its population. Some countries have much larger populations than others. For example, in 2012 the recorded population of China was 1.351 billion, much larger than any other country in the world. China's population is more than ten times the size of Japan, whose population was 1.276 million in 2012 (World Bank, 2013b). China has the largest education system in the world as a result. There are approximately 192,000,000 children enrolled in over 400,000 primary and secondary schools with 10,000,000 teachers (Open University, 2008). On June 2013 there were 9.12 million students taking the National Higher Education Entrance Examination (Gao Kao – taken at the end of compulsory schooling for university entry) in China (China Education Center, 2013). In contrast to the UK, there were only 861,819 A-level exam entries in 2012 (CEER, 2012). When comparing what national governments spend on education, it is necessary to take a country's population into consideration both in terms of enrolment and how much is spent per student.

The amount countries spend on education per student varies significantly. In 2008, spending per student from primary through tertiary ranged from $4,000 per student or less in Argentina, Brazil, Chile, China and Mexico, to more than $10,000 per student in Austria, Belgium, Denmark, Ireland, the Netherlands, Norway, Sweden and the United Kingdom. The United States and Switzerland spent the most at nearly $15,000 per student (OECD, 2011b).

When comparing educational spending between countries, it is also important to look at where money is spent. It is necessary to identify how much is spent on teacher's salaries, teaching materials, school administration, buildings, transport, meals, and teacher pensions. For example, teacher salaries are highest in Luxembourg where a lower secondary school teacher with at least 15 years of experience can expect to receive a salary in excess of $100,000, while those with equivalent experience in Hungary, Indonesia and the Slovak Republic can expect to receive a salary less than $15,000 (OECD, 2011b). Other factors that can affect expenditure are the size of classes and the number of hours spent on teaching.

Activity 4.3   Education spending and PISA

Choose two countries from Table 4.1. Compare how much they spend on education to their latest PISA results. Is there a link between how much countries spend on education and performance levels? What are the limitations of comparing in this way?

The share of GDP spent on education in Europe is static compared with other countries and emerging economies, such as Brazil in particular (Vassiliou, 2011). In 2012, Brazil adopted the National Plan for Education which aims to increase spending on education to 10% of GDP by 2020 (Education International, 2012). However, spending more money on education does not necessarily equal better quality provision (OECD, 2013). Even though Brazil spends a larger percentage of GDP than Mexico, Chile, India and Indonesia, which have similar demographic profiles, this has not necessarily increased the quality of education provision (Bruns et al., 2012).

Activity 4.4   Education spending and quality

Can you think of reasons why the quality of education might not improve despite an increase in expenditure?

A key reason that Brazil is spending more money on education is its commitment to investing in its human capital. Human capital theory sees people as a resource: 'Education and training are the most important investments in human capital' (Becker, 1993, p. 17). Moreover, 'human capital analysis assumes that schooling raises earnings and productivity

Figure 4.2   Effects of market forces

mainly by providing knowledge, skills, and a way of analysing problems' (Becker, 1993, p. 19). Therefore, an increase in education spending should lead to an improved standard of education and economic growth.

However, the relationship between education and economic growth has been difficult to prove (Allen, 2011). This will be further discussed in Chapter 5 in the context of developing countries. Despite this, 'human capital theory is the most influential economic theory of Western education, setting the framework of government policies since the early 1960s' (Fitzsimons, 1999, p. 1).

Another key economic principle that has been applied to education is that of market forces. 'Markets are places (literally or figuratively) where buyers and sellers come together to establish purchase of goods and services at an agreed upon price' (Levin & Belfield, 2003, p. 623).

 Activity 4.5   The effects of free market forces

Looking at Figure 4.2, why do some governments apply free market principles to education and schooling in particular? What do you think the advantages and disadvantages are?

Some argue that 'very competitive markets are desirable for consumers because they are able to choose between many producers who are selling similar goods, with good information about prices and quality, and with the constant threat of new suppliers forcing existing suppliers to keep prices and profits low' (Allen, 2011, p. 100). Why, therefore, do governments apply market principles to public education?

The two main reasons are a demand for better school performance (increase in quality) and the need to be decrease costs (efficiency) (Söderqvist, 2007). Economists believe that when schools compete for pupils this will encourage them to provide the best-quality education at the lowest possible cost. 'Economists argue that competition for pupils can incentivize these schools to use their resources, such as buildings, materials and teachers, to maximize pupils' achievement because this is the school output that parents value the most' (Allen, 2011, p. 100). Competition also forces schools to produce the type of education that is most desired by parents, also known as allocative efficiency (Allen, 2011). The schools with the most desirable type of education or the right mix of curriculum, extra-curricular activities, philosophy, and so forth, will attract the most pupils. The ability to choose your school is pivotal in this process.

Parental choice can be achieved through policies that include abolishing catchment areas, creating voucher programmes and setting up charter or 'free' schools (Waslander et al., 2010). Around the world, many governments have provided choice in the form of vouchers. The idea of voucher schemes was first introduced by the American Nobel Prize winning economist Milton Friedman in the 1950s. He believed that they would improve the quality of schools and at the same time make them more efficient (Friedman, 1955). Some of the countries that have introduced vouchers schemes include Chile, Sweden, the USA and Pakistan.

The marketisation of education has been heavily criticised for a number of reasons. In a review of research conducted on the effects of markets in education, the findings concluded that there is very little evidence to suggest that policies aimed at increasing parental choice and school competition are effective (Waslander et al., 2010). In fact, some have argued that market forces are disadvantageous to the poor and actually widen inequalities in society (Ball, 1993). Few markets are perfectively competitive. This can potentially lead to unfair practices and variations in quality. The marketisation of education can have political connotations (discussed in the next section) and therefore be underpinned by ideology that not everyone subscribes to.

Political factors

'Education is not a neutral concept' and 'constructing the detail of an educational experience is a highly problematized, political activity' (Bartlett & Burton, 2012, p. 132). What makes it a political activity? 'First, it is an object of policy development and implementation in the formal institutions of the state such as Parliament; and second, formal education is a human activity conducted in places like schools and universities where decisions have to be made and implemented on a daily basis' (Reid, 2010, p. 133). The political context must be understood when comparing educational systems, particularly when explaining differences, for example school organisation, pupil achievement and the underpinning values that form the core philosophical ideals. This next section will explore what these political forces are that shape education.

 Activity 4.6   The politics of education

Why is education 'not a neutral concept'? Who 'constructs the detail of an educational experience'? How and why? Why is education 'a highly problematized activity'?

If education is an 'object of policy development', then we need to consider who writes policy and for what purpose. Comparing educational policies and policy borrowing has always constituted a large part of comparative education research. 'Politicians often use international comparisons, for example of attainment in assessment [see Chapter 2], to justify educational reform' (Bates et al., 2010, p. 40). Moreover, '[s]imilarly, for political purposes, politicians will often use the fact that a particular policy initiative has been successfully implemented in one country as a rationale for change in their own, assuming that the policy will transfer from one context to another' (Bates et al., 2010, pp. 40–41). We know that educational transfer is a highly complex matter and that '[o]ne of the tasks of comparativists is to unravel the processes which are involved in all aspects of educational transfer between nations, and to highlight the problems and warnings implicit in them' (Phillips & Schweisfurth, 2008, p. 19).

To begin with, what is policy? Policy has been described as a 'complex concept' and is difficult to define (Rui, 2007). However, for the purpose of clarity, 'education policy refers to the raft of laws and initiatives that determine the shape and functioning of educational systems at both a national and local level' (Bates et al., 2010, p. 39).

⊞ Activity 4.7   Education policy

Can you identify any contemporary education polices? When were they written, by whom and for what purpose?

Who makes education policy? Practitioners, professional organisations, pressure groups and think tanks, politicians, select committees, civil servants, influential academics, parents and children are the most influential groups in the policy-making process (Bates et al., 2010). However, the most influential group in the mix is probably those who form the government.

Who is in power has a tremendous influence on education. The ideology of the dominant political party is often reflected in national educational policy. It is important to consider political ideologies when looking at education policy 'as it is these wider beliefs about society from which the education ideologies spring' (Bartlett & Burton, 2012, p. 134).

A good example of this can be found in the policies in the UK introduced by the Conservative government of the 1980s and the first half of the 1990s under the leadership of Margaret Thatcher. During this time, there were two main ideologies within the Conservative party: neo-liberalism, the belief in the importance of a free market economy, and neo-conservatism, the belief in the importance of upholding standards and traditional values (Bartlett & Burton, 2012). Although these ideologies were quite different, the former emphasising freedom of choice and market forces and the latter acknowledging the need for control, political groups within the party came together to form what was coined the 'New Right' (Bartlett & Burton, 2012).

This coming together of New Right ideology is most evident in the 1988 Education Act. 'The central purpose of the 1988 Education Act was that power should be gathered to the centre and, at the same time, devolved on to schools and parents' (Chitty, 2011, p. 43). One of the goals of the 1988

Education Act was to give parents greater control over which school their child attended. The Act also created the local management of schools (LMS), which gave schools greater autonomy and control over their budget. 'It was hoped that these changes would make schools more responsive to their clients, be they parents, children or local employers' (Wood, 2011, p. 11). Lastly, as part of the Act, the national curriculum was to be assessed through standardised testing and the results published in league tables. 'The changes from 1988 onwards were brought into existence by a Conservative government which subscribed to neo-liberal tenets believing that the introduction of free market competition in education would produce greater choice for parents, greater efficiency in the spending of state money and improved examination results' (Wood, 2011, p. 12).

 Activity 4.8   Political ideology and education

Can you make a list of political ideologies, for example, conservatism? How might these manifest themselves in education? Have a look at some political party websites, such as the Democratic Party of which the US President Obama is a member. It is available at: www.democrats.org/issues/education. What are the values of the Democratic Party and how are these visible in its education policy?

Social forces

Since the turn of the twentieth century, many comparative education scholars, such as Michael Sadler, Issac Kandal and Nichola Hans, have been interested in the relationship between education and society in their work. Before making the link between the two, it is important to understand what sociology is.

Although '[s]ociologists are not agreed on the purposes of their study' (Meighan & Harber, 2007, p. 8), they are generally interested in studying the world in which we live. Anthony Giddens, a prominent British sociologist, has defined sociology as 'the scientific study of human social life, groups and societies' and 'the scope of sociological study is extremely wide, ranging from the analysis of passing encounters between individuals on the street to the investigation of global social processes such as the rise of Islamic fundamentalism' (Giddens, 2006, p. 4).

Sociologists are interested in a wide variety of topics. Table 4.2 lists some key topics in sociology.

In the UK, the sociological study of education can be traced back to the 1950s (Waller, 2011). 'For nearly half a century, comparative educational research has been influenced by the discipline of sociology and by the sub-field of sociology of education' (Ramirez, 2006, p. 431). Expanding

Table 4.2 Key sociological themes

Gender	Race	Ethnicity	Poverty	Inequality
Social class	Disability	Family	Immigration	Identity
Sexuality	Religion	The media	Education	Politics
Work & economic life	Crime & deviance	Institutions & organisations	Age	Global issues

on the ideas of Lauder et al. (2009), Waller (2011, p. 107) developed a list of ten key questions pertaining to the sociology of education:

1. What is the purpose of schooling?

2. How does education affect the life chances of different groups in society?

3. Why do some social groups generally 'win' in terms of educational outcomes and others lose?

4. What causes individual members of such groups to vary from these norms?

5. How can educational processes be understood?

6. What do pupils learn at school along with the official curriculum?

7. Does education liberate people or control them?

8. How are educational outcomes and economic success related for individuals and the wider society?

9. How do people's educational experiences affect their sense of identity?

10. What role does post-compulsory education play in society?

Often considered one of the founding fathers of sociology, the French sociologist Emile Durkheim has played a key role in the scholarship pertaining to the relationship between society and education (see Waller, 2011). Durkheim was particularly interested in the purpose of schooling (Walford & Pickering, 1998) and believed that education is 'only the image and reflection of society' (Durkheim, 1897, in Walford & Pickering, 1998, p. 4).

Durkheim's work on the purpose or function of schooling is often known as the 'functionalist' approach. For him and other functionalists, 'society was best understood as an organised system made up of interlocking and interdependent parts', much like the human body (Curtis & Pettigrew, 2009, p. 87). Social institutions, such as education, the family, religion, work and the government, are the 'organs' and to understand these institutions you had to identify the role or function of each with respect to the whole society (Curtis & Pettigrew, 2009).

What role, then, does education play in society? The primary role or function of education, for Durkheim, was to socialise children (Giddens, 2006; Waller, 2011). In order for society to function or keep order and stability, children need to internalise the social rules necessary to perpetuate its existence. Through education and learning about history, in particular, Durkheim believed children gained an understanding of common societal values, which include religious and moral beliefs and a sense of self-discipline (Giddens, 2006). Acquiring common values was essential in 'uniting a multitude of separate individuals' (Giddens, 2006, p. 686).

Meighan and Harber (2007, p. 288) point out that '[i]f the education system functions to transmit these values, it too must work towards solidarity and integration rather than towards differentiation and managed pluralism'. In other words, schools should foster homogeneity or similarities among their pupil in order to ensure the smooth functioning of society. How can schooling do this?

From Durkheim's perspective, then, some key considerations would include questions such as:

1. What should be taught in schools? (The curriculum.)

2. What are the responsibilities of the teachers? (The role of the teacher.)

3. What is the pupil's 'purpose' in school? (The role of the pupil.)

4. How should teachers and pupils relate? (Interpersonal relations.)

(Meighan & Harber, 2006, p. 288)

Part of the answers to the questions above will inevitably be found in a country or society's culture. However, as we have seen in Chapter 3, it can be quite difficult to know what values societies hold. Recent changes in technology, migration patterns and so forth have changed the way we live. How have these changes affected our values and beliefs? Is Durkheim's framework for understanding the relationship between society and education adequate in light of these changes?

The influence of the sociology of education can be seen in the research surrounding academic achievement and educational and occupational mobility (Ramirez, 2006). In developed countries, increases in social policies that include equality and access have led to a corresponding increased interest in the social factors and their relationship to educational achievement. 'Perhaps the most significant and enduring achievement of recent studies in relation to social factors in education has been to put questions of class, culture, gender, and ethnicity at the centre of descriptions of educational processes and systems' (Bartlett & Burton, 2012, p. 254). In other words, do social factors such as race, ethnicity, gender and socio-economic status affect individuals' opportunities and therefore educational achievement?

As we saw in Chapter 2, PISA is one of the most influential international surveys that assess student achievement. The PISA studies examine certain social factors, such as gender (discussed in Chapter 6) and the impact of socio-economic background on student achievement across participant nations (see OECD, 2010). Three key findings from the 2009 PISA results are:

- Immigrant students often have to overcome multiple barriers at once in order to succeed at school.

- Across most OECD countries, poor performance among immigrant students relative to other students is strongly related to social disadvantage at school, as reflected in the proportion of students whose mothers have low levels of education.

- The concentration, in a school, of immigrant students or of those who do not speak the language of instruction at home is not as strongly related to poor performance. (OECD, 2012b)

 ## Activity 4.9 Immigrant barriers

One of the key findings above suggests that immigrant students often face multiple barriers in order to succeed at school. What do you think those barriers might be?

Historical contexts

When comparing current education systems, an understanding of how they have evolved over time is very important. How do we know where we are now and possibly heading into the future if we don't know where we have been and why? For example, why do some countries have a national curriculum (for example, the UK) while others don't (for example, the USA) and how has this evolved? The answers can only be found in the historical context of a nation's education system. As we saw in Chapter 3, culture plays an important role in shaping education. History forms part of the larger cultural picture (Wren, 2012).

Nicholas Hans was a prominent scholar in the field of comparative education and he advocated a historical approach to understand differences in education systems (see Hans, 1959). In a book on Russian education, Hans (1963, p. 1) writes: 'English education is different from French, as German education is different from Russian.' Furthermore, he believed that 'to disregard differences in education because human nature is shared by all men is as futile as to overlook the differences in ability, special talents, and particular interests between individual children. For Hans, national features of each educational system are a historical fact which could not be analysed away.

A key message from the work of Hans is that in order to understand differences in education we need to examine the historical factors that have led to its current position. Other prominent scholars, for example Michael Sadler, have argued the same. More recently, Kazamias (2001) reasoned that the rise of positivism in the 1960s and 1970s led to methodological approaches that were lacking in historical perspective or context. This is a criticism and limitation of the major international studies (IEA and PISA) discussed in Chapter 2. Kazamias (2001, p. 447) has called for a reinvention of the historical dimension in comparative education, stating that, 'in arguing for the reclamation of the disappearing historical legacy in comparative education, I would like to conclude this essay by reminding ourselves that history is also a humanistic episteme'. He goes on to say that 'it deals with the human condition, with human beings as subjects and not as commodities or numbers, with human cultures as wholes and not as narrowly economic cultures, and with human values, in short with humanistic and humanising knowledge, in the broad meaning of the term'. In other words, Kazamias believes that the reinvention of the historical dimension in researching other countries will humanise comparative education. This is particularly pertinent in a world that is increasing governed by statistics, surveys and international league tables.

So how can you, the student use the historical approach in your research? In Chapter 2, we learned that Finland has consistently ranked at the top in all the PISA assessments since 2000 (OECD, 2011a). Simola (2005) considers that in order to understand this success we need to delve into Finnish history. Simola maintains that Finnish culture is different from other Nordic and European cultures. 'There is something archaic, something authoritarian, possibly even something eastern, in the Finnish culture and mentality' and that 'there is also something collective that, in a distinctive way, permeates the Finnish schooling culture' (Simola, 2005, p. 458). In order to understand how Finnish people are today and why they are different, we need to look at Finland's recent history.

First, Finland is a relatively young nation state. It was part of Sweden until it was taken over by the Russian Empire in the early 1800s. It declared independence in 1917 in the wake of the Russian revolution and a bloody civil war ensued between the left-wing 'Reds' and the right-wing 'Whites'. The civil war lasted around three months and more than 20,000 people out of a population of 3.1 million lost their lives (Casanova, 1999). Jääskeläinen (1999) writes about the effects of the civil war and the national trauma that still haunts the collective consciousness of the Finnish people. 'In the Civil War many atrocities happened, which have haunted the whole society and single families since the war, like nightmares. Those traumas have often been so strong that they received the nature of a taboo; things that happened in the war and right after it were simply not discussed.'

Situated between Sweden and Russia, Finland's geography is different from most other European countries. It lies on the border between the East and the West so it would be fair to see elements of the East in Finnish culture. Simola (2005, p. 458) supports this view: 'The fact that Finnish Social Democracy retains some eastern authoritarian, or even totalitarian, flavour, compared with versions in other Nordic countries, is just one indication. At least heuristically, there is nothing strange in finding Finland together with nations such as Korea and Japan in some international comparisons.'

Furthermore, there was rapid social change as a result of industrialisation after the Second World War. In fact, in 1945, 70% of the Finnish population lived in rural areas, and nearly 60% were employed in agriculture (Simola, 2005). However, after the war, the pace of urbanisation was incredible and took approximately 25 years (National Board of Antiquities, 2013). During this time, the agriculture sector decreased and people moved to the cities to work in factories and also the service sector (National Board of Antiquities, 2013).

During this time, the number of school children grew and by the 1970s, the old school system was reformed into a comprehensive school system, and the vocational education and the university network developed (National Board of Antiquities, 2013). The implementation of Finland's comprehensive school system has been described as rapid, systematic and even 'totalitarian' (Simola, 2005). Therefore: 'All this is witness to the fact that the Finnish success story in education is historically very recent. Whereas almost 70% of the younger generation now aims to obtain a higher education degree, among their grandparents about the same proportion received the full elementary school certificate' (Simola, 2005, p. 458).

 Activity 4.10   The Finnish success and its historical context

The last section describes significant events in Finnish history. How might these events have influenced the education system? What evidence could there be to support your assertions?

Conclusion

It would be almost impossible to understand an educational system without examining some of the factors that shape it. While these factors have been discussed separately in this chapter, they do at times overlap and cannot necessarily be viewed in isolation. Some of the answers to key educational questions may reveal themselves when we adopt a deeper understanding of the role that various forces (economic, political, social and historic) play in relation to education.

📁 Case Study 4   The Australian curriculum

The Australian government adopted the Melbourne Declaration on Educational Goals for Young Australians on 5 December 2008. It sets the direction for Australian schooling for the next ten years (MCEECDYA, 2009). The Melbourne Declaration sets out learning and subject areas to be covered in the first ever Australia-wide curriculum currently being developed by the Australian Curriculum, Assessment and Reporting Authority (ACARA) (DfE, 2011). The curriculum will cover from Kindergarten to Year 12 (ages 5–18).

The opening paragraph of the Melbourne Declaration states: 'In the 21st century Australia's capacity to provide a high quality of life for all will depend on the ability to compete in the global economy on knowledge and innovation. Education equips young people with the knowledge, understanding, skills and values to take advantage of opportunity and to face the challenges of this era with confidence' (MCEECDYA, 2008, p. 4). The Declaration goes on to describe how important schools are for promoting the intellectual, physical, social, emotional, moral, spiritual and aesthetic development and well-being of Australian youth. Again it reiterates the importance of schools in 'ensuring the nation's on-going economic prosperity and social cohesion'. The government believe that in order for this to be achieved there must be a shared responsibility between schools and other stakeholders, such as parents, the community and business.

Key questions:

Go on to read the full document at: www.mceecdya.edu.au/verve/_resources/National_Declaration_on_the_Educational_Goals_for_Young_Australians.pdf

- Why is the purpose of schooling in Australia as stated above?

- How would you analyse the opening paragraphs from a Durkheimian perspective?

- What economic, social and political factors might this new curriculum be a response to?

- Why hasn't Australia had a nationwide curriculum before now?

- What societal values are evident in the development of a new curriculum?

Suggested reading 📖

Dufour, G. & Curtis, W. (eds) (2011) *Studying Education: An Introduction to Key Disciplines in Education Studies.* Maidenhead: Open University/McGraw Hill Introduces students to key themes in Education Studies and has chapters on the history, politics, philosophy, economics, sociology and psychology of education in addition to a chapter specifically on comparative education.

Phillips, D. & Schweisfurth, M. (2008) *Comparative and International Education: An Introduction to Theory, Method, and Practice.* London: Continuum
This book will cement your understanding of many of the key themes discussed in this book.

References

Allen, R. (2011) The economics of education, in G. Dufour & W. Curtis (eds), *Studying Education: An Introduction to Key Disciplines in Education Studies.* Maidenhead: Open University/McGraw Hill

Ball, S. (1993) Education markets, choice and social class: The market as a class strategy in the UK and the USA. *British Journal of Sociology of Education,* 14(1), 3–19

Bartlett, S. & Burton, D. (2012) *Introduction to Education Studies.* London: Sage

Bates, J., Lewis, S. & Pickard, A. (2010) *Education Policy, Practice and the Professional.* London: Continuum

Becker, G. (1993) *Human Capital: A Theoretical and Empirical Analysis with Reference to Education* (3rd edition). Chicago, IL: The University of Chicago Press

Bruns, B., Evans, D. & Luque, J. (2012) *Achieving World-Class Education in Brazil: The Next Agenda.* Washington, DC: The World Bank

Casanova, J. (1999) *Civil Wars, Revolutions and Counterrevolutions in Finland, Spain and Greece (1918–1949): A Comparative Analysis.* Available online at: http://kellogg.nd.edu/publications/workingpapers/WPS/266.pdf

CEER (Centre for Education and Employment Research) (2012) *A-Levels 2012.* Available online at: www.buckingham.ac.uk/research/ceer/publications

China Education Center (2013) *China Education.* Available online at: www.chinaeducenter.com/en/cedu.php

Chitty, C. (2011) The politics of education, in G. Dufour & W. Curtis (eds), *Studying Education: An Introduction to Key Disciplines in Education Studies.* Maidenhead: Open University/McGraw Hill

Curtis, W. & Pettigrew, A. (2009) *Learning in a Contemporary Culture.* Exeter: Learning Matters

DfE (2011) *Review of the National Curriculum in England: Report on Subject Breadth in International Jurisdictions.* London: Department for Education. Available online at: www.education.gov.uk/publications/eOrderingDownload/DFE-RR178a.pdf

Education International (2012) *Brazil: March to Strengthen Public Education.* Available online at: www.ei-ie.org/en/news/news_details/2229/

Fitzsimons, P. (1999) Human capital theory and education, in M. Peters, P. Ghiraldelli, B. Žarnić & A. Gibbons (eds), Encyclopaedia of Philosophy of Education. Available online at: www.ffst.hr/ENCYCLOPAEDIA

Friedman, M. (1955) The role of government in public education, in R.A. Solo (ed.), *Economics and the Public Interest.* New Brunswick, NJ: University of Rutgers Press

Giddens, A. (2006) *Sociology* (5th edition). Cambridge: Polity Press

Hans, N. (1959) The historical approach to comparative education. *International Review of Education,* 5(3), 299–309

Hans, N. (1963) *The Russian Tradition in Education*. London: Routledge & Kegan Paul

HM Treasury (2006) *User's Guide: Background Information on GDP and GDP Deflator*. Available online at: www.hm-treasury.gov.uk/data_gdp_backgd.htm

Jääskeläinen, S. (1999) *Political Taboos and National Trauma in Finland Caused by the Civil War 1918*. Available online at: www.kuwi.europa-uni. de/de/lehrstuhl/sw/sw2/forschung/tabu/weterfuehrende_informationen/ studentische_arbeiten/Political_Taboos_in_Finland.pdf

Kandel, I. (1933) *Studies in Comparative Education*. London: George Harrap & Co

Kazamias, A. (2001) Re-inventing the historical in comparative education: Reflections on a *protean episteme* by a contemporary player. *Comparative Education*, 37(4), 439–449

Lauder, H., Brown, P. & Halsey, A.H. (2009) Sociology of education: A critical history and prospects for the future. *Oxford Review of Education*, 35(5), 569–585

Levin, H. & Belfield, C. (2003) The marketplace in education, in H. Lauder, P. Brown, J. Dillabough & A.H. Halsy (eds) (2006), *Education, Globalization and Social Change*. Oxford: Oxford University Press, pp. 620–653

MCEECDYA (2008) *Melbourne Declaration on Educational Goals for Young Australians*. Available online at: www.mceecdya.edu.au/verve/_resources/ National_Declaration_on_the_Educational_Goals_for_Young_Australians.pdf

MCEECDYA (2009) *Melbourne Declaration*. Available online at: www.mceecdya. edu.au/mceecdya/melbourne_declaration,25979.html

Meighan, R. & Harber, C. (2007) *A Sociology of Educating*. London: Continuum

National Board of Antiquities (2013) *Constructing the Finnish Welfare State since 1945*. Available online at: www.nba.fi/en/cultural_environment/built_herit-age/built_welfare_project/heritage_of_tomorrow

OECD (2010) PISA 2009 Results: Overcoming Social Background: Equity in Learning Opportunities and Outcomes (Volume II). Available online at: www. oecd.org/pisa/pisaproducts/pisa2009/pisa2009resultsovercomingsocialback-groundequityinlearningopportunitiesandoutcomesvolumeii.htm

OECD (2011a) Lessons from PISA for the United States, Strong Performers and Successful Reformers in Education. Available online at: www.oecd-ilibrary. org/education/lessons-from-pisa-for-the-united-states_9789264096660-en

OECD (2011b) Education at a Glance. Available online at: www.oecd.org/educa-tion/skills-beyond-school/48630868.pdf

OECD (2012a) Education at a Glance 2012: OECD Indicators – Chapter B: Financial and Human Resources Invested in Education – Indicators. Available online at: www.oecd.org/edu/educationataglance2012oecdindicators-chap-terbfinancialandhumanresourcesinvestedineducation-indicators.htm

OECD (2012b) How Do Immigrant Students Fare in Disadvantaged Schools? Available online at: www.oecd.org/pisa/pisainfocus/

OECD (2013) *Education Indicators in Focus*. Available online at: www.oecd.org/ education/skills-beyond-school/educationindicatorsinfocus.htm

Open University (2008) Chinese Education: How Do Things Work? Available online at: www.open.edu/openlearn/society/international-development/ international-studies/chinese-education-how-do-things-work

Phillips, D. & Schweisfurth, M. (2008) *Comparative and International Education: An Introduction to Theory, Method, and Practice*. London: Continuum

Ramirez, F. (2006) Beyond achievement and attainment studies: Revitalizing a comparative sociology of education. *Comparative Education*, 42(3), 431–449

Reid, A. (2010) The politics of educational change, in J. Arther & I. Davies (eds), *The Routledge Education Studies Textbook*. Abingdon: Routledge

Rui, Y. (2007) Comparing policies, in M. Bray, B. Adamson & M. Mason (eds), *Comparative Education Research: Approaches and Methods*. Hong Kong: Comparative Education Research Centre

Simola, H. (2005) The Finnish miracle of PISA: Historical and sociological remarks on teaching and teacher education. *Comparative Education*, 41(4), 455–470

Söderqvist, B. (2007) *School Leaders' View on Market Forces and Decentralisation: Case Studies in a Swedish Municipality and an English County*. Available online at: http://su.diva-portal.org/smash/get/diva2:197636/FULLTEXT01

Vassiliou, A. (2011) *Investing Effectively in Education and Training in a Time of Crisis*. Available online at: http://europa.eu/rapid/press-release_ SPEECH-11-818_en.doc

Walford, G. & Pickering, W.S.F. (eds) (1998) *Durkheim and Modern Education*. London: Routledge

Waller, R. (2011) The sociology of education, in G. Dufour & W. Curtis (eds), *Studying Education: An Introduction to Key Disciplines in Education Studies*. Maidenhead: Open University/McGraw Hill

Waslander, S., Pater, C. & van der Weide, M. (2010) *Markets in Education: An Analytical Review of Empirical Research on Market Mechanisms in Education*. Education Working Paper No. 52. Available online at: http:// search.oecd.org/officialdocuments/displaydocumentpdf/?cote=EDU/ WKP%282010%2915&docLanguage=En

Wood, K. (2011) *Education: The Basics*. London: Routledge

World Bank (2013a) *GDP (Current US$)*. Available online at: http://data.world-bank.org/indicator/NY.GDP.MKTP.CD?order=wbapi_data_value_2011+wbapi_ data_value+wbapi_data_value-last&sort=asc

World Bank (2013b) World Development Indicators. Available online at: http:// databank.worldbank.org/data/views/reports/tableview.aspx

Wren, T. (2012) Conceptions of Culture: What Multicultural Educators Need to Know. Plymouth: Rowman & Littlefield

CHAPTER 5

EDUCATION AND THE DEVELOPING WORLD

This chapter explores:

- What is meant by 'development';
- International development policy;
- Theoretical explanations for 'underdevelopment' and inequality;
- Barriers to education and possible solutions.

 Activity 5.1   Barriers for the poor

Make a list of social, economic and political barriers that people living in poverty around the world may face.

Global inequalities

Recent estimates indicate that approximately 1 billion people around the world will be living on an income of less than $1.25 a day in 2015 and four out of five living in extreme poverty will live in sub-Saharan Africa and southern Asia alone (United Nations, 2012). Around 2.5

billion people, nearly half of the population in the developing world, lack access to proper sanitation facilities and are therefore at greater risk of contracting infectious diseases and suffering from ill health. In developing countries, '195 million children under 5 – one in three – experience malnutrition, causing irreparable damage to their cognitive development and their long-term educational prospects' (UNESCO, 2011, p. 1), and a third of all child deaths are linked to hunger (World Food Programme, 2013).

 Activity 5.2   Development

What does the word 'development' mean to you? What do you think the difference is between a developed and a developing country? Make a list.

Why do global inequalities such as the ones described above exist and what can be done about it? What are the long-term educational prospects for those living in developing countries or regions? What is the link between education and economic growth? This chapter seeks to explore what is meant by development, how we measure inequality (socially, politically and economically) and what role education plays in economic growth and poverty reduction?

Education and development studies

Many Western scholars believe that the study of development began after the Second World War and has its roots in US President Harry Truman's 1949 Inaugural Address, where he urged Western nations to use their scientific and industrial progress to help those living in 'underdeveloped' areas of the world (Chant & McIlwaine, 2009; Potter et al., 2012; Shields, 2013).

 Activity 5.3   Truman's 1949 Inaugural Address

Access the full speech from the internet at: http://avalon.law.yale.edu/20th_century/truman.asp

At first glance, Truman's speech appears to be quite charitable and motivated by 'doing good' in the world. However, what was the political context in which the speech was made? Was there a possible ulterior motive? Also, whose way of life appears to be superior in this speech? What do you think Truman meant by 'progress'?

Development studies emerged in the 1950s as post-war reconstruction efforts were being made, and where the emphasis was on rebuilding national economies. Many former colonies gained independence in the 1950s and 1960s and foreign policy efforts were geared towards assisting newly independent nations. Development education, as defined in Chapter 1 by Halls (1990, p. 24), is 'the production of information and plans to assist policymakers, particularly in "new nations", the development of appropriate educational methods and techniques, and the training of personnel to implement programmes'. Much of the work surrounding development education has been concerned with helping developing countries to achieve economic, political and social modernisation (Parkyn, 1977; Little, 2000).

What is a developing country?

Over the years, many terms have been used to describe 'underdeveloped' countries, with most being highly contentious and problematic for their inferior connotations or inaccurate representations. Some of the terms that have been used are: the Third world; the Global South; less developed or least developed country (LDC); the minority world; and non-industrialised. For a good discussion on the origins and debates surrounding these terms have a look at Chapter 1: Defining, conceptualising and measuring development, in Chant and McIlwaine (2009), or Chapter 1: What is Development, in Sumner and Tribe (2008).

The World Bank defines a developing country as 'one in which the majority lives on far less money – with far fewer basic public services – than the population in highly industrialized countries' (World Bank, 2012). The World Bank also estimate that 5 million of the world's 6 billion people live in developing countries where incomes are usually less than $2 per day and a significant portion of the population lives in extreme poverty (earning less than $1.25 per day). Other characteristics of developing countries are listed below.

The World Bank (2012) states that 'a developing country may be:

- largely rural or with a population that is migrating to poorly equipped cities, with a low-performing economy that is based primarily on agriculture and where non-agricultural jobs are scarce and low-paying;

- where the populace is often hungry and sorely lacks education, where there is a large knowledge gap and technological innovation is scarce;

- where health and education systems are poor and/or lacking and where transportation, potable water, power and communications infrastructure is also scarce;

- where the amount of government debt is unsustainable;

- where the land mass, population, and domestic markets are small and far disbursed, often on remote islands or in island groups, susceptible to natural disasters, with limited institutional capacity, limited economic diversification; and/or

- where government has collapsed and armed conflict has left a fragile state with weak institutions and policies, either unwilling or unable to provide basic social services, especially for the poor. It is estimated that a third of people living in absolute poverty around the world live in fragile states in a vicious cycle of poverty and conflict.'

To summarise, developing countries are typically characterised by having low income based primarily on agriculture and poor infrastructure (both physical, e.g. roads, and institutional, e.g. education system). They have a large number of poor people who are often hungry and lack access to education. These countries also tend to have high debt and poor governance.

 Activity 5.4   World Bank: Countries and economies

Look at the World Bank's website at: http://data.worldbank.org/country. Which countries are classified as low income, middle income and high income? What are the limitations of measuring development according to economic criteria?

Many recognise that there is more to an individual's development and well-being than income. Furthermore, traditional measures of GDP/GDP per capita (see Chapter 4) and GNI/GNI per capita (Gross National Income, which is GDP plus income from abroad) do not take into account the distribution of wealth within a country. Many people in high-income countries are poor, while there are growing numbers of rich people in less wealthy countries (Giddens, 2006).

Based on the work of Amartya Sen, Mahbub ul Huq, Richard Jolly, Frances Stewart and Meghnad Desai at the United Nations Development Programme (UNDP), the Human Development Index (HDI) was created in 1990 as an alternative way of measuring development (Sumner & Tribe, 2008). From its inception, the HDI, while not completely dismissing economic factors in development, aims to put people at the centre of development: 'People are the real wealth of a nation' (UNDP, 1990).

The HDI measures development by using three indicators: life expectancy, educational attainment and command over the resources needed for a decent standard of living (GNI per capita), or income in other words (UNDP, 2013). The education element is measured by mean years of schooling for adults aged 25 and expected years of schooling for children entering school age.

The top five countries with very high human development are: Norway, Australia, the United States, the Netherlands and Germany. The countries with the lowest human development are: Niger, the Democratic Republic of the Congo, Mozambique, Chad and Burkina Faso. Norway ranks number one on the HDI, with an average life expectancy of 81 years, and the average adult receiving 12.6 years of schooling and earning an annual income of $48,688. Compared to Norway, Niger has the lowest ranking HDI score, with an average life expectancy of 55 years, and the average adult receiving 1.4 years of schooling and earning an annual income of a mere $701 (UNDP, 2013).

Activity 5.5   Low human development

Choose a country with low human development from the HDI ranking list at: http://hdr.undp.org/en/statistics/ You can create your own tables and explore human development indicators over the last 30 years. Look back at the World Bank characteristics of developing countries earlier in this chapter. Compare this to your chosen country. Does your country display some of the characteristics? What are the possible causes for low human development?

Education for All

In the same year the HDI was launched (1990), delegates from 155 countries, in conjunction with a number of other governmental and non-governmental organisations, met in Jomtien, Thailand, at the World Conference on Education for All (UNESCO, 2012a). The aim was to make primary education accessible to all children and significantly reduce illiteracy before the end of the decade. The delegates adopted a World Declaration on Education for All, which confirmed that education should be seen as a fundamental human right and urged countries to strengthen efforts to address the basic learning needs of all. The Education for All (EFA) goals included: universal access to learning; a focus on equity; an emphasis on learning outcomes; broadening the means and the scope of basic education; enhancing the environment for learning; and strengthening partnerships by 2000 (UNESCO, 2012a). While the EFA goals have not been reached, the Jomtien Declaration was very important in the establishment of education for all as a fundamental item on the international development agenda and it signified a shift towards a rights-based perspective on development (Shields, 2013).

In April 2000, the international community met again, this time in Dakar, Senegal. There, delegates adopted the Dakar Framework for Action, which reaffirmed their commitment to education for all by 2015. The EFA goals have contributed to the Millennium Development Goals (discussed in the next section). They identified six key education goals:

Goal 1 Expanding and improving comprehensive early childhood care and education, especially for the most vulnerable and disadvantaged children.

Goal 2 Ensuring that by 2015 all children, particularly girls, children in difficult circumstances and those belonging to ethnic minorities, have access to, and complete, free and compulsory primary education of good quality.

Goal 3 Ensuring that the learning needs of all young people and adults are met through equitable access to appropriate learning and life-skills programmes.

Goal 4 Achieving a 50 per cent improvement in levels of adult literacy by 2015, especially for women, and equitable access to basic and continuing education for all adults.

Goal 5 Eliminating gender disparities in primary and secondary education by 2005, and achieving gender equality in education by 2015, with a focus on ensuring girls' full and equal access to and achievement in basic education of good quality.

Goal 6 Improving all aspects of the quality of education and ensuring excellence of all so that recognized and measurable learning outcomes are achieved by all, especially in literacy, numeracy and essential life skills.

(UNESCO, 2000)

Millennium Development Goals

In 2000, world leaders met at the United Nations headquarters in New York in what was called the Millennium Summit, where they adopted the United Nations Millennium Declaration. The Millennium Declaration demonstrated a commitment to reducing extreme poverty and guaranteeing basic human rights (United Nations, 2000). It set out eight goals with measurable targets to be achieved by 2015. They are now known as the Millennium Development Goals (MDGs) and are listed below:

1. Eradicating extreme poverty and hunger

2. Achieving universal primary education

3. Promoting gender equality and empowering women

4. Reducing child mortality rates

5. Improving maternal health

6. Combating HIV/AIDS, malaria, and other diseases

7. Ensuring environmental sustainability

8. Developing a global partnership for development

▦ Activity 5.6   MDGs

Have a look at the MDGs and their targets at: www.un.org/millennium
goals/poverty.shtml. Are the goals going to be met by 2015? Are there any
reasons why the goals may fail to be met by this date? Can the MDGs be
achieved without increased investments in education?

However, the MDGs are not without criticism, the first being that they are
unrealistic and many countries around the world will not meet the targets
(see Chant & McIlwaine, 2009). The second has revolved around questions as to the reasons why these targets will not be met. Many have
criticised the lack of resources needed to achieve them. In the *EFA Global
Monitoring Report 2012* (UNESCO, 2012b), it was estimated that aid to
low-income countries for basic education has stagnated in recent years
and was insufficient for securing universal primary education (UPE) by
2015. Moreover, high-income countries, in particular the G8 countries
(Canada, France, Germany, Italy, Japan, Russia, the UK and the USA),
have failed to fulfil their promise made in 2005 to increase aid by US$50
billion by 2010 (UNESCO, 2012b). Nevertheless, the MDGs are an important recognition of the plight of millions of people in the developing
world. Why is there so much inequality?

Theories of development

Modernisation theory

Numerous theories have been applied to the study of development,
many of which try to unpick the reasons for some of the problems facing
poor countries. In the 1950s, the predominant theory was modernisation
theory, led by the American economist Walt Rostow. In Rostow's classic
text, *The Stages of Economic Growth: A Non-communist Manifesto* (1960),
he proposed that there were five stages of economic growth. In his
model, economic development is based on the internal factors and social
changes which are necessary so countries can move from a traditional
society to a modern one. Development is seen as a linear process where
developing countries should copy developed ones.

However, modernisation theory soon faced a number of criticisms.
First, a traditional society is defined as a negative opposite to a modern
one, where traditional aspects of societies (for example, strong belief in
superstitions or an individual's status in society is based on their position in the family) should be superseded by modern ones (for example,
consumerism and social mobility) (Bernstein, 1971). Lack of development is therefore the fault of the developing countries for not changing

these internal factors which are necessary for economic growth (Chant & McIlwaine, 2009). Furthermore, Rostow classified all traditional societies into one category and assumed they were all the same. There will indeed be great variation and diversity between so called 'traditional' societies; no two countries are ever the same. Above all, modernisation theory is based on how Western countries developed and is largely seen as ethnocentric (Bernstein, 1971; Chant & McIlwaine, 2009). Some question whether growth is linear or sequential, as in Rostow's model, while others see the model as description, lacking in empirical evidence. Nevertheless, modernisation theory has left a huge impact on development studies (Shields, 2013).

Dependency theory

In the 1960s dependency theory emerged among social scientists who denounced modernisation theory as being imperialistic (Schuurman, 2008). It emanated from the work of Latin American scholars, led by Andre Gunder Frank, and drew on Marxist or Neo-Marxists perspectives. Rather than the failure to develop being the fault of developing countries, dependency theory proposes that the reasons for underdevelopment lie in external factors. Using a historical basis, dependency theorists believed that developing countries or 'satellites' have been exploited by wealthy capitalist countries or 'metropoles' (Frank, 1966). This exploitation began during colonialism with the extraction of raw materials and continues today, whereby multinational companies seek out cheap labour and raw materials in poorer countries in order to make profits. Poorer countries are locked into a situation from which they cannot escape.

Dependency theory has been criticised for being too simplistic (ignoring huge differences between countries), with just the satellite/metropole dichotomy, and for failing to identify specific causes of underdevelopment (Chant & McIlwaine, 2009). There were also no clear policy solutions other than socialist revolution, according to Frank. However, it has been important for raising awareness of the West's part in maintaining what many would argue is a dominant and advantageous position over many poorer countries.

 Activity 5.7   Dependency theory and comparative education

Read the following article by Noah and Eckstein (1988) at: http://home.iitk.ac.in/~amman/soc748/noah_eckstein_dependency_theory_in_comparative_education.html. What are some of the criticisms (or twelve lessons) of dependency theory not mentioned above?

World systems theory

Leading on from the dependency model is world systems theory, led by the American scholar Immanuel Wallerstein and developed in the mid-1970s and 1980s. World systems theory was borne out of an attempt to meet some of the criticisms of dependency theory (Greenberg & Park, 1994). Wallerstein (1976) believed the world to be an 'organism' and as such should be viewed as a single entity. This single world system, based on capitalism, came into existence in sixteenth-century Europe. Countries are integrated into this world system based on their capital accumulation. Instead of a simple two-tiered dichotomy of metropoles and satellites, Wallerstein divided the system into three layers: the wealthy capitalist core; the poorest and least industrialised parts of the world, called the periphery; and the newly industrialised countries (NICs) of Brazil, South Korea and Singapore, known as the semi-periphery. Countries are integrated into the world system unequally, with core countries becoming wealthy at the expense of those in the periphery through the exploitation of resources and keeping wages low. Countries can lose their dominant position over time, as was the case with the Italian city-states of Venice and Genoa nearly five centuries ago (Giddens, 2006). Researchers in comparative education, who adopt a world systems framework, analyse how education in the periphery is manipulated to serve the interests of the capitalist core (see Arnove, 1980; Clayton, 1998).

Like dependency theory, world systems theory has attracted criticism for over-generalisation (Chant & McIlwaine, 2009) and not looking at internal factors such as corruption and mismanagement (Potter et al., 2008). Both world systems and dependency theory suggest that the only way to advance is to delink from the global economy. Is this really possible or desirable when countries are becoming increasingly interdependent as a result of globalisation?

 Activity 5.8   World Systems theory

Make a list of countries that you think belong in the core, semi-periphery and periphery tiers. Justify your choices.

Post-colonial theory

'In 1921, 84 per cent of the surface of the earth had been colonized since the sixteenth century ... [and] though by the mid-1960s most colonies were, at least formally, independent, the experience of subsequent decades showed how much the ghost of colonization still loomed over the post-colonial world' (Chiriyankandath, 2007, p. 36). Generally speaking, post-colonial theory examines the impact of colonialism from the perspective of those who were formerly colonised (Crossley & Tikly, 2004). This approach seeks to 'destabilize the dominant discourse of imperial Europe (e.g. history, philosophy, linguistics and "development"), which are unconsciously ethnocentric, rooted in European cultures and reflective of a dominant Western world view' (McEwan, 2008, pp. 124–125). Edward Said (1978) argued in his classic text *Orientalism* that Western ideas of the Middle East were far from the reality. The West, as a result of its dominant position, which began during the colonial era, has perpetuated negative stereotypes of the Orient through art and literature ever since. Indigenous people were considered 'backward', morally and culturally empty, but through the process of colonisation could become civilised (McEwan, 2009). This was how the West was able to justify its power and authority over those who were seen to need Western assistance.

Many of the education systems in the developing world have roots in the colonial era when Western forms of education spread along with the acquisition of land, peoples and territories. What colonial legacies are still visible in current education systems? '[M]any existing education systems still bear the hallmarks of the colonial encounter in that they remain elitist, lack relevance to local realities and are often at variance with indigenous knowledge systems, values and beliefs' (Crossley & Tikly, 2004, p. 149). Furthermore, many post-colonial theorists contend that even though formal colonial empires have dissipated, their power has resurfaced in new forms through the work of intergovernmental organisations, multinational corporations and trade agreements (Spring, 2009). From a post-colonial perspective, education is seen as a vehicle to serve the interests of rich nations and powerful companies through the promotion of market economies, human capital education, and neo-liberal school reforms (for example, the marketisation of education discussed in Chapter 4).

Critics of post-colonial theory have argued that it is 'too theoretical and not rooted enough in material concern' and 'is ignorant of the real problems characterizing everyday life in the Global South' (McEwan, 2008, p. 127). However, there is immense potential for applying a post-colonial perspective in comparative education research, as evidenced by a number of recent studies (Phillips & Schweisfurth, 2008).

Barriers to education

There are numerous barriers that children and young people face in accessing education in the developing world. As mentioned at the beginning of this chapter, poverty, poor health and lack of basic necessities (for example, proper sanitation) are only some of the key challenges standing in the way of individuals receiving an education. The next sections discuss other barriers, including armed conflict, HIV/AIDS and child labour.

Armed conflict and education

'Countries affected by armed conflict are among the farthest from reaching the Education for All goals, yet their education challenges go largely unreported' (UNESCO, 2011, p. 6). In the last decade, 35 countries (30 were low-income and lower middle-income countries) experienced armed conflict, with the average conflict lasting 12 years. The consequences of conflict are devastating. UNESCO (2011, p. 6) reports that 'in conflict-affected poor countries, 28 million children of primary school age are out of school … and are twice as likely to die before their fifth birthday as children in other poor countries'. Education systems have been directly affected, as schools, their teachers and pupils are seen as legitimate targets.

Not only have millions of young people witnessed violence and horrific war crimes first-hand, but also an increasing number of children are being recruited to fight as soldiers. UNESCO (2011) stated that there are reports of child soldiers from 24 countries, including the Central African Republic, Chad, the Democratic Republic of the Congo, Myanmar and the Sudan. War Child (2013), a charity helping those affected by conflict, estimate there are 250,000 child soldiers in the world, and 40% of them are girls. In Sierra Leone, approximately 40,000 children (defined by the UN Convention on the Rights of the Child as being below the age of 18) were engaged in fighting during a civil war lasting just over ten years (1991–2002) (Maclure & Denov, 2006).

How do children become actively engaged in armed conflict? Many children are vulnerable to recruitment due to extreme poverty and hunger, while others are abducted from their homes and forced into becoming soldiers (War Child, 2013). The Coalition to Stop the Use of Child Soldiers (2008, p. 26) report that: 'Children in refugee camps, the internally displaced, children separated from their families and children among the rural poor and in urban slums are at higher risk.' They also suggest that education has become part of the problem as schools, particularly in Bangladesh, Pakistan and Southern Thailand, have become places where armed groups seek to indoctrinate children and identify them for recruitment.

HIV/AIDS

UNAIDS (2011) estimate that there are around 34 million people living with HIV worldwide, with the majority (68%) residing in sub-Saharan Africa. AIDS has claimed at least 1 million lives annually in sub-Saharan Africa alone since 1998. As a result, approximately 15 million children under the age of 18 have become orphaned (UNICEF, 2006) and the effects on HIV/AIDS orphans' education are enormous, to say the least.

For many orphaned children, household duties shift to them and schooling is simply not an option due to lack of time and money (Kakooza & Kimuna, 2006). Orphaned children cannot afford to pay school fees and other expenses, such as uniforms. 'Although in the short term opting out of school may help with cash needs, in the long term, it entrenches the households' poverty and puts the children at greater risk of becoming infected with the HIV virus' (Kakooza & Kimuna, 2006, p. 67). Education plays a huge role in combatting HIV/AIDS (see Coombe, 2004). UNESCO (2011) report that women with secondary education are more likely to be aware of the measures that prevent mother-to-child transmission of HIV, and in Malawi, 60% of mothers with secondary education or higher were aware that drugs could reduce the risk of transmission, compared with 27% of women with no education.

 Activity 5.9   Child labour

Before reading the next section, think about the following points:

1) How would you define child labour?

2) Why might children go to work rather than school?

3) What kind of work do children undertake in the world?

Child labour

The International Labour Organisation (ILO) estimate that there are approximately 215 million child labourers worldwide, with over half of them involved in hazardous work (ILO, 2013a). They define child labour as 'work that deprives children of their childhood, their potential and their dignity, and that is harmful to physical and mental development' (ILO, 2013b). It refers to work that is mentally, physically, socially or morally dangerous and harmful to children, and interferes with their schooling by:

- depriving them of the opportunity to attend school;

- obliging them to leave school prematurely; or

- requiring them to attempt to combine school attendance with excessively long and heavy work.

Over half of all child labourers are involved in agriculture, hunting, forestry or fishing, while approximately a quarter are found in the service sector (ILO, 2013b). Many children experience the worst forms of child labour, such as forced labour, slavery, sexual exploitation and human trafficking. An estimated 1.2 million children are trafficked worldwide every year (UNICEF, 2011).

In a study conducted in Ghana and the Gambia, Chant and Jones (2005) found that low-income young people became involved in a variety of work activities from a relatively young age, many starting in primary school. They found that almost all the children around the ages of 7 or 8 began unpaid work, mainly consisting of domestic chores, and by around the age of 11–12 many reported to have taken on part-time work. Girls take on the bulk of domestic work, including cooking, cleaning, washing, sewing and looking after the younger children in the family. Paid work is typically characterised by low wages and requires few skills. Examples include assisting relatives on market stalls or in small family businesses or running errands. Lastly, they found that hours of work vary but, on average, consist of weekends and one or two hours before or after school.

Why do so many children work? Poverty is the root cause of why millions of children work rather than go to school (ILO, 2013a). There are around 61 million children in the world who are out of school, with Nigeria topping the list with a total of 10.5 million (UNESCO, 2012b). In a recent multi-country poll on nutrition, it was found that three in ten parents have allowed their children to miss school in order to work and help pay for the family's food, and more so in Nigeria than in any other country (Globescan, 2012). There is a high demand for child labourers in many low-income countries, especially for girls who work in the home and provide childcare or look after the sick (Pyke, 2012). Other reasons why children remain out of school include poor health. UNESCO (2012b) estimate that worldwide around 171 million children are affected by moderate or severe stunting (being short for one's age), which is one of the clearest signs of malnutrition. Even though many countries have abolished school fees, there are still high costs associated with sending children to school. Poor-quality education is also holding many children back. The lack of trained teachers is a major obstacle and millions of children are failing to learn the basics (UNESCO, 2012b).

Solutions

What can be done to remove barriers such as poverty in the developing world? Many countries are plagued by what Collier (2007) calls the 'poverty trap'. Collier argues that there are approximately 1 billion people in the world who are caught in this trap, living in abject poverty in around 60 countries. The poverty trap lies in four areas: conflict, a lack of natural resources, being landlocked with poor neighbours, and bad governance. In order to break free from the trap, some of Collier's solutions include military intervention, revision to international laws, transforming aid and liberalising trade policies.

Economists such as Jeffrey Sachs (2005) argue that extreme poverty can be ended by cancelling the debt owed by poor countries and increasing aid from rich countries to the poor. However, others, such as William Easterly (2006) and Dambisa Moyo (2009), claim that aid does more harm than good. In fact, Moyo writes: 'The notion that aid can alleviate systemic poverty, and has done so, is a myth. Millions in Africa are poorer today because of aid; misery and poverty have not ended but increased' (Moyo, 2009, p. xix). Key arguments are that people become dependent on aid and this reliance on aid stops them from initiating strategies to help themselves. Bolton (2007) contends that in order for aid to be effective, people need to take ownership, have the capacity to use it and, above all, aid must be sustainable: 'Aid needs to fit with people's experience, expectations and cultural habits' (Bolton, 2007, p. 85).

Is debt relief the answer? The Jubilee Debt Campaign (JDC) estimate that '[t]he poorest 90 countries have debts totalling US$1.3 trillion, whilst for the poorest 144 countries, it is over US$4.9 trillion' (JDC, 2013). This means that they pay around $23 million every day to the rich world. It is believed that this debt worsens poverty and is preventing some countries from reaching the Millennium Development Goals. However, the good news is that there has been some debt relief. In 2005, the G8 countries signed the Multilateral Debt Relief Initiative (MDRI), which pledged to provide 100% debt relief for those countries which complete the Heavily Indebted Poor Countries (HIPC) initiative (International Monetary Fund, 2013). The MDRI covers debts from the International Monetary Fund (IMF), the World Bank and the African Development Fund (AFDF). To date, 35 countries have qualified and the total cost of MDRI to the IMF alone is estimated to be around $3.4 billion. 'Aid, no matter how good, can do no more than help create the conditions for development. It can't deliver it. Only trade – and the economic growth it brings – can do that' (Bolton, 2007, p. 169). So is the answer trade?

 Activity 5.10   Aid, trade or debt relief?

What should Western nations do, if anything, to assist 'the bottom billion'? Should we give more aid and cancel debts? Should we make it easier for countries to trade with us? Are we part of the problem rather than the solution?

Is education the answer?

What is the role of education in development? Much of the discourse on development is dominated by economics rather than education (McGrath, 2010). There is evidence to suggest that despite an increase in spending on education in the developing world, there is little connection between growth in schooling and economic growth (Easterly, 2001). Furthermore, many individuals from developing countries, once educated, leave their country of birth and migrate to places where they can earn more in what is called the 'brain drain' (Spring, 2009). Overall, the role of education in development is a complex matter and 'the relative marginalisation of educational accounts in mainstream development thinking is a major challenge to which international and comparative education needs to respond' (McGrath, 2010, p. 237).

Conclusion

No matter how you measure development, the world is an unequal place. Whatever your perspective on education and development, there is no denying that basic education and the ability to read and write can potentially free individuals from oppression and enable them to make real choices and have a say to what happens to them. Wealthy nations do not have large populations of unskilled, uneducated individuals. In short, education benefits nations by contributing to economic productivity and socially through improving individuals' prospects and life chances.

 Case Study 5   Uganda

Uganda is a landlocked country in Eastern Africa, west of Kenya and east of the Democratic Republic of Congo. Uganda ranks 161 out of 186 in terms of human development, making it low in comparison to other countries (UNDP, 2013). The United Nations Development Programme also report that the average life expectancy is 54.5 years and the mean years of schooling that an adult receives is 4.7 years. The GNI per capita is $1,168 and Uganda has a population of just over 35 million.

   The Central Intelligence Agency (CIA, 2013) reports that the most important sector of the economy is agriculture, where over 80% of the workforce is employed, and its primary export is coffee. Approximately 1.2 million people are living with HIV/AIDS.

Politics

Uganda gained independence from the United Kingdom in 1962. Political instability ensued in the years following independence. The dictatorial regime of Idi Amin (1971–79) was responsible for the deaths of some 300,000 opponents, and under Milton Obote (1980–85) at least another 100,000 lives were lost due to guerrilla war and human rights abuses. Since 1986, there has been relative stability and economic

(Continued)

(Continued)

growth to Uganda. However, 'Uganda is subject to armed fighting among hostile ethnic groups, rebels, armed gangs, militias, and various government forces that extend across its borders' (CIA, 2013).

Key questions:

- Why is Uganda considered to have low human development?

- From a post-colonial perspective, what impact do you think Uganda's colonial past has had on its current development situation?

- Why do you think the average number of years of schooling an adult has is only 4.7 years?

Suggested reading

Chant, S. & Mcllwaine, C. (2009) *Geographies of Development in the 21st Century.* Cheltenham: Edward Elgar
This is an excellent starting point for students new to ideas, concepts and theories pertaining to development. It is an accessible text with a range of topics, including urbanisation, gender, poverty and health.

McEwan, C. (2009) *Postcolonialism and Development.* Abingdon: Routledge
Provides an in-depth account of the origins of post-colonialism, what postcolonial theory is and how it relates to development.

McGrath, S. (2010) The role of education in development: An educationalist's response to some recent work in development economics. *Comparative Education*, 46(2), 237–253
An excellent article which puts the role of education in development into perspective.

References

Arnove, R. (1980) Comparative education and world-systems analysis. *Comparative Education Review*, 24(1), 48–62

Berstein, H. (1971) Modernization theory and the sociological study of development. *Journal of Development Studies*, 7(2), 141–160

Bolton, G. (2007) *Aid and Other Dirty Business.* Reading: Ebury Press

Chant, S. & Jones, G. (2005) Youth, gender and livelihoods in West Africa: Perspectives from Ghana and the Gambia. *Children's Geographies*, 3(2), 185–199

Chant, S. & Mcllwaine, C. (2009) *Geographies of Development in the 21st Century.* Cheltenham: Edward Elgar

Chiriyankandath, J. (2007) Colonialism and post-colonial development, in P. Burnell & V. Randall (eds) (2008), *Politics in the Developing World.* Oxford: Oxford University Press

CIA (Central Intelligence Agency) (2013) *The World Factbook*. Available online at: www.cia.gov/library/publications/the-world-factbook/geos/ug.html

Clayton, T. (1998) Beyond mystification: Reconnecting world-system theory for comparative education. *Comparative Education*, 42(4), 479–496

Coalition to Stop the Use of Child Soldiers (2008) *Child Soldiers: Global Report 2008*. London: Bell & Bain

Collier, P. (2007) The Bottom Billion. New York: Oxford University Press

Coombe, C. (ed.) (2004) *The HIV Challenge to Education: A Collection of Essays*. Available online at: http://unesdoc.unesco.org/images/0013/001376/137638e.pdf

Crossley, M. & Tikly, L. (2004) Postcolonial perspectives and comparative and international research in education: A critical introduction. *Comparative Education*, 40(2), 147–156

Easterly, W. (2001) *The Elusive Quest for Growth*. Cambridge, MA: MIT Press

Easterly, W. (2006) *The White Man's Burden: Why the West's Efforts to Aid the Rest Have Done so Much Ill and so Little Good*. Oxford: Oxford University Press

Frank, A.G. (1966) The development of underdevelopment. *Monthly Review*, 18.

Giddens, A. (2006) *Sociology* (5th edition). Cambridge: Polity Press

Globescan (2012) *Multi-Country Nutrition Poll 2011 Topline Report*. Available online at: www.savethechildren.org.uk/sites/default/files/docs/Nutrition-poll.pdf

Greenberg, J. & Park, T. (1994) Political ecology. *Journal of Political Ecology*, 1, 1–12

Halls, W.D. (ed.) (1990) *Comparative Education: Contemporary Issues and Trends*. London: Jessica Kingsley/UNESCO

ILO (2013a) *World Report on Child Labour: Economic Vulnerability, Social Protection and the Fight against Child Labour*. Geneva: International Labour Office

ILO (2013b) *What is Child Labour?* Available online at: www.ilo.org/ipec/facts/lang--en/index.htm

International Monetary Fund (2013) The Multilateral Debt Relief Initiative. Available online at: www.imf.org/external/np/exr/facts/mdri.htm

Jubilee Debt Campaign (2013) The Debt Crisis. Available online at: www.jubilee debtcampaign.org.uk/?lid=98

Kakooza, J. & Kimuna, S.R. (2006) HIV/AIDS orphans' education in Uganda. *Journal of Intergenerational Relationships*, 3(4), 63–81

Little, A. (2000) Development studies and comparative education: Context, content, comparison and contributors. *Comparative Education*, 36(3), 279–296

Maclure, R. & Denov, M. (2006) 'I didn't want to die so I joined them': Structuration and the process of becoming boy soldiers in Sierra Leone. *Terrorism and Political Violence*, 18(1), 119–135

McEwan, C. (2008) Post-colonialism, in V. Desai & R. Potter (2008) *The Companion Guide to Development Studies* (2nd edition). London: Hodder & Stoughton

McEwan, C. (2009) *Postcolonialism and Development*. Abingdon: Routledge

McGrath, S. (2010) The role of education in development: An educationalist's response to some recent work in development economics. *Comparative Education*, 46(2), 237–253

Moyo, D. (2009) *Dead Aid: Why Aid is Not Working and How There is Another Way for Africa*. London: Penguin

Noah, H.J. & Eckstein, M.A. (1988) Dependency theory in comparative education: Twelve lessons from the literature, in J. Schriewer & B. Holmes (eds),
Theories and Methods in Comparative Education. Frankfurt: Peter Lang

Parkyn, G.W. (1977) Comparative education research and development education. *Comparative Education*, 13(2), 87–93

Phillips, D. & Schweisfurth, M. (2008) *Comparative and International Education:
An Introduction to Theory, Method, and Practice*. London: Continuum

Potter, R., Binns, T., Elliot, J. & Smith D. (2008) *Geographies of Development: An
Introduction to Development Studies* (3rd edition). Harlow: Pearson/Prentice-
Hall

Potter, R., Conway, D., Evans, R. & Lloyd-Evans, S. (2012) *Key Concepts in
Development Geography*. London: Sage

Pyke, A. (2012) Understanding and invoking rights: Education and development, in
C. Regan (ed.), *80:20 Development in an Unequal World* (6th edition). Pretoria:
UNISA Press

Rostow, W. (1960) *The Stages of Economic Growth: A Non-communist Manifesto*.
Cambridge: Cambridge University Press

Sachs, J. (2005) *The End of Poverty*. London: Penguin

Said, E.W. (1978) *Orientalism*. London: Pantheon Books

Shields, R. (2013) *Globalization and International Education*. London:
Bloomsbury

Shuurman, F.J. (2008) The impasse in development studies, in V. Desai &
R. Potter (eds), *The Companion Guide to Development Studies* (2nd edition).
London: Hodder & Stoughton

Spring, J. (2009) *Globalization of Education: An Introduction*. Abingdon:
Routledge

Sumner, A. & Tribe, M. (2008) *International Development Studies: Theories and
Methods in Research and Practice*. London: Sage

UNAIDS (2011) *World AIDS Day Report 2011*. Available online at: www.unaids.
org/en/media/unaids/contentassets/documents/unaidspublication/2011/
JC2216_WorldAIDSday_report_2011_en.pdf

UNDP (1990) Human Development Report 1990. Oxford: Oxford University
Press. Available online at: http://hdr.undp.org/en/reports/

UNDP (2013) Human Development Report 2013: The Rise of the South: Human
Progress in a Diverse World. New York/Oxford: Oxford University Press.
Available online at: http://hdr.undp.org/en/reports/

UNESCO (2000) *The Dakar Framework for Action: Education for All: Meeting
Our Collective Commitments*. Paris: UNESCO

UNESCO (2011) *EFA Global Monitoring Report 2011: The Hidden Crisis: Armed
Conflict and Education*. Paris: UNESCO

UNESCO (2012a) *Education for All*. Available online at: www.unesco.
org/new/en/education/themes/leading-the-international-agenda/
education-for-all/the-efa-movement/

UNESCO (2012b) *EFA Global Monitoring Report 2012: Youth and Skills: Putting
Education to Work*. Paris: UNESCO

UNICEF (2006) *Africa's Orphaned and Vulnerable Generations: Children Affected
by AIDS*. Available online at: www.unicef.org/publications/files/Africas_
Orphaned_and_Vulnerable_Generations_Children_Affected_by_AIDS.pdf

UNICEF (2011) Facts on Children. Available online at: www.unicef.org/early-
childhood/9482.html

United Nations (2000) *The Millennium Declaration*. Available online at: www. un.org/millennium/declaration/ares552e.pdf

United Nations (2012) *The Millennium Development Goals Report 2012*. Available online at: www.un.org/millenniumgoals/pdf/MDG%20Report% 202012.pdf

Wallerstein, I. (1976) The Modern World-System: Capitalist Agriculture and the Origins of the European World-Economy in the Sixteenth Century. New York: Academic Press

War Child (2013) Child Soldiers. Available online at: www.warchild.org.uk/ issues/child-soldiers

World Bank (2012) About Development. Available online at: http://web.world bank.org/WBSITE/EXTERNAL/EXTSITETOOLS/0,,contentMDK:20147486~me nuPK:344190~pagePK:98400~piPK:98424~theSitePK:95474,00.html

World Food Programme (2013) Hunger Facts. Available online at: www.wfp.org/ share-a-hunger-fact?icn=hungerfacts&ici=homepage-link

CHAPTER 6

GENDER AND EDUCATION

This chapter explores:

- The relationship between gender inequality and education in the developing world;
- Global gender patterns in participation and achievement;
- Cultural explanations for gender patterns.

As we saw in the last chapter, many individuals in the developing world face multiple sources of inequalities, such as poor health and sanitation, lack of access to education and other basic necessities, all compounded very often by poverty. However, it is women and children who face the greatest social, economic and political disadvantage. How does being female affect women's social and economic prospects? In many parts of the world, 'they are less well-nourished than men, less healthy, and more vulnerable to physical violence and sexual abuse. They are much less likely than men to be literate, and still less likely to have pre-professional or technical education' (Nussbaum, 2000, p. 219).

Measuring gender inequality

Before moving on to gender inequality, it is important to understand what gender means and how it is different from someone's sex. '"Sex" refers to the biological and physiological characteristics that define men and women while "Gender" refers to the socially constructed roles, behaviours, activities, and attributes that a given society considers appropriate for men and women' (WHO, 2013a). The idea that women should cover themselves up (for example, wearing a burqa) in some countries is gendered and not a female characteristic. A female characteristic would be to have a vagina, which is biological and something men do not have.

The United Nations Development Programme (UNDP) measures the disadvantage of women and girls using the Gender Inequality Index or GII (UNDP, 2013b). The GII is based on the same principles as the HDI (discussed in Chapter 5) and shows the loss in human development due to inequality between female and male achievements in three dimensions: reproductive health, empowerment and the labour market. The health component is calculated using maternal mortality ratios and adolescent fertility rate. The empowerment component is calculated by the share of parliamentary seats held by each sex and by secondary and higher education attainment levels (see Figure 6.1). The labour component is measured by women's participation in the workforce. The index ranges from 0 (men and women are equal) to 1 (men and women are not equal) so the higher the score, the more discrimination women face.

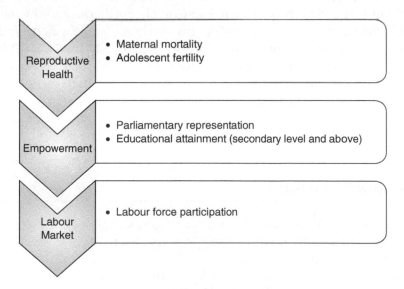

Figure 6.1   The components of the Gender Inequality Index

Source: Adapted from UNDP, 2013b

There are no countries with perfect gender equality and the world average is 0.463 or 46.3% (UNDP, 2013a). The region with the greatest inequality between men and women is sub-Saharan Africa at 0.577 or 57.7%, followed by South Asia with 0.568 or 56.8% and then the Arab states at 0.555 or 55.5%. Countries with the highest gender inequality include Yemen (0.747 or 74.7%), Afghanistan (0.712 or 71.2%) and Niger (0.707 or 70.7%). Countries with the lowest inequality are the Netherlands (0.045 or 4.5%), Sweden (0.055 or 5.5%), Switzerland and Denmark (0.057 or 5.7%). The United Kingdom has a score of 0.205 or 20.5% and the United States 0.256 or 25.6%.

 Activity 6.1   Limitations of measuring gender inequality

Before reading the next section, what do you think are the limitations of measuring gender inequality and of the GII in particular? Are there any alternative ways?

Limitations of the GII

The United Nations Development Programme recognises that there are limitations to the GII. The empowerment dimension is measured by national representation in parliament and does not take into account participation in government at a local level. Furthermore, 'the labour market dimension lacks information on incomes, employment and on unpaid work [which is] mostly done by women' (UNDP, 2013b). The GII does not take into consideration household chores such as caring for elders or infants, cleaning, cooking, and so forth. Other issues omitted are asset ownership, gender-based violence and involvement in community decision making. This lack of data is one of the main reasons why it is difficult to obtain a true picture of gender inequality.

Women and health

Reproductive health is a good indicator of gender inequality. 'Every year more than half a million women die as a result of complications during pregnancy and childbirth, 99% in developing countries' and '[a] further 300 million women worldwide (25% of the developing world's adult women) currently live with avoidable ill health and disability as a result of pregnancy' (Conway & Waage, 2010, p. 180). Some of the issues include infertility, uterine prolapse (where the womb falls into the vagina) and obstetric fistula (a hole between the vagina and the bladder or rectum that causes leakage of faeces and/or urine into the vagina. As a result, many women become socially excluded from their communities or shunned by their husbands because of the unpleasant odour and their inability to have children (Fistula Foundation, 2012). The World Health Organisation (WHO) estimates that between 50,000 and 100,000 women are affected by fistula each year (WHO, 2010a).

Millennium Development Goal (MDG) number 5 is aimed at improving maternal health, with targets to reduce the maternal mortality ratio by three-quarters and achieve universal access to reproductive health. Maternal mortality has decreased globally, nearly by half since 1990, but it is still fifteen times higher than in developing regions (United Nations, 2013). Despite this positive step, the rate has not decreased enough to suggest that the MDG goal can be met by 2015.

Promoting gender equality and empowering women

Having equal access to quality education for both boys and girls is vital in order to achieve economic, political and social equality. MDG number 3 is aimed at promoting gender equality and empowering women, with a target to eliminate gender disparity in primary and secondary education. There are now roughly the same numbers of boys and girls enrolled in primary school in the developing world, with the exception of southern and western Asia and sub-Saharan Africa. However, at secondary level, girls have even greater barriers accessing education. Girls face significant challenges in sub-Saharan Africa where there are only 82 girls enrolled for every 100 boys (United Nations, 2012).

One of the consequences of not having access to education is illiteracy. 'In 2010, there were still 122 million people between 15 and 24 years of age – 74 million women and 48 million men – who were unable to read and write a short, simple statement about their everyday life' (United Nations, 2012, p. 19). Furthermore, in data collected from 146 countries from 2005 to 2010, it was found that in 81 countries more women than men are illiterate and of these countries, 21 display extreme gender disparity, with fewer than seven literate women for every ten literate men (UNESCO, 2012).

Barriers to girls' education

There are many social, cultural, political and economic barriers that girls face accessing education in the developing world. These barriers will vary across and within countries but, generally speaking, many girls face similar challenges. Various societies value boys' education over that of girls (Nussbaum, 2000; Atchoarena & Gasperini, 2003; Shabaya & Konadu-Agyemang, 2004). If families cannot afford the direct costs of schooling (fees, clothing, books, and so forth), they may have to choose between sending a boy or a girl to school. The boy is usually given preference. Often, educating a girl is seen as a waste of time and money because in some countries (for example, India) when a girl marries she becomes the property of her husband's family. Sometimes girls are married at a young age, which can be a factor in them dropping out of school once they are enrolled. Pregnant girls and young mothers are often prohibited from attending school (Lloyd & Mensch, 1999; UNICEF, 2011). Furthermore, girls often undertake domestic chores such as cooking, cleaning and looking after younger siblings, keeping them at home rather than at school.

For many girls, going to school can be a dangerous activity. Action Aid International, a children's charity, believes that violence is a major barrier to education for millions of girls around the world (Action Aid International, 2004). Their research has found that violence against girls takes place in schools, on the way to school and around schools. The violence itself takes many forms, which include sexual violence, sexual harassment, intimidation, teasing and the threat of violence. Parents are also less likely to allow daughters to attend school if they have to travel long distances as they may fear for their safety (UNICEF, 2011).

In many schools around the world, girls suffer abuse at the hands of their teachers. In research conducted on sexual violence against school girls in Zambia, 60 of the 105 girls interviewed (57%) said that they knew about teachers at their current or former school who had sexually harassed or abused female students (Ballinger et al., 2012). The research also found that in order to coerce girls into participating in sexual activities, teachers would often bribe students with money for food, school fees or uniform. Teachers would also leak exam answers, known as 'leakages', in exchange for sexual favours. Lastly, girls often encounter sexist attitudes from their teachers, making them 'feel uncomfortable, unwanted or stupid' (UNICEF, 2011).

Outside school, violence against women is widespread and occurs in many forms, including honour killings, female genital mutilation, forced or early marriages, sexual violence (including conflict-related sexual violence), and trafficking (WHO, 2013b). However, the most common type of violence, whether physical, sexual or emotional, experienced by women is that committed by their partner or husband. The World Health Organisation estimates that one in three women will experience this type of violence at some point in her life.

The disadvantage, sexual harassment and violence that girls face in education mirror the position of women in society at large. In many developed and developing countries around the world, the notion of male privilege and female subordination (known as patriarchy) exists to varying degrees. Patriarchy is reflected in law, in public policies and in public institutions. It is demonstrated in societies where women face the greatest inequalities in education, employment and health.

Honour crimes are typically found in patriarchal cultures. In the most extreme cases, such crimes involve murder. An honour killing is the murder of a person who has been seen to bring 'shame' on their family. Although it is very difficult to arrive at a true picture, in 2000, the United Nations Population Fund (UNPFA) estimated that there were around 5,000 women and girls worldwide who were killed by a family member for 'dishonouring' their family (UNPFA, 2000). Many of the victims are accused of having pre-marital sex, committing adultery or simply being 'too Western'. While this cultural practice is widespread and cases have been found in the UK, the USA and Brazil, the majority of killings occur in countries where the population is predominately Muslim. However, in a recently published study into teenage attitudes towards honour killings in Jordan, researchers found that those who supported honour killings did so not because of their religious belief but because of their collectivist, patriarchal worldviews and a belief in the importance of female chastity (Eisner & Ghuneim, 2013). The respondents also displayed a more general belief that violence against others is morally justified. From the 856 students surveyed, almost half of boys (40%) and one in five girls (20%) believe that killing a daughter, sister or wife who has 'dishonoured' or shamed the family is justified. A third of all teenagers involved in the research advocated honour killing. It was found that attitudes in support of honour killing are far more likely in adolescent boys with low education backgrounds.

Dowry deaths are another example of violent crimes committed against women. According to the Indian National Crimes Record Bureau (NCRB), there were 8,618 dowry deaths in 2011 (NCRB, 2012). A dowry death is where a woman is murdered or driven to suicide as a result of her inability to pay a dowry (money or other items that a woman brings to a marriage) as demanded by her husband or in-laws. Dowry crimes are typically found in India, despite being prohibited by law since 1961. According to Mishra (2011), education has always been one of the highest social indicators for the middle and upper-middle classes in India. Therefore, in addition to a family's status and wealth, a man's educational qualifications play an important role in how much dowry is given to a groom's family. The higher a man's qualification, the larger the dowry they can demand from the bride's family. Mishra reports that, apparently, '[a] groom with a good MBA can command a dowry of Rs6 million (US$132,000) from his prospective bride's family'. However, women with an education can offset high dowry demands: 'Parents of highly educated financially independent women say they need to find a much lower or even no dowry when a match is agreed' (Mishra, 2011).

Another barrier to education for women and girls in developing regions is female genital mutilation or FGM. FGM, as defined by the World Health Organisation (WHO, 2010b, p. 1), 'refers to all procedures involving partial or total removal of the external female genitalia, or other injury to the female genital organs for non-medical reasons'. FGM can be found across the globe, but is most prevalent in 28 countries in Africa and some countries in Asia and the Middle East. Health workers in the UK and USA have seen an increase in cases due to a rise in immigration from countries where FGM is practised (see Dave et al., 2011). WHO (2010b) estimates that more than 90 million women and girls over the age of 10 have undergone FGM in African countries, and some 3 million girls are at risk of undergoing the procedure each year. Reasons for FGM will vary across countries but include maintaining social status, religion, hygiene, better marriage prospects, and preservation of a girl's virginity (GIZ, 2011b).

FGM has serious consequences on girls' schooling. In Kenya, for example, FGM is part of an initiation ritual that can last for several months (GIZ, 2011a). During this time, girls will be absent from school and often never return because once FGM is performed girls are eligible for marriage. As a result, they can lose interest in school, or are expected to manage the home instead of attending school, or become pregnant. However, in Guinea (West Africa), FGM is increasingly performed by trained medical staff and occurs independently from initiation rituals (GIZ, 2011b). Due to having low incomes, parents will often have to choose between paying for a daughter's schooling and having the procedure done; many choose the latter.

Women and work

'Should [women] attempt to enter the workplace, they face greater obstacles, including intimidation from family or spouse, sex discrimination in hiring, and sexual harassment in the workplace – all, frequently, without effective legal recourse' (Nussbaum, 2000, pp. 119–220). Furthermore, women are far more likely than men to be engaged in vulnerable employment (United Nations, 2012). Work is considered to be vulnerable when there is no employer (people are self-employed) or no formal arrangements, such as work contracts or formal terms of employment or work conditions. Vulnerable employment is poorly paid or often un-paid if, for example, the work is carried out in the family home.

Many women also experience what Nussbaum (2000) describes as the 'double day'. This happens when they work outside the home but still have full responsibility for housework and childcare. All their time is taken up with work so that they have limited opportunities for activities that develop their creative and cognitive capabilities. 'All these factors take their toll on emotional well-being: women have fewer opportunities than men to live free from fear and to enjoy rewarding types of love – especially when, as often, they are married without choice in childhood and have no recourse from a bad marriage' (Nussbaum, 2000, p. 220).

Women and politics

Women also face similar challenges in their participation of the political arena. While women are gaining representation in parliaments, the rate and the overall number of women MPs is still low. In 1995, women held 11.3% of parliamentary seats worldwide, but by the end of January 2012 this number had increased to 19.7% (United Nations, 2012). Women's representation is greatest in the Nordic countries and, in the developing world, Latin America and the Caribbean rank the highest with an average of 23%, followed closely by sub-Saharan Africa with 20% representation. Countries with very low female representation are Oceania (3%), Western Asia (11%) and Northern Africa (11%). In the 2012 Egyptian elections, the number of women holding parliamentary seats plummeted from 12.7% to just below 2%, with only 10 out 508 members being a woman.

Women also have fewer legal rights than men. 'In many nations, women are not full equals under the law: they do not have the same property rights as men, the same rights to make a contract, the same rights of association, mobility, and religious liberty' (Nussbaum, 2000, p. 220). In many parts of the world, until women have more political power to ensure that their rights are upheld, many will continue to been seen as second-class citizens in the eyes of the law.

Impact of education on life chances

'Educated women are also better equipped to enter the paid labour force, which is critical to the survival of the many female-headed households in developing countries' (Shabaya & Konadu-Agyemang, 2004, p. 399). In a study on the relationship between education and gender equality in the labour market, it was found that educated people (both men and women) have greater access to better-paid occupations. However, the extent to which education and skills raises earnings in employment is significantly greater for women than for men (Aslam & Kingdon, 2012). They also tend to have fewer children than their non-educated counterparts. According to the United Nations, a mother's education is a powerful determinant of equity: 'Children of educated mothers – even mothers with only primary schooling – are more likely to survive than children of mothers with no education' (United Nations, 2012, p. 28).

Article 26 of the Universal Declaration of Human Rights states that everyone has the right to education. When women and children are unable to attend school, their human rights are being denied. 'Basic education is, and always has been, the key to freedom from subjugation, fear and want. Education is an effective weapon to fight poverty. It saves lives and gives people the chance to improve their lives. It gives people a voice.

And it increases a nation's productivity and competiveness, and is instrumental for social and political progress' (UNESCO, 2000).

 Activity 6.2   Feminism

What do you think feminism is? How might it potentially affect education? Drawing from your own experience of school, do you think boys and girls experience schooling differently and how might this affect their learning?

Gender and education in the developed world

The previous sections have explored women's and girls' education and the disadvantages they face in the developing world. However, the situation in some of the developed, industrialised countries with high human development is significantly different. In recent years, there has been much literature written in the UK, Australia and elsewhere about boys' underachievement and strategies for raising attainment (Epstein, 1998; Skelton, 2001; Younger et al., 2005; Wilson, 2007). In the UK, girls have been outperforming boys in many subjects, as measured by their achievement in national tests and assessments at the end of Key Stage 2 (between ages 7 and 11) and at GCSE level (ages 14–16) (Younger et al., 2005; Sundaram, 2010).

The so-called gender gap is also evident in PISA scores (discussed in Chapter 2). The gender gap measures the difference between the performance of boys and girls in each subject. In PISA 2009 and PISA 2012, out of all the countries and economies that participated (65 in total), girls outperformed boys in reading (OECD, 2010, 2013). Since 2000, the gender gap in reading has actually widened, particularly in Bulgaria, France and Romania. Finland, which has consistently ranked at the top of the PISA scores, also demonstrated a fairly significant gender gap. Even high-performing countries are struggling with equitable outcomes for both boys and girls.

In mathematics, however, the picture is slightly different, with boys outperforming girls in 35 out of the 65 countries and economies that participated in PISA 2009 (OECD, 2010) and in 37 out of the 65 countries and economies that participated in PISA 2012 (OECD, 2013). Unlike in reading, where girls outperformed boys in every country, in five countries girls outperformed boys in both PISA 2009 and PISA 2012. The country with the largest gender gap in 2012 was Jordan, where girls scored significantly higher than boys. The gender gap is smaller in maths than in reading, and on average boys and girls perform about the same in science. However, boys outperformed girls in science in the UK, Costa Rica, Denmark and Japan (OECD, 2013).

Activity 6.3   Cultural values and education

Look back at Chapter 3 and Hofstede's cultural dimensions. How does national culture affect children's schooling? In other words, how does a masculine society influence how boys and girls behave in school, how they are taught, what they are taught, and by whom? How might this lead to gender inequality? Also, can you make a list of subjects which may be considered masculine or feminine?

Many attribute the current success that girls are experiencing in education to the rise of feminist thinking in the 1960s (Meighan & Harber, 2007; Wood, 2011; Bartlett & Burton, 2012). While there are many strands of feminist theory, they all wish to explain how women experience the world. 'Feminism takes the ideological perspective that women are placed at a disadvantage to men in society by virtue of their gender. Feminists seek to study, explain and highlight these disadvantages with a view to creating change in future power/gender relationships' (Bartlett & Burton, 2012, p. 270). A turning point for women in the UK was the Sex Discrimination Act 1975. This Act made it illegal to discriminate on the basis of gender in areas of education, training and employment and aimed to promote equality between men and women.

Boys and literacy

Considering the PISA scores of the UK, why is it then that boys are performing better in maths and science while girls are faring much better in literacy? The answer may lie in the curriculum. Paechter (2013) believes that different subjects are associated with masculinity and femininity. Mathematics, science and technology are seen as masculine and enjoying a high status in society, while humanities and languages, both national and foreign, are linked with femininity and are accorded with having a lower status. 'The big problem with this is that girls and young women are less likely to study mathematics, science and technology, closing the door on high-status and better-paid careers later on. Similarly, boys are more likely to opt out of the humanities and modern foreign languages, closing down other options' (Paechter, 2013). This is evident despite more woman participating in tertiary education (post-secondary) in Europe overall. The number of men studying science, maths and computing at this level is significantly higher. In fact, men represent around 60–70% of students in this field (EACEA, 2009).

Conversely, why do girls outperform boys in reading and have better literacy skills (reading, writing, listening and speaking)? There is little doubt that reading plays an important role in learning and active citizenship so why is it seen as a feminine activity? Reading fiction, in particular, is seen by many boys as something women and girls do (Wilson, 2006). The number of girls who read for enjoyment is greater than that of boys. According to the OECD (2011, p. 4), this gap has widened between 2000 and 2009: 'In 2000, 60% of boys and 77% of girls read for enjoyment; by 2009, these percentages had dropped to 54% and 74%, respectively.' This could be one of the reasons why girls appear to be doing better in literacy.

Another factor could be the age at which reading and writing is introduced. In countries such as Bulgaria, Estonia, Finland, Latvia, Lithuania, Poland, Serbia, and Sweden, children do not start compulsory primary education until the age of 7, while others in Cyprus, England, Malta, Scotland and Wales start at the age of 5 (Eurydice, 2013). Northern Ireland has the lowest statutory age of school entry at 4 years old. The majority of European countries have a starting age of 6 years old. There is a question about whether boys are experiencing failure in literacy early on in their education because many may not be ready for formal schooling at such a young age. McClure (2008, p. 63) asserts that 'at the beginning of their school career boys are likely to be approximately a year behind girls of the same age, particularly in literacy and social skills'. Finland has one of the highest PISA scores in Europe for reading, even though children start compulsory schooling much later than in the UK. Would starting school later be an advantage for boys in particular? Some, like McClure (2008), argue that parents should be given the choice when a child starts school, depending on their readiness.

To make matters worse for boys, research suggests that children born in the summer (in Northern hemisphere countries) are more likely to have lower attainment throughout their schooling years than their older peers (DfE, 2010). While this is potentially limiting for both boys and girls, it could put boys born in July or August at a particular disadvantage.

 Activity 6.4   Barriers to boys' achievement

In the previous section, some barriers to boys' achievement have already been mentioned. Before reading the next section, can you make a list of other possible barriers? Do you think there are any biological or innate differences in boys and girls that affect their learning?

It is important to note that not all boys and girls will experience school in the same way. However, many practitioners and scholars have argued that boys and girls do experience school differently and therefore will have different challenges. Table 6.1 lists some of these barriers. Do you agree?

Both McClure's (2008) statement regarding boys' developmental delay on entering school and Wilson's (2006) belief that boys have different

Table 6.1   Boys' barriers to attainment

Lack of independence prior to starting school	Less developed linguistically on entry to school
Forced to read and write before physically or emotionally ready	Playtimes tend to be hyperphysical and 'boysterous'
Many writing activities perceived as irrelevant and unimportant	Difficulty with structuring work
Reticence about spending time on planning and preparation	Reading fiction perceived as a female province
Teacher talk and teacher expectations: gender bias	Emotional intelligence issues
Mismatch of teaching styles to preferred ways of learning	Lack of opportunities for reflection
Pupil grouping	Inappropriate seating arrangements
Ineffective group work	Peer pressure
Inappropriate reward systems and lack of positive achievement culture	The laddish culture
The influence of street culture	Mismatch between assessment/examination methods and preferred ways of working
Lack of positive role models	The use of non-performance enhancing drugs
Low self-esteem and limiting self-beliefs	Lack of engagement with the life of the school
Homophobic bullying	Parents' lack of understanding of the role they can play
Intervention occurring too late	Teachers' lack of awareness of the barriers to boys' learning

Source: Adapted from Wilson, 2006

learning approaches could suggest that there are innate or biological differences between boys and girls. This notion is widely debated and often contested in the literature. Some believe, as McClure does, that girls' and boys' brains are wired differently. As an example, girls are said to have more than one centre for acquiring, producing and interpreting language, whereas boys have only one (in the left hemisphere). This could account for why some boys find it harder to multi-task and listen to more than one thing at a time (McClure, 2008).

Others believe that any difference in achievement between boys and girls is down to social factors rather than biological ones. 'However, we know of no neurological evidence to suggest that boys' cognitive processing approaches or ways of learning are any different from girls', or that any particular learning or thinking styles could be gender specific' (Bartlett & Burton, 2012). One could also argue that when considering the barriers listed in Table 6.1, these do not pertain only to boys. Some girls also have low self-esteem and limiting self-beliefs, for example. The issues and debates surrounding gender and education are both complex and numerous. The biggest risk we face when analysing gender issues in education is seeing male and female achievement at the expense of the other. Through inclusive education and removing barriers for all children, while also taking into consideration not only sex, but race and social background, can we perhaps close the gender gap and create a fully equitable and fair system for all? Is this realistic and, more to the point, is it possible?

Conclusion

Gender inequality exists throughout both the developing and developed world. However, the nature and direction of it is markedly different. Many girls in the developing world face barriers in accessing education, unlike girls who live in the Global North. The challenges they face are often deep-rooted in social and cultural practice and are compounded by high levels of poverty. They also face higher levels of violence both in school and outside. More research into the lives of the poor, and especially girls and women, is sorely needed if we are to fully understand the strategies needed to empower them. On the other hand, girls in the developed world have excelled in education in recent years. This just shows what can be done when barriers are removed and efforts are made to provide more equal and fairer access to education for all, for both boys and girls.

🗁 Case Study 6   One hundred million missing

Women make up the majority of the world's population. The reason can be explained by the fact that when women and men receive equal nutrition and medical care, women tend to live longer. They are also more resistant to disease in infancy. However, Sen (1990) noticed that the number of women to men was lower in Asia (in China and India, in particular) and North Africa compared to Europe, the USA and Japan. For example, it is estimated that by 2020, there will be 30 million more men than women reaching adulthood in China (Brooks, 2013). Why are there so many more men than women?

In some countries, there is a historical preference for boys. Boys are needed for physical labour to contribute to the family income. Women have fewer legal rights so may not be able to inherit land. In some countries a woman becomes the property of her husband's family upon marriage and so will not be able to look after her own parents in old age. In China, for instance, families are only allowed one child and they usually want a son. With cheap ultrasounds, they are able to abort unwanted girls and try again for a boy (see *The Economist*, 2010). Women in many parts of the world do not have equal access to health care and adequate nutrition, resulting in a higher death rate for women than men. And many women are simply abused, killed or neglected so as to cause death. Sen (1990) estimated the number of 'missing' women and girls to be around 100 million.

Note: This case study is based on an article written in 1990 by the Nobel prize-winning economist Amartya Sen. The article, entitled 'More than 100 Million Women Are Missing', appeared in the *New York Review of Books* and can be accessed at: www.nybooks.com/articles/archives/1990/dec/20/more-than-100-million-women-are-missing/

Key questions:

- How can countries raise the value of girls in order to decrease the number of 'missing' women?

- How can female education help?

- What are the future implications of the current trend in the sex ratio?

Suggested reading

Fennell, S. & Arnot, M. (eds) (2008) *Gender Education and Equality in a Global Context: Conceptual Frameworks and Policy Perspectives*. Abingdon: Routledge
Contains articles written by experts in the field and links with many other topics in this book.

Spade, J. & Valentine, C. (eds) (2013) *The Kaleidoscope of Gender: Prisms, Patterns, and Possibilities* (4th edition). London: Sage
Provides a wide range of gender-related articles with a distinct cross-cultural outlook.

References

Action Aid International (2004) *Stop Violence against Girls in Schools*. Available online at: www.actionaid.org.uk/sites/default/files/doc_lib/125_1_stop_violence_against_girls.pdf

Aslam, M. & Kingdon, G. (2012) Can education be a path to gender equality in the labour market? An update on Pakistan. *Comparative Education*, 48(2), 211–229

Atchoarena, D. & Gasperini, L. (eds) (2003) *Education for Rural Development: Towards New Policy Responses*. Rome: Food and Agriculture Organisation of the United Nations

Ballinger, G., Brundige, E., Furstenau, D., McClendon, K., Lugtong, P., Pradhan, M., Roman, E., Rudin, S., Teredesai, R. & Tofigh, S. (2012) *They are Destroying Our Futures: Sexual Violence against Girls in Zambia's Schools*. Available online at: www.lawschool.cornell.edu/womenandjustice/Conferences-and-Events/upload/Sexual-Violence-Against-Girls-in-Zambia-s-Schools.pdf

Bartlett, S. & Burton, D. (2012) *Introduction to Education Studies* (3rd edition). London: Sage

Brooks, R. (2013) *China's Biggest Problem? Too Many Men.* Available online at: http://edition.cnn.com/2012/11/14/opinion/china-challenges-one-child-brooks

Conway, G. & Waage, J. (2010) *Science and Innovation for Development.* London: UK Collaborative on Development Sciences (UKCDS)

Dave, A., Seithi, A. & Morrone, A. (2011) Female genital mutilation: What every American dermatologist needs to know. *Dermatologic Clinics*, 29(1), 103–109

DfE (2010) *Month of Birth and Education.* Schools Analysis and Research Division. London: Department for Education. Available online at: www.gov.uk/government/uploads/system/uploads/attachment_data/file/182664/DFE-RR017.pdf

EACEA (2009) *Key Data on Education in Europe 2009.* Available online at: http://eacea.ec.europa.eu/education/eurydice/documents/key_data_series/105en.pdf

Eisner, M. & Ghuneim, L. (2013) Honor killing attitudes amongst adolescents in Amman, Jordan. *Aggressive Behaviour*, 9999, 1–13

Epstein, D. (1998) *Failing Boys? Issues in Gender & Achievement.* Buckingham: Open University Press

Eurydice (2013) *Compulsory Age of Starting Schooling European Countries: 2013.* Available online at: www.nfer.ac.uk/shadomx/apps/fms/fmsdownload.cfm?file_uuid=3B48895C-E497-6F68-A237-BCD7AB934443&siteName=nfer

Fistula Foundation (2012) *Fast Facts and FAQs.* Available online at: www.fistula-foundation.org/whatisfistula/faqs.html

GIZ (2011a) *Female Genital Mutilation and Education.* Available online at: www.giz.de/Themen/de/dokumente/giz-fgm-EN-bildung-2011.pdf

GIZ (2011b) *Female Genital Mutilation in Guinea.* Available online at: www.giz.de/Themen/de/dokumente/giz-fgm-EN-guinea-2011.pdf

Lloyd, C.B. & Mensch, B.S. (1999) Implications of formal schooling for girls' transitions to adulthood in developing countries, in C. Bledsoe, J.B. Casterline, J.A. Johnson-Kuhn & J.G. Haaga (eds), *Critical Perspectives on Schooling and Fertility in the Developing World.* Washington, DC: National Academy Press, pp. 80–104

McClure, A. (2008) *Making It Better for Boys.* London: Continuum

Meighan, R. & Harber, C. (2007) *A Sociology of Educating* (5th edition). London: Continuum

Mishra, A. (2011) *INDIA: Degrees Replace Dowries for Educated Classes.* Available online at: www.universityworldnews.com/article.php?story=20111125211736183

National Crime Records Bureau (2012) *Chapter 5: Crime against Women.* Available online at: http://ncrb.nic.in/CD-CII2011/cii-2011/Chapter%205.pdf

Nussbaum, M. (2000) Women's capabilities and social justice. *Journal of Human Development*, 1(2), 219–247

OECD (2010) *PISA 2009 Results: What Students Know and Can Do – Student Performance in Reading, Mathematics and Science (Volume I).* Available online at: www.oecd.org/pisa/pisaproducts/48852548.pdf

OECD (2011) *Do Students Today Read for Pleasure?* Available online at: www.oecd.org/pisa/pisainfocus/48624701.pdf

OECD (2013) *PISA 2012 Results: What Students Know and Can Do – Student Performance in Mathematics, Reading and Science (Volume I).* Available online at: www.keepeek.com/Digital-Asset-Management/oecd/education/pisa-2012-results-what-students-know-and-can-do-volume-i_9789264201118-en#page3

Paechter, C. (2013) *Curriculum.* Available online at: www.genderandeducation.com/resources/pedagogies/curriculum/

Sen, A. (1990) More than 100 Million Women Are Missing. *New York Review of Books.* Available online at: www.nybooks.com/articles/archives/1990/dec/20/more-than-100-million-women-are-missing/

Shabaya, J. & Konadu-Agyemang, K. (2004) Unequal access, unequal participation: Some spatial and socio-economic dimensions of the gender gap in education in Africa with special reference to Ghana, Zimbabwe and Kenya. *Compare: A Journal of Comparative and International Education,* 34(4), 395–424

Skelton, C. (2001) *Schooling the Boys: Masculinities and Primary Education.* Buckingham: Open University Press

Staudt, K. (2011) Women and gender, in P. Burnell, V. Randall & L. Rakner (eds), *Politics in the Developing World* (3rd edition). Oxford: Oxford University Press

Sundaram, V. (2010) Gender and education, in J. Arthur & I. Davies (eds), *Education Studies.* London: Routledge

The Economist (2010) The Chinese are coming, Vol. 394, Issue 8672, March 6th 2010.

UNDP (2013a) *Human Development Report 2013: The Rise of the South: Human Progress in a Diverse World.* New York: UNDP

UNDP (2013b) *Gender Inequality Index (GII).* Available online at: http://hdr.undp.org/en/statistics/gii/

UNESCO (2000) *Education for All.* Available online at: www.un.org/cyberschoolbus/briefing/education/education.pdf

UNESCO (2012) *EFA Global Monitoring Report 2012: Youth and Skills: Putting Education to Work.* Paris: UNESCO

UNFPA (2000) *State of the World Population 2000.* Available online at: www.unfpa.org/swp/2000/english/index.html

UNICEF (2011) *Promoting Gender Equality through UNICEF-supported Programming in Basic Education.* Available online at: www.unicef.org/gender/files/BasicEducation_Layout_Web.pdf

United Nations (2012) *The Millennium Development Goals Report 2012.* Available online at: www.un.org/millenniumgoals/pdf/MDG%20Report%202012.pdf

United Nations (2013) *The Millennium Development Goals.* Available online at: www.un.org/millenniumgoals/

WHO (2010a) *10 Facts on Obstetric Fistula.* Available online at: http://www.who.int/features/factfiles/obstetric_fistula/en/

WHO (2010b) *Global Strategy to Stop Health-care Providers from Performing Female Genital Mutilation.* Available online at: http://whqlibdoc.who.int/hq/2010/WHO_RHR_10.9_eng.pdf

WHO (2013a) *Gender, Women and Health.* Available online at: www.who.int/gender/whatisgender/en/

WHO (2013b) *Violence against Women: The Health Sector Responds.* Available online at: http://apps.who.int/iris/bitstream/10665/82753/1/WHO_NMH_VIP_PVL_13.1_eng.pdf

Wilson, G. (2006) *Breaking through Barriers to Boys' Achievement: Developing a Caring Masculinity.* London: Continuum

Wilson, G. (2007) *Raising Boys' Achievement.* London: Continuum

Wood, K. (2011) *Education: The Basics.* London: Routledge

Younger, M., Warrington, M., with Gray, J., Rudduck, J., McLellan, R., Bearne, E., Kershner, R. & Bricheno, P. (2005) *Raising Boys' Achievement.* Norwich: HMSO

PART 2

INTERNATIONAL EDUCATION

CHAPTER 7

UNDERSTANDING INTERNATIONAL EDUCATION

This chapter explores:

- What international education is;
- How it has developed over the years;
- Why it is important to study it.

 Activity 7.1   Defining international education (1)

Before beginning this chapter, can you write down a definition of what you think international education is? List what you see as aspects of international education. At the end of the chapter, reflect on your definition. Is international education what you thought? How it is different from comparative education, as outlined in Chapter 1, and where might these two fields overlap?

As previously stated in Chapter 1, comparative education is often used interchangeably with international education. These so-called 'twin' fields (Bray, 2010) certainly overlap but are two distinct areas of study. This chapter seeks to define key concepts associated with international education and provide a rationale for studying it. International education is concerned with a broad range of subjects, extending from curriculum matters to inclusive teaching. So then, how do we exactly explain what it is? How is it different from comparative education? Why is it important to study it?

What is international education?

Mary Hayden, a well-known scholar in the field of international education, asserts that, like comparative education, there is no easy way to characterise international education either. She writes, '...there is no simple definition of international education to which all would subscribe' (Hayden, 2006, p. 5). This difficulty is echoed by a number of writers in the field and debates surrounding terminology have been around for decades (Marshall, 2007). Dolby and Rahman (2008) contend that international education is used as an 'umbrella term' and, as a result, there are many varied definitions. 'The diversity of our world makes a "one size fits all" model of international education impossible' (Tate, 2012, p. 207). Simandiraki (2006, p. 35) also states that 'international education is a field collectively understood by the academics and practitioners involved in it, but still difficult to define universally. As a result, there are many definitions of international education, which make difficult not only its description, but also the description of its relationship with other elements of practice'. Cambridge (2012, p. 230) adds to this by maintaining that 'it remains controversial whether "international education" constitutes an academic subject in its own right, or whether it is a hybrid field comprising international extensions to a variety of other cognate areas of inquiry. The term "international education" can be used in a variety of contexts.'

Epstein (1992) believed that international education was distinct from, but related to, comparative education. As previously stated in Chapter 1, Epstein (1992, p. 409) argued that international education 'refers to organized efforts to bring together students, teachers, and scholars from different nations to interact and learn about and from each other'. He also maintained that 'practitioners of international education are experts on international exchange and interaction. What makes them expert is based in part on a knowledge of comparative education. Comparativists, however, are scholars first and foremost, interested in *explaining* how and why education relates to the social factors and forces that form its context than in merely knowing about other people's cultures and their education' (Epstein, 1992, p. 409).

International education is often used together with international schooling in the literature. While much of the literature does deal with international schools, it is important to note that we cannot substitute one for the other. International schooling is only a part of what constitutes international education. Some international schools (it is important to note that not all) are involved in international education. International schooling will be discussed in Chapter 11.

International education is closely linked with 'international mindedness' (Cambridge, 2012). What is 'international mindedness'? Hill (2012) believes international mindedness is the product of a successful international education. It is about pursuing knowledge and understanding of cultural differences and global issues and how they affect us all. It is also about being able to critically analyse those issues in order to propose solutions. More than that, Hill also believes international mindedness is a value proposition: 'it is about putting the knowledge and skills to work in order to make the world a better place through empathy, compassion and openness – to the variety of ways of thinking which enrich and complicate our planet' (Hill, 2012, p. 246). Fundamental to international mindedness is the appreciation of cultural diversity within and between nations and the multiple perspectives which arise from it. International mindedness lies closely at the heart of the aim and purpose of many schools worldwide.

An appreciation of cultural diversity is important if we are to include all individuals in the participation of society. Nowadays, many of us, particularly in the UK, live in a multicultural society. 'The term multicultural describes the culturally diverse nature of human society. It not only refers to elements of ethnic or national culture, but also includes linguistic, religious and socio-economic diversity' (UNESCO, 2006, p. 17). What does this mean for educators?

'Multicultural education uses learning about other cultures in order to produce acceptance, or at least tolerance, of these cultures' (UNESCO, 2006, p. 18). It is very much rooted in national systems of education where the aim is to respond to the needs of migrant children (Hill, 2007a). Multicultural education can include bilingual education, immersion programmes, minority education and community education (Husén and Postlethwaite, 1994, in Hill, 2007a). According to Fujikane (2003, p. 137), '…the meanings of multicultural education, the times when it became important, and the practices implemented in schools all varied from country to country'. Hill (2007a) also points out that the term 'multicultural education' is not used consistently and is often used interchangeably with 'intercultural education'.

What, then, is intercultural education? 'Intercultural education aims to go beyond passive coexistence, to achieve a developing and sustainable way of living together in multicultural societies through the creation of understanding of, respect for and dialogue between the different cultural groups' (UNESCO, 2006, p. 18). This is discussed further in Chapter 11, but for the purpose of this chapter it is important to know that multicultural and intercultural education can play an important role in international education.

One way that international education can be promoted is through the curriculum. Many international schools and some national schools follow the International Baccalaureate (IB) curriculum which defines international education according to a set of criteria, listed below:

- Developing citizens of the world in relation to culture, language and learning to live together

- Building and reinforcing students' sense of identity and cultural awareness

- Fostering students' recognition and development of universal human values

- Stimulating curiosity and inquiry in order to foster a spirit of discovery and enjoyment of learning

- Equipping students with the skills to learn and acquire knowledge, individually or collaboratively, and to apply these skills and knowledge accordingly across a broad range of areas

- Providing international content while responding to local requirements and interests

- Encouraging diversity and flexibility in teaching methods

- Providing appropriate forms of assessment and international benchmarking. (IBO, 2013a)

The International Baccalaureate began in 1968 as a not-for-profit organisation and offers four programmes from ages 3 to 19. In 2013, the IB worked with 3,521 schools in 144 countries to over 1,078, 000 students (IBO, 2013b). The IB will be discussed further in relation to international schools in Chapter 11.

 Activity 7.2   The International Baccalaureate

How many schools can you find near you that offer the IB? Use the following website: www.ibo.org/general/where.cfm

---

Globalisation and international education

Globalisation has played a key role in shaping international education over the past couple of decades. The nature and extent to which it has done so is widely debated and will be explored in Chapter 8. Definitions of globalisation vary and it is 'a complex and highly contested term – and one that is widely used but open to multiple interpretations' (Crossley & Watson, 2003, p. 53). However, in order to provide clarity for the purpose of this book, the following definition will be used: 'Globalization may be thought of initially as the widening, deepening and speeding up of worldwide interconnectedness in all aspects of contemporary social life, from the cultural to the criminal, the financial to the spiritual' (Held et al., 1999, p. 2).

In this definition, 'all aspects of contemporary social life' refers to the economic, political, social and cultural spheres that global forces have touched. These spheres influence education (and vice versa) in various ways and to varying degrees. Moreover, 'worldwide interconnectedness' means individuals, societies and nations are linked economically, politically, socially and culturally. We are linked socially through the media and telecommunications; culturally through movements of people; economically through trade; environmentally through sharing one planet; politically through international relations and systems of regulation (Oxfam, 2006, p. 2). Because we are 'interconnected' or 'linked', what happens in other parts of the world on a global level, in turn, affects us on a local level.

How has this worldwide interconnectedness influenced education both nationally and internationally? Some academics argue that globalisation has created greater standardisation in norms of teaching and learning internationally (Phillips & Schweisfurth, 2008; Spring, 2009). Globalisation has also played a role in the internationalisation of higher education in institutions worldwide. Internationalisation at the national/sector/institutional level is defined as 'the process of integrating an international, intercultural or global dimension into the purpose, functions or delivery of post-secondary education' (Knight, 2004, p. 11). The internationalisation of higher education will be discussed in Chapter 12.

The political, economic, technological and cultural trends that have emerged as a result of globalisation have given rise to a growing interest in global citizenship education (Ibrahim, 2005). According to Phillips and Schweisfurth (2008, p. 46): 'Global Citizenship Education (GCE) explicitly seeks to inculcate in learners an international outlook and a sense of belonging to, and responsibility towards the global community.' Oxfam (2006, p. 3) defines a global citizen as someone who:

- is aware of the wider world and has a sense of their own role as a world citizen

- respects and values diversity

- has an understanding of how the world works

- is outraged by social injustice

- participates in the community at a range of levels, from the local to the global

- is willing to act to make the world a more equitable and sustainable place

- takes responsibility for their actions.

In this sense, global citizenship education deals with learning about others, preparing young people for the challenges and issues they are currently facing and the ones they may potentially face in the future. Global citizenship education aims to support young people in dealing with the 'interconnectedness' we now face.

> ### ⊞ Activity 7.3 Global citizenship education
>
> Using the Oxfam (2006) criteria, are you a global citizen? If yes, what examples could you give to provide evidence to support this claim?

Sylvester (2005) regards Robert Hanvey's model of 'education for a global perspective' as a key point in the history of defining international education. Originally written in 1976, Hanvey (2004, p. 1) describes education for a global perspective as:

> Learning which enhances the individual's ability to understand his or her condition in the community and the world and improves the ability to make effective judgments. It includes the study of nations, cultures, and civilizations, including our own pluralistic society and the societies of other peoples, with a focus on understanding how these are all interconnected and how they change, and on the individual's responsibility in this process. It provides the individual with a realistic perspective on world issues, problems and prospects, and an awareness of the relationships between an individual's enlightened self-interest and the concerns of people elsewhere in the world.

Hanvey's definition has subsequently been one of the most frequently cited works relating to international education in the last 30 years (Sylvester, 2005).

The United Nations Educational Scientific Organisation (UNESCO) has been involved in international education since its creation in 1945. They define international education as '…education for international understanding' (Martínez de Morentin, 2004, p. 5). What does international understanding mean? International understanding is arrived at through education which is based on respecting human rights, maintaining peace and respecting others culture. 'This international understanding promotes learning about diversity; about the richness of cultural identities; of the existence of individuals, races, nations and cultures with the capacity to communicate, share and cooperate with others; of the acceptance of difference as an opportunity to act with interest towards others; and understanding' (Martínez de Morentin, 2004, p. 98).

For UNESCO, a key component of education is concerned with promoting democratic coexistence, or peace, in other words. According to Martínez de Morentin (2011, p. 598): 'Peace, from today's point of view, involves general well-being, equal opportunity to enjoy a society's benefits, and mutual respect. It results when everyone involved has rights and freedoms and when humans live in harmony with their environment'. UNESCO maintains that international education is an important concept that must be integrated into all the processes that develop and form human beings.

Like UNESCO, Thompson (in Hayden & Thompson, 1998, p. 278) refers to the ultimate objectives of international education as being 'related to the achievement of greater levels of mutual respect and harmonious coexistence among nations'. Education, and therefore international educational, plays a key role in developing human beings who can live together harmoniously, through respecting not only one another but their environment as well.

International education can also refer to the educational experiences of students of one country studying in another (Cambridge, 2012). This can include those students on exchange programmes such as Erasmus (European Community Action Scheme for the Mobility of University Students). 'Exchanges play a key role in creating the international scholar' (Phillips & Scweisfurth, 2008, p. 44). In 2012, Erasmus celebrated its twenty-fifth anniversary and over 3 million students have participated since it began (European Commission, 2013). The Erasmus programme is part of the EU's Lifelong Learning Programme, which is administered by the European Commission, the executive body of the European Union. The European Commission (2013) believe that Erasmus 'not only enriches students' lives in the academic and professional fields, but can also improve language learning, intercultural skills, self-reliance and self-awareness'. Lastly, Epstein (1992, p. 409) refers to international education as 'organised efforts to bring together students, teachers, and scholars from different nations to interact and learn about and from each other'. 'Organised efforts' can include both student and staff exchanges, which clearly play a vital role in international education.

 Activity 7.4   'Organised efforts' in international education

Using Epstein's (1992) definition of international education, can you think of any other ways, apart from formal exchange schemes, that students, teachers and scholars can be brought together 'to interact and learn about and from each other'?

The term 'international education' has also been applied when researching education in developing countries. Crossley and Watson (2003, p. vii) point out that '[h]istorically, the label international education has often been used to describe the work of scholars from industrialised countries who have studied education in less developed countries'. Phillips and Schweisfurth (2008, p. 51) support this view, stating that '[t]raditionally, particularly in the UK, the term international education has been strongly associated with the study of education in developing countries'. However, as stated in Chapter 1, in order to gain clarity of the 'twin fields' and for the purpose of this book,

Halls' (1990) classification of international education will be used. A brief reminder is necessary here in order to define the field. Halls subdivides international education into 'international pedagogy' and 'Study of the work of international educational institutions'. 'International pedagogy is the study of teaching multinational, multi-cultural and multiracial groups, e.g. in international schools, transnational schools (such as those of the European community), or the education of linguistic or ethnic minorities'. In other words, international pedagogy is not only about how we teach diverse groups of individuals, either in an international or national context, but also how we respond to the needs of particular groups of learners. 'It is also the study of such subjects as education for international understanding, peace education, international population and ecological studies'. Within this area, Halls (1990) also includes the resolution of intra-national differences regarding the teaching of controversial subject-matter, efforts to 'objectivize' textbooks, the harmonisation of curricula and the establishment of international teaching norms. This partly refers to curriculum matters such as global citizenship education and sustainability, and also to the similarities found between schools across contexts (Phillips & Schweisfurth, 2008). Many would argue that the standardisation of education internationally is a result of glo-balisation (see Spring, 2009). The relationship between globalisation and education will be discussed further in Chapter 8.

The second component of international education, according to Halls, is the 'Study of the work of international education institutions'. Although this overlaps with international pedagogy, it 'is more concerned with policy matters, such as the establishment of international acceptability of qualifications, the promotion of educational exchanges and the initiation of cultural agreements'. A good example of this is the Bologna Process (to be discussed in Chapter 12) and those organisations and people involved, such as the European Commission, Council of Europe and UNESCO-CEPES (Centre Européen pour l'Enseignement Supérieur).

Again, there is no agreement among scholars as to the usage of these terms and many, perhaps, would argue that international education is not a subfield of comparative education, as Halls has proposed.

Activity 7.5   Defining international education (2)

Find some books or journal articles with 'international education' in the title. Look at the table of contents. Can you identify the main topics? What is the book or article about? How do these topics relate to the various definitions described in this chapter?

Historical development of international education

Hill (2012) writes that the historical roots of international education date back to John Comenius, a Czech teacher, philosopher and writer in the seventeenth century. Comenius drew up numerous plans for international cooperation and Piaget (1993, p. 12) regarded him '...as a great forerunner of modern attempts at international collaboration in the field of education, science and culture'. Comenius wrote about the establishment of Collegium Lucis in his *Treatise on the Universal Improvement of Human Affairs* (Goormanghtigh, 2004). The Collegium Lucis was to be a sort of international ministry of education that would foster international collaboration through, among other activities, student exchanges, textbooks using a standard language, and creative teaching methods (Hill, 2012). One of Comenius's most important ideas was his philosophy of pansophism. His pansophic view of education was basically a form of universal education where everything is taught to everyone (both boys and girls). Because of his ideas on education for everyone, Comenius's ideas may be regarded as one of the precursors to UNESCO (Piaget, 1993; Sturm & Groenendijk, 1999). When UNESCO began 1946, it had 120 member countries and was tasked with promoting cooperation in the fields of education, science and culture. In fact, Goormanghtigh (2004, p. 3) asks, 'was it to become the *Collegium Lucis* that John Comenius had envisaged three centuries earlier? Would it be the embryo of the ministry of education that he had in mind?'

Crossley and Watson (2003) credit the origins of international education to César Auguste Basset, a French professor of literature who eventually became the director of education at the Ecole Normale in Paris. Basset published a book in 1808 called *Essais sur l'organisation de quelques parties de l'instruction publique; ou, Réflexions sur les inspecteurs généraux de l'université et ceux des académies et observations concernant l'éducation en general* (which translates as *Essays on the organization of some parts of public education; or, Reflections on the inspectors general of the university and those academies and observations on education in general*). Despite the long and complex title, the book was only 97 pages in length. In it, Basset wrote about 'the usefulness of making observations in foreign countries about education and instruction in general' (1808, cited in Brickman, 2010, p. 47) and called for the Université de France to send a scholar who was free from bias and prejudices to go abroad and make these observations (Brickman, 2010). Basset's work was a few years before Marc-Antoine Jullien's book, *Esquisse d'un ouvrage sur l'éducation comparée* or (*Sketch and Preliminary Views on Comparative Education*) in 1817. Perhaps it is possible that Marc-Antioine Jullien, the 'father' of comparative education, was influenced by Basset's work and if this is the case, then could it be argued that comparative education was influenced by initial developments in international education? In fact, Epstein (1992, p. 409) purports that '[a]lthough they are now concurrent pursuits, comparative education grew out of and was inspired by international education'.

This coincides with Noah and Eckstein's (1969) third stage of comparative education, as discussed in Chapter 1. The third stage occurred around the middle of the nineteenth century when scholars travelled to foreign countries not necessarily in the interest of advancing their own country's education but in order to promote international understanding. Perhaps, key events in international education were the catalysts for growth in the field of comparative education?

Sylvester (2007) believes that the beginnings of international education grew from the first world fair, the London Universal Exposition in 1851. The London Universal Exposition was originally called 'The Great Exhibition of the Works of Industry of All Nations' and is sometimes referred to as the Crystal Palace Exhibition, after the place in which it was held. There were 6,039,195 visitors, 17,062 exhibitors and 28 participating nations (Mattie, 1998). 'The first international world exhibition was born out the hope that all peoples of the world might live in harmony, and, more prosaically, out of a desire to tap new potential markets for British products' (Mattie, 1998, p. 12). In other words, the aim of the fair was twofold: first, to stimulate trade and industry, and, secondly, to foster international cooperation.

At the 'Great Exhibition', an educational conference on kindergarten and other topics was held with representatives from Europe and the USA (Sylvester, 2007). This set the scene for international meetings on education to be held at subsequent world fairs in 1855 (Paris), 1862 (London), 1873 (Vienna) and 1876 (Philadelphia, PA).

Sylvester (2002) argues that there were serious efforts to establish international schools from the mid-1800s to the late 1920s. However, Stewart (1972, cited in Sylvester, 2002, p. 6) believes that the establishment of Spring Grove School (its official name was the London College of the International Education Society) in London in 1886 was the 'one genuine and successful attempt at international education in the nineteenth century'. International schools began a slow rise with the opening of the Odenwald School in Germany and the International School of Peace in Boston in 1910, followed by schools in Geneva and Yokohama in 1924 (Sylvester, 2007). However, it was not until after the First World War (1914–1918) that a sizeable rise in international schooling began to happen worldwide (Hill, 2007b). This was largely due to the perception 'that the school could be effectively used as a medium of international understanding' (Arora, Koehler & Reich, 1994, p. 11).

In 1921, the League of Nations was created in the aftermath of the First World War to maintain peace and security between nations. One way in which it promoted international cooperation was by calling for the revision of textbooks to remove nationalistic biases and the glorification of wars

(Arora et al., 1994). The League of Nations lasted 27 years and was replaced by the United Nations in 1945.

Since its establishment in 1945, UNESCO, a specialised agency of the United Nations, has played a key role in fostering educational coopera- tion between nations. UNESCO was set up 'to contribute to peace and security by promoting collaboration among nations through education, science and culture in order to further universal respect for justice, for the rule of law and for the human rights and fundamental freedoms which are affirmed for the peoples of the world, without distinction of race, sex, language or religion' (UNESCO, 1945). Its early activities included sup- porting the growth in international schools. In 1949, UNESCO organised a 'Conference of Principals of International Schools', which was attended by the heads of 15 schools 'wishing to develop an international outlook' (Hill & Hayden, 2010). In 1950, UNESCO financed a 'Course for teachers interested in international education' at the International School of Geneva to discuss how schooling could be made more international in terms of content and methodology (Hill, 2001). There were 50 participants from 18 countries. Hill (2001) believes that, while on this course, participants devised the first known definition of international education.

> It should give the child an understanding of his past as a common heritage to which all men irrespective of nation, race, or creed have contributed and which all men should share; it should give him an understanding of his present world in which peoples are interdependent and in which cooperation is a necessity.
>
> In such an education emphasis should be laid in a basic attitude of respect for all human beings as persons, understanding of those things which unite us and appreciation of the positive values of those things which may seem to divide us, with the objective of thinking, free from fear or prejudice.
>
> (Final Report of the Course for Teachers Interested in International Education, 1950: Section I, in Hill, 2001, p. 38).

There are a number of institutes and centres, both globally and region- ally, that work as part of UNESCO's education programme to support countries in dealing with some of the issues they are facing in educa- tion. The International Bureau of Education (IBE), founded in 1925, was originally a private non-government organisation and the first intergov- ernmental organisation in the field of education (UNESCO, 2012). In 1969, the IBE became an integral part of UNESCO but still operates autonomously. The IBE focuses particularly on curriculum development and on the contents, methods and structures of education in order to support its overall aim, which is the attainment of quality Education for All (UNESCO, 2008). The IBE also produces a quarterly journal entitled *Prospects* (published in English, French, Spanish, Arabic, Chinese and Russian) in the field of comparative education. Other UNESCO institutes include the International Institute for Educational Planning (IIEP), which helps countries to 'design, plan and manage their education systems', the Institute for Lifelong Learning (UIL) and the Institute for Information Technologies in Education (IITE).

Marshall (2007) believes that key developments in the UK since the 1980s and early 1990s have led to a second phase in 'global' rather than international education. The first phase, beginning in the nineteenth century, originated from the peace movements in the USA, Britain and continental Europe. However, Marshall (2007) summarises some key themes now affecting the field as result of the global agenda being firmly placed in the public eye. These include a growing interest and concern over the relationship between globalisation and education; and new threats, such as terrorism, evoking fresh calls for global education and understanding.

 Activity 7.6   International education: Product or process?

Have you received an international education? If yes, how do you know this? Is international education a product or a process? If not, explain why.

Conclusion

The concept of international education is complex and can mean different things to different people. However we choose to define it, common themes can be found. Respect for others, appreciation of cultural diversity, knowledge of global issues, and learning to live together are just some of these common themes. At its simplest, international education is learning about others. What we learn, how we learn and why we learn depend on the context in which our learning takes place. You can find international education in publicly or privately funded national or 'international' schools, colleges or higher education institutions.

International education is delivered through policy initiatives, the curriculum, and the teaching and learning strategies employed by those involved in international education. As we continue to become further interconnected in the next decades to come, international education may play an even more important role in creating harmony, peace and justice among individuals, societies and nations.

To summarise, international education, depending on the context, can refer to:

• Education for global citizenship
• Education for 'international understanding'

- Education for 'international mindedness'
- Education for sustainable development
- Human rights education
- Intercultural education
- International curricula, such as the International Baccalaureate (IB)
- International schooling
- International student and staff exchange
- Multicultural education
- Peace education
- The teaching and learning of diverse groups of individuals in a national or international context
- The teaching and learning of indigenous and ethnic minority groups

 Case Study 7   Genocide and international education

Throughout history, man has been the perpetrator of some of the most vicious crimes against humanity. This has resulted in the mass killings of hundreds and thousands of innocent men, women and children around the world. The Convention on the Prevention and Punishment of the Crime of Genocide, which was adopted by the United Nations General Assembly in 1948, defines genocide as any of the following acts committed with intent to destroy, in whole or in part, a national, ethnical, racial or religious group, as such:

a)   killing members of the group;

b)   causing serious bodily or mental harm to members of the group;

c)   deliberately inflicting on the group conditions of life calculated to bring about its psychical destruction in whole or in part;

d)   imposing measures intended to prevent births within the group;

e)   forcibly transferring children of the group to another group.

According to the Peace Pledge Union, a non-government organisation formed in 1934 to promote peace, there have been eight genocides in the twentieth century (Melicharova, 2002), as follows:

- 1904 Namibia

- 1915 Armenia

- 1932 Ukraine

- 1933–45 The Holocaust

- 1975 Cambodia

(Continued)

(Continued)

- 1982 Guatemala
- 1994 Rwanda
- 1995 Bosnia

The Holocaust refers to the period (1933–45) when Adolf Hitler, leader of the Nazi Party, killed approximately 6 million Jewish men, women and children (Gitlin, 2011). The Nazis believed that they were the 'master race', and therefore superior, and that the Jews were subhuman and enemies of Germany (Gitlin, 2011). They also murdered a number of Soviet prisoners of war, Polish intellectuals, Romani (gypsies), homosexuals and people with physical and mental disabilities (Tonge, 2009). The Jews were systematically exterminated in concentration or 'death' camps in Poland and Germany. If not directly killed, many were illtreated, used as slave labour and died from lack of adequate food, exhaustion or disease.

Key questions:

- Did you learn about genocide in school? Should subjects such as the Holocaust be taught, and if so how (see Hirsch & Kacandes, 2004)?

- How do you think key historical events, such as war crimes, are dealt with in different countries? Is history always treated in a factual, nonbiased manner? If not, why might this be the case?

- What is the role of international education in eliminating prejudice and hatred?

- Can international education achieve peace, tolerance of others and justice for all, or is it just an ideal?

Suggested reading

Hayden, M., Levy, J. & Thompson, J. (eds) (2007) *The Sage Handbook of Research in International Education*. London: Sage
An essential book for anyone wishing to extend their knowledge of international education. It contains numerous articles by well-known scholars in the field. The book contains critical discussions on the origins, current interpretations and contributions of international education.

Singh, J.P. (2010) *United Nations Educational, Scientific, and Cultural Organization (UNESCO): Creating Norms for a Complex World*. Abingdon: Routledge
This book is ideal if you would like a better understanding of the role of UNESCO in the world and its history.

References

Arora, G.L., Koehler, W. & Reich, B. (1994) International education – past and present, in B. Reich & V. Pivovarov (eds), *International Practical Guide on the Implementation of the Recommendation concerning Education for International Understanding, Co-operation and Peace and Education relating to Human Rights and Fundamental Freedoms*. Paris: UNESCO

Bray, M. (2010) Comparative education and international education in the history of boundaries, overlaps and ambiguities. *Compare: A Journal of Comparative and International Education*, 40(6), 711–725

Brickman, W. (2010) Comparative education in the nineteenth century. *European Education*, 42(2), 46–56

Cambridge, J. (2012) International education research and the sociology of knowledge. *Journal of Research in International Education*, 11(3), 230–244

Crossley, M. & Watson, K. (2003) *Comparative and International Research in Education: Globalisation, Context and Difference*. Abingdon: Routledge

Dolby, N. & Rahman, A. (2008) Research in international education. *Review of Educational Research*, 78(3), 676–726

Epstein, E.H. (1992) Editorial. *Comparative Education Review*, 36(4), 409–416

European Commission (2013) *The ERASMUS Programme – Studying in Europe and More*. Available online at: http://ec.europa.eu/education/lifelong-learning-programme/erasmus_en.htm

Fujikane, H. (2003) Approaches to global education in the United States, England and Japan. *International Review of Education*, 49(1–2), 133–152

Gitlin, M. (2011) *The Holocaust*. Minnesota: ABDO Publishing Company

Goormanghtigh, J. (2004) *From the Collegium Lucis to the International Baccalaureate*. Peterson Lecture. Available online at: www.intbac.org/council/peterson/goormaghtigh/documents/goormaghtigh_lecture.pdf

Halls, W.D. (ed.) (1990) *Comparative Education: Contemporary Issues and Trends*. London: Jessica Kingsley/UNESCO

Hanvey, R.G. (2004) *An Attainable Global Perspective*. New York: American Forum for Global Education

Hayden, M. (2006) *Introduction to International Education*. London: Routledge

Hayden, M. & Thompson, J. (eds) (1998) *International Education: Principles and Practice*. Abingdon: Taylor & Francis

Held, D., McGrew, A., Goldblatt, D. & Perraton, J. (1999) *Global Transformations*. Cambridge: Polity Press

Hill, I. (2001) The beginnings of the international education movement, Part II. *European Council of International Schools*, 21(1), 35–48

Hill, I. (2007a) Multicultural and international education: Never the twain shall meet? *Review of Education*, 53, 245–264

Hill, I. (2007b) International education as developed by the International Baccalaureate Organisation, in M. Hayden, J. Levy & J. Thompson (eds), *The Sage Handbook of Research in International Education*. London: Sage

Hill, I. (2012) Evolution of education for international mindedness. *Journal of Research in International Education*, 11(3), 245–261

Hill, I. & Hayden, M. (2010) *The International Baccalaureate: Pioneering in Education*. Woodbridge: John Catt Educational

Hirsh, M. & Kacandes, I. (eds) (2004) *Teaching the Representation of the Holocaust*. New York: The Modern Language Association of America

IBO (International Baccalaureate Organisation) (2013a) *Four Programmes at a Glance*. Available online at: www.ibo.org/programmes/index.cfm

IBO (International Baccalaureate Organisation) (2013b) *About the International Baccalaureate*. Available online at: www.ibo.org/general/who.cfm

Ibrahim, T. (2005) Global citizenship education: Mainstreaming the curriculum? *Cambridge Journal of Education*, 35(2), 177–194

Knight, J. (2004) Internationalization remodeled: Definition, approaches, and rationales. *Journal of Studies in International Education*, 8(1), 5–31

Marshall, H. (2007) The global education terminology debate: Exploring some of the issues, in M. Hayden, J. Levy & J. Thompson (eds), *The Sage Handbook of Research in International Education*. London: Sage

Martínez de Morentin, J.I. (2004) *What is International Education?* Paris: UNESCO

Martínez de Morentin, J.I. (2011) Developing the concept of international education: Sixty years of UNESCO history. *Prospects*, 41(4), 597–611

Mattie, E. (1998) *World's Fairs*. New York: Princeton Architectural Press

Melicharova, M. (2002) *Genocide*. Available online at: www.ppu.org.uk/genocide/index1a.html

Noah, H. & Eckstein, M. (1969) *Toward a Science of Comparative Education*. New York: Macmillan

Oxfam (2006) *Education for Global Citizenship: A Guide for Schools*. Available online at: www.oxfam.org.uk/~/media/Files/Education/Global%20Citizenship/education_for_global_citizenship_a_guide_for_schools.ashx

Phillips, D. & Schweisfurth, M. (2008) *Comparative and International Education: An Introduction to Theory, Method and Practice*. London: Continuum

Piaget, J. (1993) Jan Amos Comenius. *Prospects*, XXIII(1/2), 173–196

Simandiraki, A. (2006) International education and cultural heritage. *Journal of Research in International Education*, 5(1), 35–56

Spring, J. (2009) *Globalization of Education*. New York: Routledge

Sturm, J. & Groenendijk, L. (1999) On the use and abuse of great educators: The case of Comenius in the Low Countries. *Paedagogica Historica: International Journal of the History of Education*, 35(1), 110–124

Sylvester, R. (2002) The 'first' international school, in M. Hayden, J. Thompson & G. Walker (eds), *International Education in Practice*. Abingdon: Routledge, pp. 3–17

Sylvester, R. (2005) Framing the map of international education (1969–1998). *Journal of Research in International Education*, 4(2), 123–152

Sylvester, R. (2007) Historical resources for research in international education (1851–1950), in M. Hayden, J. Levy & J. Thompson (eds), *The Sage Handbook of Research in International Education*. London: Sage

Tate, N. (2012) Challenges and pitfalls facing international education in a post-international world. *Journal of Research in International Education*, 11(3), 205–217

Tonge, N. (2009) *The Holocaust*. New York: The Rosen Publishing Group

UNESCO (1945) *Conference for the Establishment of the United Nations Educational, Scientific and Cultural Organisation*. Available online at: http://unesdoc.unesco.org/images/0011/001176/117626e.pdf

UNESCO (2006) *UNESCO Guidelines on Intercultural Education*. Available online at: http://unesdoc.unesco.org/images/0014/001478/147878e.pdf

UNESCO (2008) *IBE Strategy 2008–2013*. Paris: UNESCO

UNESCO (2012) *History of IBE*. Available online at: www.ibe.unesco.org/en/about-the-ibe/who-we-are/history.html

GLOBALISATION AND EDUCATION

This chapter explores:

- What is meant by globalisation;
- How globalisation has influenced education both nationally and internationally;
- English as a global language.

 Activity 8.1   Defining globalisation (1)

Before beginning this chapter, what do you think globalisation might mean? Write down a definition and then try to think how it might be linked to education.

What is globalisation?

Globalisation has been a key theme and hotly debated topic in business, academia and the media since the 1980s. So what exactly is it and how has it come to influence education? Before considering the concept of globalisation, it has to be stated that 'no single universally agreed definition of globalization exists' (Held & McGrew, 2000, p. 3) and it also 'is one of the most charged issues of the day' (Donnellan, 2002, p. 14).

The International Monetary Fund (IMF) refers to globalisation as an economic process which is the result of human innovation and technological advancement. Globalisation is 'the increasing integration of economies around the world, particularly through trade and financial flows. The term sometimes also refers to the movement of people (labor) and knowledge (technology) across international borders' (IMF, 2000).

This definition focuses on the economic dimension of globalisation while others are more inclusive and all-encompassing. For example, 'globalization may be thought of initially as the widening, deepening and speeding up of worldwide interconnectedness in all aspects of contemporary social life, from the cultural to the criminal, the financial to the spiritual' (Held et al., 1999, p2). This definition includes the social, cultural, political and economic dimensions of globalisation. The main tenet is the notion of interconnectedness. As stated in the previous chapter, individuals, societies and nations are linked socially through the media and telecommunications; culturally through movements of people; economically through trade; environmentally through sharing one planet and politically through international relations and systems of regulation (Oxfam, 2006, p. 2).

Another way of looking at it is: 'globalisation can thus be defined as the intensification of worldwide social relations which link distant localities in such a way that local happenings are shaped by events occurring many miles away and vice versa' (Giddens, 1990, p. 64). A good example of this was the financial crisis (2007–2009) that began in the United States in the mortgage lending industry. This affected economies around the world, particularly in Europe, with governments having to bail out banks. The financial crisis which had its roots in the USA led to a worldwide recession.

▦ Activity 8.2   Defining globalisation (2)

Eric Beerkens, a Dutch academic, compiled a list of definitions of globalisation. You can access the list at: www.beerkens.info/files/globalisation.pdf Can you pick out some common themes?

There is also no agreement on when globalisation began. Some scholars, such as Anthony Giddens (1990), believe the process of globalisation has its origins in the nineteenth century. For Giddens and others, it is a modern phenomenon emanating from the industrial revolution, advances in technology and the rise of capitalism as the dominant way of organising economies. Immanuel Wallerstein (1976) maintains that globalisation has its roots in the formation of sixteenth-century European markets and the creation of a modern world economy. Others, such as Lemert et al.

(2010), claim that globalisation goes back even further to the empires of ancient civilisation (approximately 1000 years BC).

Disagreement on the starting point of globalisation also extends to the direction of globalisation and its effects. There are three main strands of globalisation theory: the hyperglobalists, the sceptics and the transformationalists (see Bray, 2003; or Martell, 2007, for concise summaries). The 'first wave' of theory is hyperglobalism, which focuses on the economic forces of globalisation. Kenichi Omhae, a Japanese business strategist, is a key hyperglobalist. In his books *The Borderless World* (1991, 1999) and *The End of the Nation State* (1996), he argued that the power of individual nations to control economic activities has decreased as we have become increasingly interlinked. In essence, the world has become a single economy without geographically defined borders. In this scenario, multinational companies have more power than nation states to make decisions and influence policy.

The 'second wave' of theorists are known as the sceptics (see Hirst & Thompson, 1996, as an example). They argue that the interconnectedness we now experience is nothing new and that there has always been economic exchange between nations and that perhaps trade between them is becoming more regionalised rather than global. For the sceptics, there is little evidence to suggest that the power of national governments is in decline and that it is merely a myth perpetuated by the West to serve its own economic interests.

The 'third wave' or transformationalists (e.g. Held et al., 1999) maintain that the effects of globalisation are less certain. Like the hyperglobalists, they recognise the world is undergoing unprecedented change, but that this change is happening unequally – some countries are integrated into the world economy and others are not.

Globalisation and education

For educationalists, the fundamental question is how might globalisation influence educational policy and practice, both nationally and internationally? Spring (2009, p. 5) asserts that there are ten key components of educational globalisation, and these are:

- The adoption by nations of similar educational practices, including curricula, school organizations, and pedagogies
- Global discourses that are influencing local and national educational policymakers, school administrators, college faculties and teachers
- Intergovernmental and nongovernment organizations that influence national and local educational practices
- Global networks and flow of ideas and practices

- Multinational corporations that market educational products, such as tests, curricula, and other school materials

- Global marketing of higher education and educational services

- Global information technology, e-learning and communications

- The effect of the world migration of peoples on national and local school policies and practices regarding multiculturalism

- The current effect of English as the global language of commerce on local school curricula and cultures

- Global models of religious and Indigenous education.

For Spring (2009, p. 1), 'Globalization of education refers to the world-wide discussions, processes, and institutions affecting local educational practices and policies. This means that events are happening on a global scale that affect national school systems'. A key component is the idea of a global education superstructure (see Figure 8.1).

How does this global education superstructure influence national systems of education and why? Ideas, practices and policies are drawn from the global education superstructure where national elites can interpret, adapt or reject them. 'Borrowing' educational policy and practice from other countries is commonplace as national governments seek to find more effective and efficient ways to organise education in order be competitive in a globalised world. Some believe, as do Rizvi and Lingard (2010, p. 3), that

Figure 8.1   Global education superstructure

Source: Adapted from Spring, 2009

'...global processes are transforming education policy around the world...' and that '...the processes that now frame education policy are often constituted globally and beyond the nation-state, even if they are articulated in nationally specific terms.' The Millennium Development Goals (MDGs) discussed in Chapter 5 are a good example of this. The MDGs constitute an international policy framework written by professionals and organisations in the global education superstructure but are implemented and interpreted on the national and local level.

 ## Activity 8.3   Global education superstructure

Do you think a global education superstructure exists? Can you find some examples of people, organisations and journals that might make up the global education superstructure? Why might governments choose to draw from this superstructure?

A key question is whether the existence of a global education superstructure leads to similar practices in national education systems across the world. In the introductory chapter of a book on global schooling, Anderson-Levitt (2003, p. 2) asks: 'Is there one global culture of schooling, or many? Are school systems around the world diverging from their original European sources, or are they converging toward a single model?' Furthermore, Altinyelken (2012, p. 203) questions, 'Why do different countries around the world seem to be engaging in a similar dialogue on how pedagogy should be reformed? Why are official discourses converging around the same pedagogical mode [constructivism]?' A key question remains as to whether globalisation has brought about the homogenisation (the increasing uniformity) of education across national boundaries. What similarities can be found in education around the world and where is the evidence?

 ## Activity 8.4   Homogenisation of schooling

Reflect on some of the questions above. How might schooling around the world be the same? Consider the structure of national education systems (early years, primary, secondary, and so forth), the school day, teaching and learning methods and the curriculum. What educational trends, if any, exist on a global level? Don't forget about what you learned about culture and education in Chapter 3.

According to world culture theorists, globalisation has a created a global or world culture which crosses national boundaries and supersedes local or national culture. If there is one world culture, then there is an educational model which everyone follows. Spring (2009) has identified four word education models (the first two are based on Anderson-Levitt's work): Human Capital World Model; Progressive Education World Model; Religious Education World Models: and Indigenous Education World Model.

The Human Capital World Model is based around the notion that the purpose of education should be to prepare students for work in the global economy. This is supported by many national leaders who see education as an investment which leads to economic growth and development. Using Anderson-Levitt's ideas, Spring (2009, pp. 16–18) proposed the following aspects of the Human Capital World Model:

- National standardization of the curriculum
- Standardized testing for promotion, entrance, and exiting from different levels of schooling
- Performance evaluation of teaching based on standardized testing of students
- Mandated textbooks
- Scripted lessons
- Teaching of world languages, particularly English
- The goal of education is educating workers to compete in the global economy
- The value of education is measured by economic growth and development.

 Activity 8.5   Human Capital World Model

What do you think are some of the criticisms of the Human Capital World Model? How would you provide evidence of the existence of such a model? Consider the last point on the list: How *does* society measure the value of education?

Benavot et al. (1991) found that national educational systems and primary curricula are similar throughout the world. They write that 'instruction in core subject areas appears in practically all national curricula and there is a great deal of similarity in the amount of time devoted to these core categories' (Benavot et al., 1991, p. 97). However, is this as a result of globalisation or something else?

The increasing popularity of international curricula, such as the International Baccalaureate (IB), the International Primary Curriculum (IPC), the European Baccalaureate (EB) and Cambridge International

Examinations (CIE), has potentially led to an increasingly standardised way of educating young people. Cambridge International Examinations, for example, 'is the world's largest provider of international education programmes and qualifications for 5 to 19 year olds' (CIE, 2013). Apparently, over 9,000 schools in over 160 countries around the world offer Cambridge qualifications. Some of the qualifications include Cambridge Checkpoint (a test for 11–14 year olds), which provides schools with international benchmarks for student performance. However, 'Cambridge IGCSE is the world's most popular international qualification for 14 to 16 year olds. It is taken in 140 countries and in more than 3700 schools around the world' (CIE, 2013). International curricula are clearly a response to the forces of globalisation but the question remains to the whether they contribute to the homogenisation of education around the world and the extent to which they influence national education systems.

Multinational education corporations

Big multinational companies (MNCs) are on the increase (Held & McGrew, 2002) and have enormous power and influence nationally and internationally in the realms of economics, society and politics (Rizvi & Lingard, 2010; Bates, 2011). According to Anderson and Cavanagh (2000), 51 of the world's top 100 economies are corporations. Royal Dutch Shell's revenues are greater than Venezuela's GDP. Using the same principles, WalMart is bigger than Indonesia; General Motors is approximately the same size as Ireland, New Zealand and Hungary combined. Furthermore, there are 63,000 transnational corporations (TNCs) worldwide with 690,000 foreign affiliates. Three-quarters of all transnational corporations are based in North America, Western Europe and Japan. Lastly, 99 of the 100 largest transnational corporations are from the industrialised countries.

There are a number of multinational education companies (MNECs) such as the ones offering the International Primary Curriculum (IPC). The IPC is offered by a company called Fieldwork Education, which is part of the World Class Learning Group (WCL). The WCL Group owns and operates schools worldwide, mainly in response to the needs of MNCs to educate their employees' children. The IPC began in the 1980s when Shell (mentioned above) introduced the English National Curriculum to its English-speaking schools located around the world (WLC, 2013). The IPE developed as a result of Shell employing a more international workforce and their need to adopt a more internationally focused primary curriculum to serve the children of that workforce. It can also be argued here that 'education is seen as a necessary vehicle for the transformation of societies and their education systems so as to produce both the skills and the disciplines required by the TNC's global expansion' (Bates, 2011, p. 11). This is aligned with the Human Capital World Model discussed above.

International educational franchises such as Montessori (see the International Centre for Montessori Education (ICME) website at: www. montessori-icme.com/mission.html) and Kumon also contribute to the global education superstructure. Headquartered in Japan, Kumon is ranked 27th in the top 100 global franchises (Franchise Direct, 2013). It offers maths and reading tuition to children in 48 countries using its own methods. Its stated aim 'is to nurture human capital who will support global society in the 21st century' (Kumon, 2013).

 ## Activity 8.6   The textbook industry

Other multinational education companies include large publishers such as Pearson and McGraw-Hill. How might these companies contribute to the global education superstructure?

Intergovernmental and non-government organisations influence national and local educational practices. An intergovernmental organisation (IGO) is one that is created by an agreement or treaty between states. Examples of IGOs discussed in this book are the United Nations, the OECD, the European Union, the World Bank and the International Monetary Fund. A non-governmental organisation (NGO) is established by individuals or groups of individuals interested in social change, and while they may receive funding from governments, they are not directly part of the structure of any government. In other words, they are not endowed with any governmental powers but can nevertheless be influential. Oxfam and Médecins Sans Frontières (MSF) are two internationally recognised NGOs noted for their humanitarian efforts. While other organisations, such as the International Baccalaureate Organisation and Cambridge International Examinations are non-profit organisations, they operate in a similar manner to large MNCs or NGOs.

Education for a knowledge economy

 ## Activity 8.7   The knowledge economy

What do you think is meant by the term 'the knowledge economy'? Think about the economies of Europe, Japan and the USA after the Second World War. In what ways have these economies changed over the years? What kind of education is needed for the knowledge based economy?

Much of what drives the global education superstructure is the knowledge economy. According to Wood (2011, p. 27): 'The term is difficult to define but it purports to describe the way advanced industrial economies are being transformed from industries dependent on raw materials and manufacturing to industries based on the creation and trading of knowledge'. What is more, it is suggested that education needs to adapt to this and the skills learners now need have shifted away from those important in manual work to problem solving and entrepreneurship, skills which are considered vital in an era of globalisation and economic competitiveness. In the knowledge economy, wealth is created through creativity, innovation and technical expertise. In order for nations to be successful, they must have a highly skilled workforce involved in wealth creation based on these principles (Bates & Lewis, 2009). Human capital, in other words, has become the engine for economic growth in the knowledge economy.

This is evident in national and international education policy such as the Lisbon Strategy (sometimes known as the Lisbon Agenda) of 2000. In 2000, European leaders adopted the strategy 'as a response to globalisation' (European Commission, 2010). This was borne out of an attempt to respond to 'global challenges such as the advancement of the US and Japan in a "new" knowledge-based economy and their domination in the field of information and communication technologies' (Samardžija & Butkovic´, 2010, p. 5). The aim was to increase employment and economic growth in Europe and committed the EU to become by 2010 'the most dynamic and competitive knowledge-based economy in the world capable of sustainable economic growth with more and better jobs and greater social cohesion, and respect for the environment' (European Communities, 2004). Key areas were to invest in human capital; research, development and innovation; a less bureaucratic environment for businesses; and a greener, more environmentally friendly economy. Many of the goals set out by the strategy were not met by 2010, but its contribution to economic and education reform and has nevertheless been significant.

ICT and the knowledge economy

 Activity 8.8   E-Learning

How has technology changed what we learn? Where we learn? And how we learn? Can you give some examples?

Innovations in technology and the advances in communication, particularly the internet, have transformed societies and the way we live. The period of history we are now living in has been called 'the information age' or 'the digital age'. Information communication technology (ICT) plays a key role in disseminating information in the knowledge economy.

The first commercial computer, the Universal Automatic Computer or UNIVAC 1, was introduced to the public in 1951, and by 1981 IBM had launched the personal computer (PC) for use in the home (Steitz, 2006). In the last 30 years, improvements in the performance of computers and other technologies, such as semi-conductors, have made the development of the internet possible. The internet is a network that connects more than 100 million computers around the world. The World Wide Web (WWW) is a system of interlinked documents accessed via the internet. Together they have 'stimulated a communications revolution that has changed the way individuals and institutions use computers in a wide variety of activities' (Mowery & Simcoe, 2002, p. 1369).

Modern technology has changed what we learn, where we learn and how we learn in most advanced industrialised countries. For example, we now have virtual learning environments (VLEs), interactive white boards and other electronic learning platforms that can enhance learning. The education sector has had to incorporate ICT in the curriculum so that pupils have the skills needed to keep up with the rapid changes in technology. ICT skills are needed for future employment as the United Nations (2013) report that 'more than 95% of jobs have a digital component'. Moreover, 'internationally, many countries have rushed to integrate ICT into their education system in order to ensure an internationally competitive workforce' (Shields, 2013, p. 93).

However, access to ICT is unequal around the world and many countries have been left behind, creating what is known as a 'digital divide'. Many countries in the developing world lack the resources necessary to make technology accessible and affordable to the majority of their population. What is more, 'there are other, less obvious factors, that keep many people from using and benefiting from ICT, simply because most ICT is designed by and for the wealthiest 30 per cent of the planet' (Cutrell, 2011). These factors include constraints in education and literacy; an incredible diversity of small language communities; political, religious, gender and other social prohibitions on use; and differences in cognitive models – that is, how individuals frame and organise information about the world. Cutrell argues that simply having access to more affordable technology will not solve some of these issues. Does this mean that for millions of people with limited ICT, the divide will continue to get bigger and bigger and access to the knowledge economy even a more distant reality?

Student achievement and the knowledge economy

Shields (2013, p. 85) points out that the 'role of education in the global knowledge economy has created a new emphasis on measuring education achievement and particularly on comparing and ranking educational achievement levels in different countries'. International surveys on student achievement were discussed in Chapter 2 but need to be briefly mentioned here in the context of globalisation. Spring (2009, p. 62) states that the 'OECD contributes to the creation of a world education culture through the development and implementation of PISA'. He believes that PISA creates global standards for the knowledge required for a global economy and 'the consequence is a trend to uniformly national curricula as school leaders attempt to prepare their students to do well on the test' (Spring, 2009, p. 62).

English as a global language

Another key component of educational globalisation is the effect that the rise of English as a global language has had on local school curricula and cultures (Spring, 2009). 'English is now the language most widely taught as a foreign language in over 100 countries, such as China, Russia, Germany, Spain, Egypt and Brazil, and in most of these countries it is emerging as the chief foreign language to be encountered in schools, often displacing another language in the process' (Crystal, 2003, p. 5).

The spread of English began in the sixteenth century as European powers expanded their wealth through imperialism (the political control of foreign lands and people) and colonialism (the control of foreign lands and people by establishing colonies or settlements). At the forefront of this expansion was the British Empire. The industrial revolution which began in Britain in the late 1700s fuelled this expansion in the quest for raw materials and new markets. And by the middle of the nineteenth century, Britain had become 'the undisputed technological leader in the industrialization process', mostly through its textiles industry but also 'it was the largest exporter and importer in the world', possessing the greatest commercial fleet at the time (WTO, 2007). Because most of the innovations during the industrial revolution were of British origin, it added tens of thousands of new words to the English language (Crystal, 2003). In order to access and benefit from these innovations, it meant having to learn English.

The case is still largely true today as English is the medium of communication around the globe. The internet originated in the USA (Mowery & Simcoe, 2002) and as a result has come to be dominated by the English language. Although estimates of how much of the internet is in English vary from over 90% to as little as 40% (Pimienta et al., 2009), a truer picture is probably closer to 60% (W3Techs, 2013). Other top languages on the internet are Russian, German, Spanish, French, Chinese and Japanese. In other words, there is more linguistic diversity on the internet than originally thought.

Nevertheless, English has become the major language of business and commerce (Neeley, 2012). Many multinational companies, such as Nokia and Airbus, have adopted English language policies in order to have a common language to facilitate communication, or a *lingua franca*. Furthermore, English plays a central role in most international meetings from the United Nations to the Olympics. English is also the official language of many science organisations, such as the African Association of Science Editors (AASE), and most academic journals are also published in English (Crystal, 2003).

As a result, there is a huge demand for English language learning globally. The number of schools, colleges and universities that use English as the medium of instruction (in countries where English is not the native language) is on the increase. It is estimated that by 2020 there will be around 4.9 million students studying in around 8,000 such schools (Brummitt, 2009, cited in Hayden & Thompson, 2011). In the English Language Teaching (ELT) sector alone (excluding further and higher education), students studying English in the UK are worth just over £1 billion to the British economy (British Council, 2007). This figure is possibly underestimated and most probably growing as well.

However, there are a number of criticisms surrounding the dominance of English as a global language. First, Phillipson (2001, p. 188) writes: 'many write loosely that English is the world language, but to describe English in such terms ignores the fact that a majority of the world's citizens do not speak English, whether as a mother tongue or as a second or foreign language'. It is often seen as elitist; not everyone has access to English except those with wealth and power. For Phillipson, the real question is whose interest does English serve: multinational corporations, Western governments and other organisations, such as the World Bank? English was introduced in many countries during colonisation (for example, in India, Ghana, Nigeria and Zambia) and is still associated with being culturally and economically imperialistic.

Another key question is whether the spread of English is at the expense of indigenous or local languages. Education First (2012) estimate that by 2020 there will be nearly 2 billion people learning English. Because of the number of individuals who are now proficient in English, they too have also come to 'own' it, just as much as the British, Americans or Australians. Many English terms and phrases have been introduced into national languages, such as Japanese, Brazilian and French. As an example, some of the words that have permeated Japanese are 'negotiation', 'literacy' and 'interactive' (French, 2002). This encroachment of English words has caused concern (Etzioni, 2008). As the study and scope of English through television, film and the media are more widespread, the world is seen to become increasingly monolinguistic. Is linguistic diversity at risk as long as the world has a global language?

Any non-native person who has studied English would probably understand how difficult it is to master. Is English really a suitable language for global communication? Smith (2005) concludes that English is a poor *lingua franca* for four main reasons: it is unpronounceable, irregular, too complex and ambiguous. Many also question whether American and British economic and political influence in the world is decreasing, while China is on the rise. Many, like Pak (2012), ask: 'Is English or Mandarin the language of the future?'

Globalisation: Good or bad?

There has been much debate about whether globalisation is a force for good or bad. Some have perceived it as 'Americanisation' or 'Western Imperialism' (Held & McGrew, 2002). In this sense, globalisation is seen as the spread of Western, and particularly American, economic, social and cultural values. In Ritzer's (2000) book, *The McDonaldization of Society*, he proposed that the principles of the American fast-food restaurant McDonald's have transformed society in the USA and other countries around the world. Ritzer also talks about the 'McUniversity', where pressure to become more efficient in an era of competition (better grades, rankings, and so forth) has led to greater predictability. Colleges and universities offer similar courses, use similar textbooks, and structure their classes in a similar fashion, leading to uniformity and therefore predictability. If you are a fast-food chain and need to ensure that every burger tastes exactly the same, then this is a good thing. However, if you are interested in diversity, then predictability is not necessarily desirable. The question remains: Has globalisation signified the end of cultural diversity?

 Activity 8.9   McDonald's

Find out more about McDonald's on the internet. When and where did it all begin? How many countries worldwide have a McDonald's? How else has American popular culture spread throughout the world and to what extent? Is this good or bad, and why?

Which direction is globalisation taking us? Is there a convergence of a single world culture? Many of you know through reading the first part of this book that in comparative education culture plays a big role in shaping national provision. Modern comparativists understand that you cannot simply copy educational ideas and practices without taking into consideration the socio-cultural context. With this in mind, culturalists believe that global ideas are often adapted by policy makers and practitioners to local conditions. Therefore, they do not believe there exists a single form of knowledge and they also reject the idea that global organisations like the World Bank and UNESCO work together to create global education uniformity (Spring, 2009).

Activity 8.10   Over to you

What do you think? Has globalisation created one world culture and, if so, is this a bad thing? Are you a culturalist? If so, why and can you provide evidence?

Conclusion

There are many actors in the global education arena: MNCs, MNECs, IGOs, NGOs, national governments, and professionals. There is some evidence of the spreading of international curricula, the importance of international student achievement surveys and the rise of English as global language in the globalisation of education. Technological innovations such as the internet and the advent of the knowledge economy are also indicators of the influence of globalisation. However, is there enough evidence to prove that these activities have led to the homogenisation of education around the world? How globalisation will shape education in the future is probably less certain than the predictability of models such as the Human Capital World Model provides. The world is surrounded by inequality. Is globalisation the cause or the potential cure?

 Case Study 8   English language education in Malaysia and Singapore

Malaysia and Singapore are two former colonies of the British Empire. As a result, English has played an important role in the region. Singapore has four official languages: Malay, Mandarin, Tamil and English. However, English is the main language used in government and administration and is also the only medium of instruction in schools (Leimgruber, 2011). After gaining independence in 1957, in order to build national identity, the Malaysian government adopted its own language, Bahasa Malaysia, also known as Malay, rather than English as the medium of instruction in education and government. English was used in some schools but phased out by the 1970s.

However, in 2003, the government adopted PPSMI, a policy which meant that mathematics and science subjects were to be taught in English. In the primary science curriculum document published by the Malaysian Ministry of Education, it states that 'the teaching of science using English as the medium of instruction enables pupils to obtain various sources of information written in English either in electronic or print forms and helps them to keep abreast of developments in science and technology. Pupils will be able to see science and technology in a wider context and learn to relate their knowledge to the world beyond their school' (Ministry of Education, Malaysia, 2003).

However, in 2009, the government decided to reverse its decision and phase out the policy from 2012. Since its inception and subsequent reversal, the policy has been subject to much debate. Many parents are unhappy at the decision and a recent BBC documentary, which can be accessed at: www.bbc.co.uk/programmes/p00nkzz7, told of parents sending their children on a two-hour bus journey to Singapore just to learn 'good' English.

Key questions:

- What do you think was the rationale for adopting PPSMI in the first place?

- Why do you think the government is phasing out the policy?

- PPSMI has divided opinion. Why might some parents be for or against it?

You can follow the debate at the following web pages: www.theguardian.com/world/2009/jul/10/malaysia-tefl; www.nst.com.my/opinion/letters-to-the-editor/english-bring-back-ppsmi-for-the-sake-of-our-students-future-1.302883; www.loyarburok.com/2012/07/04/ppsmi-choice/

Suggested reading

Breidlid, A. (2013) *Education, Indigenous Knowledges and Development in the Global South*. Abingdon: Routledge
This text explores indigenous education in the developing world. Due to colonialism and Western capitalist expansion, a Eurocentric knowledge system has come to dominate and 'the people of the South have been marginalised and subalternized' as a result. Indigenous World Education Models, according to Spring (1990, see below), 'openly reject world models of schooling based on Western education'.

Spring, J. (2009) *Globalization of Education: An Introduction*. New York: Routledge
This is an excellent text on the globalisation of education. It goes into much further detail of some of the main concepts introduced in this chapter.

References

Altinyelken, H. (2012) A converging pedagogy in the developing world? Insights from Uganda and Turkey, in A. Verger, M. Novelli & H. Altinyelken (eds), *Global Education Policy and International Development: New Agendas, Issues and Policies*. London: Bloomsbury
Anderson, S. & Cavanagh, J. (2000) *Top 200: The Rise of Corporate Global Power*. Washington, DC: Institute for Policy Studies

Anderson-Levitt, K. (ed.) (2003) *Local Meanings, Global Schooling: Anthropology and World Culture Theory*. New York: Palgrave Macmillan

Bates, J. & Lewis, S. (2009) Education and employability, in J. Sharp, S. Ward & L. Hankin (eds), *Education Studies: An Issues-Based Approach* (2nd edition). Exeter: Learning Matters

Bates, R. (ed.) (2011) *Schooling Internationally: Globalisation, Internationalisation and the Future of International Schools*. Abingdon: Routledge

Benavot, A., Cha, Y.K., Kamens, D., Meyer, J. & Wong, S. (1991) Knowledge for the masses: World models and national curricula, 1920–1986. *American Sociological Review*, 56(1), 85–100

Bray, M. (2003) Comparative education in the era of globalisation: Evolution, missions and roles, *Policy Futures in Education*, 1(2), 209–224

British Council (2007) *Global Value*. Available online at: http://globalhighered.files.wordpress.com/2007/09/britishcouncil.pdf

CIE (Cambridge International Examinations) (2013) *Media Information 2013*. Available online at: www.cie.org.uk/docs/profiles/media/CIE%20media%20factsheet%20v1.13.pdf

Crystal, D. (2003) *English as a Global Language* (2nd edition). Cambridge: Cambridge University Press

Cutrell, E. (2011) *Context and Design in ICT for Global Development*. Available online at: www.un.org/wcm/content/site/chronicle/home/archive/issues2011/thedigitaldividend/contextanddesigninictforglobaldevelopment

Donnellan, C. (ed.) (2002) *Globalisation: Issues*. Cambridge: Independence

Education First (2012) *English Proficiency Index*. Available online at: www.ef.co.uk/__/~/media/efcom/epi/2012/full_reports/ef-epi-2012-report-master-lr-2

Etzioni, A. (2008) A global, community-building language? *International Studies Perspectives*, 9, 113–127.

European Commission (2010) *Lisbon Strategy for Growth and Jobs*. Available online at: http://ec.europa.eu/archives/growthandjobs_2009/objectives/index_en.htm

European Communities (2004) *Facing the Challenge: The Lisbon Strategy for Growth and Employment*. A report from the High Level Group chaired by Wim Kok. Luxembourg: Office for Official Publications of the European Communities. Available online at: http://ec.europa.eu/research/evaluations/pdf/archive/fp6-evidence-base/evaluation_studies_and_reports/evaluation_studies_and_reports_2004/the_lisbon_strategy_for_growth_and_employment__report_from_the_high_level_group.pdf

Franchise Direct (2013) *Top 100 Global Franchises – 2013 Rankings*. Available online at: www.franchisedirect.com/top100globalfranchises/rankings/

French, H. (2002) *To Grandparents, English Word Trend Isn't 'Naisu'*. Available online at: www.nytimes.com/2002/10/23/international/asia/23TOKY.html

Giddens, A. (1990) *The Consequences of Modernity*. Cambridge: Polity Press

Hayden, M. & Thompson, J. (2011) Teachers for the international school of the future, in R. Bates (ed.), *Schooling Internationally: Globalisation, Internationalisation and the Future for International Schools*. Abingdon: Routledge

Held, D. & McGrew, A. (eds) (2000) *The Global Transformations Reader: An Introduction to the Globalization Debate*. Cambridge: Polity Press

Held, D. & McGrew, A. (2002) *Globalization/Anti-Globalization*. Cambridge: Polity Press

Held, D., McGrew, A., Goldblatt, D. & Perraton, J. (1999) *Global Transformations*. Cambridge: Polity Press

Hirst, P. & Thompson, G. (1996) *Globalization in Question*. Cambridge: Polity Press

IMF (2000) *Globalization: Threat or Opportunity?* Available online at: www.imf. org/external/np/exr/ib/2000/041200to.htm

Kumon (2013) *Spreading Globally*. Available online at: www.kumongroup.com/ eng/world/index.html?ID=eng_method

Leimgruber, J. (2011) Singapore English. *Language and Linguistics Compass*, 5(1), 47–62.

Lemert, C., Elliot, A., Chaffee, D. & Hsu, E. (eds) (2010) *Globalization : A Reader*. Abingdon: Routledge

Martell, L. (2007) The third wave in globalization theory. *International Studies Review*, 9(2), 173–196

Ministry of Education, Malaysia (2003) *Integrated Curriculum for Primary Schools: Science Syllabus*. Available online at: www.moe.gov.my/bpk/kbsr_ kbsm/sp/sp_science_primary.pdf

Mowery, C. & Simcoe, T. (2002) Is the internet a US invention? An economic and technological history of computer networking. *Research Policy*, 31(8–9), 1369–1387

Neeley, T. (2012) *Global Business Speaks English*. Available online at: http://hbr. org/2012/05/global-business-speaks-english

Ohmae, K. (1991, 1999) *The Borderless World: Power and Strategy in the Interlinked Economy*. New York: Harper Collins

Ohmae, K. (1996) *The End of the Nation State: The Rise of the Regional Economies*. New York: Harper Collins

Oxfam (2006) *Education for Global Citizenship: A Guide for Schools*. Available online at: www.oxfam.org.uk/~/media/Files/Education/Global %20Citizenship/education_for_global_citizenship_a_guide_for_schools.ashx

Pak, J. (2012) *Is English or Mandarin the Language of the Future?* Available online at: www.bbc.co.uk/news/magazine-17105569

Phillipson, R. (2001) English for globalisation or for the world's people? *International Review of Education*, 47(3–4), 185–200

Pimienta, D., Prado, D. & Blanco, A. (2009) *Twelve Years of Measuring Linguistic Diversity in the Internet: Balance and Perspectives*. Paris: UNESCO

Rizvi, F. & Lingard, R. (2010) *Globalizing Education Policy*. Abingdon: Routledge

Ritzer, G. (2000) *The McDonalization of Society*. Newbury Park, CA: Pine Forge Press

Samardžija, V. & Butković, H. (2010) *From the Lisbon Strategy to Europe 2020*. Available online at: www1.zagreb.hr/euzg/eu_publikacije/From_the_lisbon_strategy_to_europe_2020.pdf

Shields, R. (2013) *Globalization and International Education*. London: Bloomsbury

Smith, R. (2005) 'Global English: gift or curse. *English Today*, 82, 21(2), 56–62

Spring, J. (2009) *Globalization of Education: An Introduction*. New York: Routledge

Steitz, B. (2006) *A Brief Computer History*. Available online at: http://people. bu.edu/baws/brief%20computer%20history.html

United Nations (2013) On 'Girls in ICT Day,' UN encourages jobs in information and communications technology. Available online at: www.un.org/apps/news/story.asp?NewsID=44758&Cr=technology&Cr1#.UfU3jY1QGDo

Wallerstein, I. (1976) *The Modern World-System: Capitalist Agriculture and the Origins of the European World-Economy in the Sixteenth Century*. New York: Academic Press

WLC (2013) *International Primary Curriculum: Our Story*. Available online at: www.greatlearning.com/ipc/about/our-story

Wood, K. (2011) *Education: The Basics*. Abingdon: Routledge

WTO (2007) *The Economics and Political Economy of International Trade Cooperation*. Available online at: www.wto.org/english/res_e/booksp_e/anrep_e/wtr07-2b_e.pdf

W3Techs (2013) *Usage of Content Languages for Websites*. Available online at: http://w3techs.com/technologies/overview/content_language/all

CHAPTER 9

GLOBAL CITIZENSHIP EDUCATION

This chapter explores:

- The concept of global citizenship and cosmopolitanism;
- Global citizenship education;
- The relationship between globalisation, citizenship education and identity.

 Activity 9.1   A global citizen

What does it mean to be a citizen? What does it mean to be a global citizen? Is this possible? Write down some global issues (social, political, economic and environmental). Are these issues everyone's responsibility?

Global citizenship

As we saw in the last chapter, the world is becoming increasingly inter-connected economically, politically, socially and culturally through the process of globalisation. This has led to what Omhae (1991, 1999) has called a 'borderless world' and extends to the notion of citizenship as well. In the past, citizenship has largely been confined to national boundaries and specific geographical locations. However, as Veugelers (2011, p. 473) rightly points out, 'the meaning of the term citizenship is also being broadened. It is no longer just connected to a particular nationality, but also to the global world. Nowadays, we speak of European citizenship and of global citizenship'. In fact, the journal *Globalisation, Societies and Education* published a special edition entitled *The Political Economy of Global Citizenship Education* in 2011. But what is global citizenship and how does education contribute to its formation?

After having read eight chapters so far, you will now be aware that there are no agreed definitions among scholars of key concepts, and what it means to be a global citizen is no exception. In Chapter 7, which introduced the second part of the book, we saw that Oxfam (1997) define a global citizen as someone who:

- is aware of the wider world and has a sense of their own role as a world citizen;

- respects and values diversity;

- has an understanding of how the world works economically, politically, socially, culturally, technologically and environmentally;

- is outraged by social injustice;

- participates in and contributes to the community at a range of levels from local to global;

- is willing to act to make the world a more sustainable place;

- takes responsibility for their actions.

This definition is problematic for a couple of reasons. Davies (2008) points out that in order to be motivated to change we have to be outraged, and that it is not enough simply to care. Are we only motivated when we feel outrage? She additionally states: 'This definition also raises the issue of whether a person in a low-income country who has little access to formal education or wide-ranging knowledge, and does not have the opportunity to participate internationally, can receive the title of a "global citizen".' Is, then, the concept of a global citizen a Western one and Eurocentric by nature? Moreover, do we always have the means or capabilities to make the world a more sustainable place? Can a global citizen only be someone with wealth or power?

The Oxfam definition talks about a more sustainable world but what other aspects should concern a global citizen? What issues of social injustice are there? Global Citizen (2014), a non-profit charity, aims 'to amplify and unite a generation's call for justice' in order 'to bring an end to extreme poverty'. In a promotional video entitled 'What is a global citizen?', it talks about creating a world that not only is sustainable but also has a lack of extreme poverty and greater equality, access, justice, freedom and health for all its citizens. Think back to Chapters 5 and 6, which discussed a number of inequalities such as lack of access to education, maternal health and gender disparity. The international community is working hard (some argue not hard enough) through the Millennium Development Goals (MDGs), with the help of NGOs and IGOs, but many of these goals will not be achieved by 2015. Can global citizens help to achieve them? Is this an ideal or a real possibility?

Global citizenship links to the idea of cosmopolitanism. There are different perspectives as to what cosmopolitan means and no single understanding exists. The term 'cosmopolitanism' is often associated with being sophisticated. The *Oxford Advanced Learner's Dictionary* (Hornby, 2000, p. 281) defines cosmopolitan (adjective) as 'containing people of different types or from different countries, and influenced by their culture' (e.g. a cosmopolitan city); or, 'having or showing a wide experience of people and things from many different countries' (e.g. a cosmopolitan person or outlook). Although not unrelated, cosmopolitanism in philosophy is likely to be more specialised (Schefflera, 1999). 'In its most basic form, cosmopolitanism maintains that there are moral obligations owed to all human beings based solely on our humanity alone, without reference to race, gender, nationality, ethnicity, culture, religion, political affiliation, state citizenship, or other common particularities' (Brown & Held, 2010, p. 1). Hankin (2009, p. 203) describes a global citizen as 'a responsible and responsive person owing allegiance to the world as much as to the nation state into which they were born'. In other words, a global citizen can also be called a world citizen.

A key thinker of this idea is Martha Nussbaum, Professor of Law at the University of Chicago. While the notion of being a world citizen can be traced back to ancient times, contemporary cosmopolitan theory is said to have begun with an article Nussbaum wrote in 1994, which sparked great debate about citizenship education in the Western world (Poulsen, 2008).

Drawing from a branch of Greek philosophy called stoicism, she suggests that we should be citizens of a world of human beings first and foremost. If we identify with the human race above that of our national identity, then we are more likely to treat others in a moral, just and right way (Nussbaum, 1994). Her central argument stems from the idea that if patriotism and national identity become our primary focus, we can become ethnocentric and lose the desire for more universal aspirations and concerns. The focus here is not on nations, cultures or societies, but on individuals, a common humanity and our moral obligation to each other.

Activity 9.2 Citizenship

How do you primarily see yourself... as a citizen of: a particular nation state (e.g. French); a nation without a state (e.g. Kurdish); or a citizen of the world? Why do you identify yourself in this way?

Can we really be a citizen of the world? Bates (2012, p. 262) says: 'Strictly and legally, global citizenship is not possible, as citizenship is a concept ineluctably associated with the nation state. Proof of citizenship is the possession of documents that guarantee that a particular state accepts the individual as a member.' In this sense, then, the only way to be a citizen of the world is if there were a single world government, which currently does not exist. However, global citizenship is not really about a formal arrangement but more about a moral obligation to ourselves and to others.

There are a number of criticisms of Nussbaum's cosmopolitanism, ranging from the philosophical to those 'who simply condemn her for proposing a stateless world society or even a world state devoid of their patriotic predilections ... [while] other critics have even described her cosmopolitanism as unimaginative' (Naseem & Hyslop-Margison, 2006, p. 56). There has also been much debate surrounding the idea that cosmopolitanism does not necessarily need to be in direct opposition with the values of nationalism.

Education for global citizenship

 Activity 9.3 Global citizenship education

What do you think a curriculum for global citizenship should be like? Think about the overall aims and philosophy underpinning it. How would go about achieving it? What are the merits and disadvantages of your envisaged curriculum?

What are the implications of global citizenship and cosmopolitanism for education? In other words, how do we go about educating our young people to be citizens of the world? Perhaps, and more importantly, the question should be whether global citizenship education is even desirable? Before answering these questions, it is important to first consider citizenship education in a national context. Education has always played an important role in the making of citizens, the building of nations and the formation of national identity (Green, 1997). Kandel (1933, p. 10) recognised that 'education has steadily assumed an increasingly important place in programs of national development'. Despite the forces of globalisation, is this still true today? The inculcating of ideas, values, beliefs and norms of national culture is a part of formal schooling (see Chapter 3). In schools, pupils learn about their own culture through a variety of informal and formal means. They study a common language, history and aspects of their own legal system and government, which help aid a sense of shared identity. In this sense, education is the glue which holds together individuals and helps to create social cohesion. Education has also played a vital role in building the economic capacity of nations through educating its future workers (human capital).

Citizenship education as part of the formal curriculum exists to varying degrees around the world. In fact, the UK was the last country in Europe, the USA and the Commonwealth not to have it as a subject in a National Curriculum (Crick, 2002). It was not until the Education Reform Act 1988 that it was made a non-statutory, cross-curricular theme of the National Curriculum. However, its impact was limited partly as a result of it being non-statutory, so it therefore had to compete with compulsory subjects for teaching time (Beck, 2012). Moreover, the 1990s in the UK saw a rise in political apathy and anti-social behaviour (Bamber, 2009). As a result, some questioned whether citizenship education was or could fulfil its original purpose in the curriculum.

In response, the government appointed Bernard Crick to lead an advisory group on citizenship education. The group's final report, entitled *Education for Citizenship and the Teaching of Democracy in Schools*, was published in 1998 and is known as the Crick Report (QCA, 1998). The Crick Report outlined a framework for citizenship education which contained three strands: social and moral responsibility, community involvement and political literacy. It defined social and moral responsibility as 'children learning from the very beginning self-confidence and socially and morally responsible behaviour both in and beyond the classroom, both towards those in authority and towards each other' (this is an essential pre-condition for citizenship) (QCA, 1998, p. 11). Community involvement is where pupils learn about and become helpfully involved in the life and concerns of their communities. This includes learning by actively participating in community service. Political literacy is where pupils learn about and how to make themselves effective in public life through knowledge, skills and values. Key concepts that students are supposed to understand by the time they reach the end of their compulsory schooling are:

- democracy and autocracy
- co-operation and conflict
- equality and diversity
- fairness, justice, the rule of law, rules, law and human rights
- freedom and order

- individual and community
- power and authority
- rights and responsibilities

(QCA, 1998, p. 44)

 Activity 9.4   The Crick Report

You can access the full report at: www.educationengland.org.uk/documents/pdfs/1998-crick-report-citizenship.pdf. Have a look at the values and dispositions to be achieved as a result of citizenship education on page 44 of the report. Reflect on these and some of the key concepts outlined above. How similar are these ideas to those found in the previous definitions of a global citizen?

The report received a number of criticisms, ranging from the language used to serious allegations of omissions in content on racism and diversity (Jerome, 2012). Nevertheless, it has been highly influential in creating discussion around the formation of citizenship education in the UK. In 2002, citizenship education became a statutory subject in the English National Curriculum at Key Stages 3 and 4 (pupils aged 11–16) and in the recent National Curriculum review (in 2013), it was declared that citizenship is to remain a separate, compulsory subject in both Key Stages (see DfE, 2013). Changes include adding human rights and international law at Key Stage 4: 'Citizenship addresses issues relating to social justice, human rights, community cohesion and global interdependence, and encourages students to challenge injustice, inequalities and discrimination' (DfE, 2013). Critics of the review feel that the teaching of citizenship should begin in primary school as the current draft contains no programmes of study for citizenship at Key Stages 1 or 2 (Moorse, 2013).

 Activity 9.5   Civics

What does the study of civics entail? What aspects of civics did you study in school?

What do we know about citizenship education elsewhere in the world? The International Association for the Evaluation of Educational Achievement (IEA) conducted a study in 2009 called the International Civic and Citizenship Education Study or ICCS. It was conducted in 38 countries and 'took place in a context characterized by significant societal change, including the rapid development of new communication technologies, increased movement of people between countries, and the growth of supranational organizations' (IEA, 2010). The data was gathered from more than 140,000 14-year-old students and 62,000 teachers in over 5,300 schools. The next survey is due to take place in 2016. The ICCS examines the ways in which countries prepare their young people to undertake their roles as citizens so it investigated student knowledge and understanding of civics and citizenship as well as their attitudes, perceptions and activities related to it.

The key initial findings of the survey were:

- Different approaches to provision of civic and citizenship education were evident in the ICCS countries. These approaches included having a specific subject, integrating relevant content into other subjects and including content as a cross-curricular theme.

- 21 of the 38 countries in ICCS included a specific subject concerned with civic and citizenship education in their curriculum. Civic and citizenship education covered a wide range of topics, including knowledge and understanding of political institutions and concepts, such as human rights, as well as newer topics covering social and community cohesion, diversity, the environment, communications, and global society.

- The study revealed considerable variation across and within participating countries in civic knowledge.

- Girls gained significantly higher civic knowledge scores than did boys in nearly all of the ICCS countries.

- Trust in civic institutions varied across the ICCS countries. Overall, the least trusted institutions were political parties.

- Active civic participation in the community was relatively rare among the students surveyed in ICCS. Civic participation at school tended to be much more frequent and also to be associated with higher civic knowledge and interest scores.

(IEA, 2010)

 Activity 9.5   ICCS findings

What do the ICCS findings suggest in light of globalisation? Are global forces homogenising education, given these findings? These findings also suggest that students are not engaged with their communities. Why might this be the case? Can citizenship education resolve issues of non-engagement?

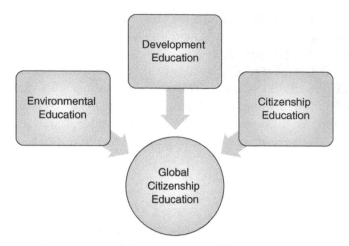

Figure 9.1   The convergence of education for global citizenship

Source: Adapted from Mannion et al., 2011

There is much variation in citizenship education so it is no surprise that not everyone agrees on what global citizenship education is or how it should be taught. The findings from the ICCS also suggest that citizenship education is starting to incorporate aspects of the global. This is also evident in the new citizenship curriculum in England, which takes effect in 2014. What then is global citizenship education? Looking at a few different ideas of what it is and how it may be taught are essential here. First, it is not usually a discrete, stand-alone subject, but is taught through cross-curricular activities or, as Figure 9.1 suggests, is incorporated into other more established subjects.

In support of the above, the Scottish government believe that 'global citizenship brings together education for citizenship, international education and sustainable development education and recognises the common outcomes and principles of these three areas. All curriculum areas can contribute to developing the skills, attributes and knowledge that will create active global citizens' (Education Scotland, 2013).

One clear and structured conception of global citizenship education comes from Scotland. The Scottish government have outlined the key principles of global citizenship for the curriculum as follows:

1. Know, respect and care for the rights, responsibilities, values and opinions of others and understand Scotland's role within the wider world.

2. Develop an awareness and understanding of engagement in democratic processes and be able to participate in critical thinking and decision making in schools and communities at local, national and international level.

3. Understand the interdependence between people, the environment, and the impacts of actions, both local and global.

4. Appreciate and celebrate the diversity of Scotland's history, culture and heritage and engage with other cultures and traditions.

5. Think creatively and critically and act responsibly in all aspects of life, politically, economically and culturally.

 Activity 9.6   Global citizenship education for the practitioner

The Scottish government has proposed a series of questions for each key principle in order to help practitioners incorporate global citizenship into their practice. You can access them at: www.educationscotland. gov.uk/learningteachingandassessment/learningacrossthecurriculum/ themesacrosslearning/globalcitizenship/about/developingglobalcitizens/ principles.asp
    Reflect on some of those questions. How can they be achieved?

In England, the advent of global citizenship can be found in a strategic document entitled *Putting the World into World-Class Education: An International Strategy for Education, Skills and Children's Services* (DfES, 2004). At the time, this was part of the Labour government's five-year strategy for children and learners. It also fed into the Lisbon Strategy mentioned in Chapter 8. The document included the then Labour government's 'world vision' as follows: 'We live in one world. What we do affects others, and what others do affects us, as never before. To recognise that we are all members of a world community and that we all have responsibilities to each other is not romantic rhetoric but modern economic and social reality' (DfES, 2004, p. 5). To that end, it defined three key goals:

Goal 1: Equipping our children, young people and adults for life in a global society and work in a global economy

Goal 2: Engaging with our international partners to achieve their goals and ours

Goal 3: Maximising the contribution of our education and training sector and university research to overseas trade and inward investment

The global dimension of the strategy centres on eight key concepts: (global) citizenship, social justice, sustainable development, diversity, values and perceptions, interdependence, conflict resolution and human rights. These concepts intersect across social, economic, environmental and political areas. However, it could be argued that the main aim of the strategy is really about improving the economic competitiveness of the UK, specifically England, rather than concerning a genuine interest in the learning about others. Furthermore, when comparing the English and Scottish policies on global citizenship education, it is easy to see the difficulty in creating a shared vision of what it should be. If two countries which share a border and are joined constitutionally (since 1707) cannot agree on a unified curriculum, then on a global level is this even possible?

Drawing from the work of Colin Wringe, Ibrahim (2005, p. 178) suggests that 'global citizenship education is about understanding the nature of global issues as well as the range of ways in which those with power and resources can be influenced to act in a globally responsible way'. If we unpick this definition, it means that we need to teach pupils not only about the issues facing the world, but also how to influence others with power (e.g. governments, IGOs, NGOs and MNCs) to act towards resolving the issues. One of the main problems with viewing global citizenship in this way is that it appears to exclude those in the developing world from participating in the resolution of the problems. It also appears to derive from a Western perspective and assumes poor people do not have any agency or ownership of the issues affecting their lives. It might suggest that they are incapable of resolving their own problems themselves. When individuals are empowered to make change, the likelihood of it happening is much more real. What is empowerment and how can governments go about empowering individuals, communities and societies in order to make real change in the world? Is global citizenship education the answer?

'Empowerment is the process of enhancing the capacity of individuals or groups to make choices and to transform those choices into desired actions and outcomes. Central to this process are actions which both build individual and collective assets, and improve the efficiency and fairness of the organizational and institutional context which govern the use of these assets' (World Bank, 2011). Ironically, this definition is offered by the World Bank, which is often criticised for its unfair policies in the developing world (see Spring, 2009). Is this rhetoric or reality? Should global citizenship, then, be more about empowering others rather than how we can become more globally competitive?

However, further to the definition above, and drawing on Osler and Vincent (2002), Ibrahim (2005, p. 178) does believe that a global citizenship education based on the principles of cooperation, non-violence, respect for human rights and cultural diversity, democracy, tolerance and a concern for social justice will 'enable young people to learn about their rights and responsibilities and equip them with skills for democratic participation, at all levels, from local to global'.

Activity 9.7   Democracy and global citizenship education

Is global citizenship education a Western concept only suitable for pupils living in advanced industrialised countries that enjoy a range of freedoms and democracy? Does it apply to those who live in dictatorships and authoritarian regimes?

Global citizenship and identity

Global citizenship challenges traditional notions of national identity. What does it mean to be Spanish, British or Japanese in the modern world? This is a complex question and no doubt you would get a variety of answers, depending on who you ask. In part, this is because we now live in much more pluralistic and multicultural societies (discussed in Chapter 10), but also because older generations will have experienced the world differently. One can be sure that many of our grandparents never would have imagined the internet and all its possibilities. The recent technological, economic, social, cultural and political changes, as discussed in Chapter 8, have transformed society and thus, in the process, how we see ourselves.

Therefore, how do we construct our identity in the age of globalisation? We can consider identity on an individual or collective level, putting ourselves or the group at the fore. Moreover, our identity is important in determining the way we behave and think. Castells (2006, p. 63) states 'identity is the process whereby people draw on cultural attributes to build meaning in their lives'. In other words, we acquire our identity through our culture. He writes: 'Evidently, I cannot awake one morning and suddenly decide to be a Hutu. Becoming a Hutu is a much more complex affair' (Castells, 2006, pp. 62–63). Identity is built upon personal experience taken from history and a culture, both having linguistic and geographic elements. For Castells, the process of constructing identity has changed as a result of globalisation. Globalisation has strengthened various cultural identities – religious, national, ethnic and geographic – due to the fact that people feel alienated from a state that no longer represents them. For example, the rise in Islamic fundamentalism and 'the construction of a religious identity in the Muslim world has arisen from: the failure of Nation-States to manage globalisation; the failure of Arab nationalism in the long-running dispute over Israel and globalisation in general; the failures of Arab or other kinds of nationalism in other parts of the Muslim world; and religious reconstruction excluding the State' (Castells, 2006, pp. 64–65). Castells calls this resistance-based identity.

Resistance-based identity occurs when groups are marginalised culturally, politically or socially. They respond by constructing an identity drawn from history and self-identification which allows them to resist assimilation by the very system that made the feel disregarded and ostracised in the first place. Castells believes that certain kinds of globalisation push people to the fringes of society and they resist it through fundamentalism, for example, because they cannot do so as citizens or because they are in a minority and cannot exercise their political rights.

 Activity 9.8   Globalisation and identity

Consider the different waves of globalisation theory (hyperglobalists, sceptics and transformationalists), as discussed in Chapter 8, and think how globalisation from these perspectives might affect identity. Do you agree with Castells' (2006) argument? Does globalisation strengthen certain identities? Destroy others?

The question remains whether globalisation and ideas about cosmopolitanism can help to create a global form of identity? Analysing the World Values Survey (which asks respondents about primary identity in terms of geographic group), Norris (2000) found that local and national identities remain far stronger than any cosmopolitan orientation. From the data, it emerged that almost half the public (47%) see themselves as belonging primarily to their locality or region of the country, while over one-third (38%) say they identify primarily with their nation. Only a small minority have a sense of a cosmopolitan identity, with one-sixth of the public (15%) feeling close to their continent or 'the world as a whole' in their primary identity. In other words, the percentage of people who see themselves as world citizens is relatively small.

With a more concerted effort to bring a global dimension to curricula, will the percentage of individuals who see themselves as world citizens increase? Is a world identity even desirable and whose identity would it really be anyway?

Conclusion

Increased interconnectedness and interdependence as a result of globalisation has changed traditional notions of citizenship based on national boundaries. This has sparked debate about what it means to be a global citizen and the role education plays in shaping citizens of the world. At the heart of global citizenship education lays a desire to get young people interested in issues that face them and others around the world. Some of the issues pertain to human rights, sustainability, social justice and understanding and respect for diversity. It is about instilling a sense of moral responsibility to ourselves, our family, friends and communities, both locally and further afield, to help resolve some of these issues. Global citizenship is often criticised for being elitist and based on Western principles and ideology. However, being human, identifying and relating to others in this way is not a Western concept. Anyone in any part of the world has the capacity to do this. Perhaps the real question is whether global citizenship education is the right means to this end.

Case Study 9   Malala Yousafzai – a global citizen?

On 9 October 2012, Malala Yousafzai, a young Pakistani schoolgirl was shot in the head and neck in an attempt by Taliban gunmen to assassinate her while returning home on a school bus. She became a target of the Taliban after campaigning for girls' rights to access education. She lived in the Northwest region of Pakistan, in the Swat Valley, which was under Taliban rule at the time. The Taliban banned girls from attending school in January 2009 and destroyed around 150 schools. At the same time, Malala, aged 11, began writing a blog for the BBC in Urdu under the pen name 'Gul Makai' about her life under the Taliban (see BBC, 2009). Her diary gives an idea of the dangers Malala and other girls faced simply by attending school.

Her diary entry on 3 January 2009 talks of her fear of the Taliban, who had recently issued an edict banning all girls from attending schools. However, Malala still attended school that day, along with 11 others (out of 27). After school on her way home, she heard a man saying that he would kill her. Luckily, this time, the man was talking on his mobile phone, threatening someone else. Subsequent diary entries talk about how she was ordered by the principal not to wear her uniform or colourful clothes to school and how fearful she was that she may never attend school again as a result of the Taliban's edict.

Peace was eventually restored in the region in 2011 with the help of the Pakistani military. This paved the way for Malala to campaign actively for girls' education in the media. Unfortunately, the media attention also drew criticism from her Taliban opponents, leading to the attempt to assassinate her in 2012. Fortunately, after her attack, she was flown to the UK and treated at the Queen Elizabeth Hospital in Birmingham where she made a full recovery.

In her first public speech since the attack, on 12 July 2013, Malala Yousafzai, aged 16, addressed the United Nations in her campaign for universal education. 12 July is now officially known as Malala Day. In her speech, she said, 'Let us pick up our books and pens. They are our most powerful weapons. One child, one teacher, one pen and one book can change the world. Education is the only solution. Education first' (Malala Yousafzai, in BBC, 2013).

(Contiuned)

(Contiuned)

In an article titled, 'Malala and global citizenship', Rafiq (2013) believes Malala is the perfect example of a global citizen. He writes: 'We saw Malala the Muslim, Malala the Pakistani, Malala the Pashtun, Malala the South Asian, Malala the young woman, and Malala the global citizen. Instead of situating herself in a single camp, Malala has embraced them all.' Rafiq urges young Pakistanis to learn from Malala's example and extend the love they have for their country outside its borders. Embracing humanity in this way will allow them to be a part of the global community.

Key questions:

- Is Malala a good example of a global citizen? Be prepared to justify your answer.

- Rafiq (2013) believes it is possible to reconcile the tensions between nationalism versus universalism. How is this achieved and is it really possible?

- Overall, what do you think of the concept of global citizenship education? Is it desirable? As discussed in the chapter, many view it as an elitist, Western pursuit. Do you think this is the case with Malala?

Suggested reading

Arthur, J. & Cremin, H. (eds) (2012) *Debates in Citizenship Education*. Abingdon: Routledge
A series of articles on contemporary key issues surrounding citizenship education. It covers a range of issues, including international comparative perspectives on citizenship education.

Brown, G.W. & Held, D. (eds) (2010) *The Cosmopolitan Reader*. Cambridge: Polity Press
This is great resource for those interested in learning more about cosmopolitanism from its origins to application in the social, cultural and political arenas.

Globalisation, Societies and Education (2011) *The Political Economy of Global Citizenship Education* (special edition), 9(3–4).
This is a special edition of the journal that focuses on the political economy of global citizenship education. There are numerous articles from academics around the world.

References

Bamber, P. (2009) Education for citizenship: Different dimensions, in W. Bignold & L. Gayton (eds), *Global Issues and Comparative Education*. Exeter: Learning Matters

Bates, R. (2012) Is global citizenship possible, and can international schools provide it? *Journal of Research in International Education*, 11(3), 262–274

BBC (2009) *Diary of a Pakistani School Girl*. Available online at: http://news.bbc.co.uk/1/hi/world/south_asia/7834402.stm

BBC (2013) Shot Pakistan schoolgirl Malala Yousafzai addresses UN. Available online at: www.bbc.co.uk/news/world-asia-23282662

Beck, J. (2012) A brief history of citizenship education in England and Wales, in J. Arthur & H. Cremin (eds), *Debates in Citizenship Education*. Abingdon: Routledge

Brown, G.W. & Held, D. (eds) (2010) *The Cosmopolitan Reader*. Cambridge: Polity Press

Castells, M. (2006) Globalisation and Identity. Available online at: www.llull.cat/rec_transfer/webt1/transfer01_foc01.pdf

Crick, B. (2002) Education for citizenship: The citizenship order. *Parliamentary Affairs*, 55(3), 488–504

Davies, L. (2008) *Global Citizenship Education*. Available online at: www.tc.edu/centers/epe/

DfE (2013) *Citizenship*. Available online at: www.education.gov.uk/schools/teachingandlearning/curriculum/secondary/b00199157/citizenship

DfES (2004) *Putting the World into World-Class Education: An International Strategy for Education, Skills and Children's Services*. Available online at: www.globalfootprints.org/files/zones/hec/DfES%20International%20strategy.pdf

Education Scotland (2013) *About Global Citizenship*. Available online at: www.educationscotland.gov.uk/learningteachingandassessment/learningacrossthecurriculum/themesacrosslearning/globalcitizenship/about/index.asp

Global Citizen (2014) About Global Citizen.org, www.globalcitizen.org/AboutUs/AboutUs.aspx?typeId=15

Globalisation, Societies and Education (2011) *The Political Economy of Global Citizenship Education* (special edition), 9(3–4)

Green, A. (1997) *Education, Globalization and the Nation State*. Basingstoke: Macmillan

Hankin, L. (2009) Global citizenship and comparative education, in J. Sharp, L. Hankin & S. Ward (eds), *Education Studies: An Issues-based Approach* (2nd edition). Exeter: Learning Matters

Hornby, A.S. (2000) *Oxford Advanced Learner's Dictionary of Current English* (6th edition). Oxford: Oxford University Press

Ibrahim, T. (2005) Global citizenship education: Mainstreaming the curriculum? *Cambridge Journal of Education*, 35(2), 177–194

IEA (2010) *Initial Findings from the IEA International Civic and Citizenship Education Study*. Amsterdam: International Association for the Evaluation of Educational Achievement

Jerome, L. (2012) *England's Citizenship Education Experiment*. London: Bloomsbury

Kandel, I. (1933) *Studies in Comparative Education*. London: George Harrap & Co

Mannion, G., Biesta, G., Priestley, M. & Ross, H. (2011) The global dimension in education and education for global citizenship: Genealogy and critique. *Globalisation, Societies and Education*, 9(3–4), 443–456

Moorse, L. (2013) DfE's updated National Curriculum misses the point. Available online at: www.democraticlife.org.uk/2013/07/08/dfes-updated-national-curriculum-misses-the-point/

Naseem, M.A. & Hyslop-Margison, E.J. (2006) Nussbaum's concept of cosmopolitanism: Practical possibility or academic delusion? *Paideusis*, 15(2), 51–60

Norris, P. (2000) Cosmopolitan citizens, in J. Nye & J. Donahue (eds), *Governance in a Globalizing World*. Washington, DC: Brookings Institution Press

Nussbaum, M. (1994) Patriotism and cosmopolitanism, in M. Nussbaum & J. Cohen (eds), *For Love of Country?* Boston, MA: Beacon Press

Ohmae, K. (1991, 1999) *The Borderless World: Power and Strategy in the Interlinked Economy*. New York: Harper Collins

Oxfam (1997) *What is Global Citizenship?* Available online at: www.oxfam.org.uk/education/gc/what_and_why/what/

Poulsen, F. (2008) *On Nussbaum, Cosmopolitanism and Patriotism (and Nationalism)*. Available online at: http://frankejbypoulsen.wordpress.com/2008/11/09/on-nussbaum-cosmopolitanism-and-patriotism-and-nationalism/

QCA (1998) *Education for Citizenship and the Teaching of Democracy in Schools*. London: QCA

Rafiq, A. (2013) Malala and global citizenship. *The Tribune*. Available online at: http://tribune.com.pk/story/587867/malala-and-global-citizenship/

Schefflera, S. (1999) Conceptions of cosmopolitanism. *Utilitas*, 11(3), 255–276

Spring, J. (2009) *Globalization of Education: An Introduction*. New York: Routledge

Veugelers, W. (2011) The moral and the political in global citizenship: Appreciating differences in education. *Globalisation, Societies, and Education*, 9(3–4), 473–485

World Bank (2011) *What is Empowerment?* Available online at: http://web.worldbank.org/WBSITE/EXTERNAL/TOPICS/EXTPOVERTY/EXTEMPOWERMENT/0,,contentMDK:20272299~pagePK:210058~piPK:210062~theSitePK:486411~isCURL:Y,00.html

CHAPTER 10

MULTICULTURAL EDUCATION

This chapter explores:

- The meaning of multiculturalism and pluralism;
- The concept of multicultural and intercultural education;
- The role of foreign language and bilingual education in understanding others.

 Activity 10.1   Multiculturalism

What do you think words like multicultural, multiculturalism and pluralism mean? How might they be similar to and different from each other? Draw a mind map linking some of your ideas together.

Migration patterns

As a result of globalisation, there has been an increased movement of people across national boundaries in the past couple of decades. 'Approximately 20 people cross an international border every second'

(Suárez-Orozco & Suárez-Orozco, 2009, p. 63). While the movement of people is not historically unprecedented, the sheer volume of people on the move in recent times is. In 2010, the total number of international migrants worldwide was estimated to be around 214 million persons, which is an increase of 58 million since 1990 (United Nations, 2011). According to new UN global migration statistics, this figure rose slightly to 232 million in 2013 (UNESCO, 2014). This means that international migrants currently represent around 3% of the total world population. As a result, UNESCO (2014) believes that international migration 'is a key feature of globalization and a central issue on the international agenda'.

Migration can be understood as 'the movement of a person or a group of persons, either across an international border, or within a State. It is a population movement, encompassing any kind of movement of people, whatever its length, composition and causes; it includes migration of refugees, displaced persons, economic migrants, and persons moving for other purposes, including family reunification' (IOM, 2011). The largest number of international migrants live in Europe (approximately 70 million), followed by Asia (61 million) and Northern America (50 million). There were 19 million international migrants living in Africa, 7 million in Latin America and the Caribbean and 6 million in Oceania. In terms of international migrants relative to the total population, Oceania had the highest percentage at 16.8%, followed by Northern America (14.2%) and Europe (9.5%). In Africa, Asia and Latin America and the Caribbean, international migrants accounted for less than 2% of the total population (United Nations, 2011).

Why do people migrate from one country to another? Suárez-Orozco & Suárez-Orozco (2009, p. 42) believe globalisation is the main reason and, more specifically:

1) Where capital flows immigrants follow.

2) New information, communication and media technologies not only further global economic production but also stimulate migration by generating new desires, tastes, consumption practices and lifestyle choices. Would be immigrants envision better lives elsewhere and with better information mobilize to achieve them.

3) Globally integrated economies are increasing structured around a need for foreign workers (both in the knowledge-intensive sector and least desirable sectors of the economy).

4) Mass transportation has become affordable, which has made the option of migration possible for millions of people.

Castles (2009: 49) echoes this: 'People move to seek economic opportunities, refuge from war and persecution, or just new ways of living'. In short, globalisation has created the conditions for greater human mobility and the movement of people both within and across national boundaries.

Activity 10.2   Migration and hyperglobalism

How does Ohmae's (1991, 1999) idea of a borderless world (discussed in Chapter 8) link to global migration patterns?

Multiculturalism

Migration has meant that many societies have become much more diverse in terms of race, ethnicity, gender, class, languages and religion. Diversity 'simply describes the existence of many different groups of people' (Koppelman, 2014, p. 316). This has led to societies being referred to as multicultural. 'The term multicultural describes the culturally diverse nature of human society. It not only refers to elements of ethnic or national culture, but also includes linguistic, religious and socio-economic diversity' (UNESCO, 2006, p. 17). However, the meaning behind the term 'multiculturalism' is something quite different. The concept of multiculturalism is often a politically charged and highly sensitive subject which has been at the centre of much debate. Many definitions have been offered by various academics, politicians and journalists over the years. Heckmann (1993, p. 245) outlined seven different uses of the term:

1) To describe social change in terms of ethnicity or societies moving from a more homogeneous population to one that is more heterogeneous.

2) In a 'normative-cognitive way' where countries should recognise the fact that they have become a destination for immigration, and they need immigration presently and in the future so therefore must accept the social and cultural consequences.

3) To describe both an attitude and a norm, multiculturalism as tolerance towards others; as friendly and supportive behaviour towards immigrants. Multiculturalism is seen as a liberal and democratic attitude based on learning from the errors and consequences of nationalism, chauvinism and ethnic intolerance.

4) As an interpretation of the concept of culture: there are no 'pure' original cultures. Each culture has incorporated elements of other cultures; cultures are the result of interaction with one another; culture is a continuous process of change; and immigrants are seen as opportunities for the enrichment of one's own culture.

5) At a superficial level, multiculturalism is an attitude that looks upon some aspects of the immigrant's culture (folklore, food, for example) and sees these as possible enrichment of 'our' culture.

6) As a political-constitutional principle which refers to ethnic identities as a major basis for political and state organisation for the distribution of rights and resources; it means the reinforcing of ethnic pluralism, ethnic autonomy, and speaks out against acculturation or assimilation, against one 'state language'.

7) As a critical category meaning multiculturalism is regarded as a well-intended, but false concept which overlooks the necessity for a common culture, language and identification to enable societal and state integration and stability. The unifying and homogenizing effects of the nation-state are looked upon as an achievement that should not be easily given up.

 Activity 10.3   Multiculturalism defined seven ways

Think back to the opening activity for this chapter and look at your definition of multiculturalism. Which category does it fit into according to Heckmann's (1993) model?

In the multicultural debate, the phrase 'pluralistic society' or 'pluralism' is often used in the context of multiculturalism. It is important to know that they do mean different things from multiculturalism. Cultural pluralism 'describes a society that allows multiple distinctive groups to function separately and equally without requiring any assimilation into the dominant society' (Gollnick & Chinn, 2013, p. 11). Another way of looking at it is: 'Pluralism describes a society in which diversity is accepted and supported. In a pluralistic society, diverse groups function together effectively, with mutual respect' (Koppelman, 2014, p. 316). Furthermore, Feinberg (1996, p. 182) states: 'Pluralism seeks a society in which people from different cultural formations and orientations are allowed, if they wish to do so, to express their way of life within a separate cultural sphere, and are treated as equal individuals in a common public sphere'. So what is the difference between pluralism and multiculturalism? Pluralism is about allowing cultural identity to flourish, while multiculturalism actively encourages it to do so (Feinberg, 1996).

Historical development of multiculturalism

In the USA, multiculturalism grew out the civil rights movement of the 1960s when African Americans began to demand equal rights in the political, economic and social spheres. This in turn paved the way for other marginalised groups to do the same (Banks, 2009). However, in the UK, multiculturalism is said not to have emanated from a political movement but from immigration, specifically from outside Europe, with the movement of non-white peoples into predominately white countries (Modood, 2007). For Modood, the UK has a much narrower meaning of multiculturalism, which focuses on the consequences of immigration.

In the 1960s, the UK government's underlying philosophy towards immigrants was based on the ideas of assimilation (Walters, 2012). Assimilation is a one-way process where 'newcomers do little to disturb the society they are settling in and become as much like their new compatriots as possible' (Modood, 2007, p. 48). When immigrants assimilate, they are expected to lose their cultural heritage (language, practices and identity) and take on the dominant culture instead.

However, by the 1970s, immigrants were settling but not always assimilating. According to Castles (2009), there were two main reasons: first, they could not assimilate because of racial or ethnic discrimination and social disadvantage led to segregation in terms of work and housing; and secondly, they simply did not want to because it meant giving up their language, religion and customs, which were essential to their identity. As a reaction to this, the underlying approach moved from assimilation to integration. By the 1990s, assimilation seemed to be on the way out and, in the UK, policies were re-labelled, with a greater emphasis on integration, social cohesion (Castles, 2009) and a more general trend towards the principles of multiculturalism.

Integration is a two-way process 'where members of the majority community as well as immigrants and ethnic minorities are required to do something; so the latter cannot alone be blamed for failing (or not trying) to integrate' (Modood, 2007, p. 48). In order for integration to be successful, it requires the institutions, including employers and the government of the established society, to take the lead. Over the years, much of the immigration debate has centred on the issues surrounding integration versus assimilation, and which approach is best for both the individual and the country as a whole. Recently, there has been some backlash against multiculturalism. This is evident in a speech made by David Cameron, the UK Prime Minister, at the Munich Security Conference in 2011, where he argued that multiculturalism had failed Britain. He stated:

> We have allowed the weakening of our collective identity under the doctrine of state multiculturalism. We have encouraged different cultures to live separate lives apart from one another and apart from the mainstream. We failed to provide a vision of society to which they feel they want to belong. We've even tolerated these communities behaving in ways that run completely counter to our values.
>
> David Cameron (BBC, 2011)

Activity 10.4   Multiculturalism: A failure?

Access the Prime Minister's speech at: http://www.bbc.co.uk/news/magazine-12381027

What is his interpretation of multiculturalism? Where does this fit in with Heckmann's (1993) definitions? What kind of multicultural society is he suggesting we have? When he talks about 'our values', whose values does he mean? Does he mean the dominant culture and, if so, which culture would that be? What does it mean to be British in this context?

Multicultural education

Activity 10.5   Multiculturalism and education

Consider some of the meanings of multiculturalism discussed in the previous section. How might these be applied to education?

How does education shape people's attitudes towards each other? Schooling has always played an important role in nation building (see Chapter 9). In the 1960s, schools in the UK played a prominent role in the assimilation of new immigrants. The melting-pot analogy is often used to describe this process. The term 'melting pot' became popularised in the USA around 1908 when immigration from parts of Europe was growing (Gloor, 2006). The idea is that when the ingredients, in this case people, in the pot heat up, they melt together. When the ingredients melt together, they come out of the pot with the same consistency, texture, and so forth. 'For years, the goal of schools was to be the fire under the melting pot' (Woolfolk et al., 2008, p. 187). Newly arrived immigrant children were expected to adapt, change and assimilate into their society by learning English and becoming mainstream citizens through schooling. In fact, 'Until 30–40 years ago, students of colour would have rarely seen themselves in textbooks or learned the history and culture of their group in the classroom. Even today, the curriculum is contested in some communities when families do not see their cultures and values represented' (Gollnick & Chinn, 2013, p. 11).

The 'melting-pot' approach has been heavily criticised for a number of reasons. 'With assimilation, the individuals lose their own culture completely and adopt the culture of the dominant group' (Domnwachukwu, 2010, p. 62). This idea comes with the expectation that immigrants must deny themselves their cultural heritage in order to be successful in their new country. Is this fair, desirable or even possible? Immigrant children were expected to change with very little effort from the school system. In fact, the problems they faced were perceived to be their fault due to their lack of assimilation and lack of English proficiency.

As stated earlier, assimilation gave way to integration in the 1970s. According to Walters (2012, p. 135), 'The expectation was still that ethnic minority pupils and their families would become absorbed into British society, but there was a shift towards recognizing the existence of cultural diversity and to an understanding that the educational support that ethnic minority pupils might need might be more that simply providing English lessons'. There was a greater understanding and awareness that cultural diversity could be beneficial to society and multicultural education for all pupils eventually became a policy approach.

However, despite this positive step, ethnic minority pupils were still underachieving in the UK. In 1977, the Commons Select Committee on Race Relations and Immigration drew attention to widespread concerns about the poor performance of West Indian (or African-Caribbean) children in schools in their report, *The West Indian Community*. The report called for an investigation into the underlying causes of this underachievement. Hence, in 1979 the government set up the Committee of Inquiry into the Education of Children from Ethnic Minority Groups, led by Anthony Rampton. In 1981, they published what became known as the Rampton Report, where 'they concluded that the main problems were low teacher expectations and racial prejudice among white teachers and society as a whole' (Rampton, 1981; Gillard, 2008). This 'confirmed what black parents had been saying all along – that racism against black children was indeed a major factor in their experience of school' (Cole, 2012, p. 88).

Not happy with the outcome, the government dismissed Rampton and commissioned another study, but this time the scope was extended to other ethnic minority groups. The report, published in 1985, is known as the Swann Report, *Education for All*, after Lord Michael Swann, who led the committee responsible for producing it. They found the same thing as the previous Rampton Report, which was that ethnic minorities were underachieving as a result of disadvantage from having low socio-economic status and suffering racial prejudice and discrimination both within school and outside. Underachievement was found not to be a result of low intelligence, as some had previously suggested. The Swann Report (1985, p. 768) states: 'Low average IQ has often been suggested as a cause of underachievement, particularly in the case of West Indians. This has long been disputed, and our own investigations leave us in no doubt that IQ is not a significant factor in underachievement.' The Report is significant because the recommendations it made have influenced multicultural education in the UK ever since. A selection of some of its recommendations is listed below:

(a) The fundamental change that is necessary is the recognition that the problem facing the education system is not how to educate children of ethnic minorities, but how to educate all children.

(b) Britain is a multiracial and multicultural society and all pupils must be enabled to understand what this means.

(c) It is necessary to combat racism, to attack inherited myths and stereotypes, and the ways in which they are embodied in institutional practices.

(d) Multicultural understanding has also to permeate all aspects of a school's work. It is not a separate topic that can be welded on to existing practices.

(Swann Report, 1985, p. 769)

The recommendations also stated that learning English should be a priority for all students, but particularly for those students from ethnic minority groups. Hence they called for the withdrawal of separate language units within schools and stated that 'the needs of learners of English as a second language should be met by provision within the mainstream school as part of a comprehensive programme of language education for all children' (Swann Report, 1985, p. 771). They did not go as far as supporting bilingual education but recognised that 'All teachers in schools with substantial numbers of pupils for whom English is not their first language have a responsibility to cater for the linguistic needs of these pupils and should be given appropriate support and training to discharge it' (Swann Report, 1985, p. 771). Lastly, they understood that there was an underrepresentation of ethnic minorities in the teaching profession.

While the Swann Report has been hugely influential in shaping multicultural education in Britain, one of its underlying principles was that if children were taught about each other's cultures, then this would help to reduce prejudice, particularly among white children (Cole, 2012). However, many like Cole feel that the Swann Report's 'predominant focus on culture set the trajectory of multicultural education along a superficial line in which children were taught about the food, the clothes, and the music of different countries, usually by white teachers, without also understanding the structural and institutional inequalities that had been at the core of community campaigns' (Cole, 2012, p. 88). Furthermore, many people have a limited and misguided view as to what multicultural education is. Banks and Banks (2013, p. 314) feel that if we reduce multicultural education down to 'isolated lessons in sensitivity training or prejudice reduction or separate units about cultural artifacts or ethnic holidays', we will do little to influence student learning. So what really should multicultural be education about?

Activity 10.6   The Swann Report (1985)

You can access the full report at: www.educationengland.org.uk/documents/ swann/swann18.html

What do you think some of the criticisms of the Swann Report might be? Are the needs of pupils with English as a Second Language (ESL) or English as an Additional language (EAL) catered for in schools? How prominently are their needs addressed in teacher education?

There are different views, if only slightly different, on what multicultural education is or should be, so looking at a few key definitions is an essential starting point. Multiculturalism in an educational context is 'a philosophical position and movement that assumes that the gender, ethnic, racial, and cultural diversity of a pluralistic society should be reflected in all of the institutionalized structures of educational institutions, including the staff, the norms and values, the curriculum, and the student body' (Banks & Banks, 2013, p. 355). Multicultural education, for Banks (2009, p. 13), goes a step further, from simply setting ideals to actively pursuing them: 'Multicultural education is an approach to school reform designed to actualize educational equality for students from diverse, racial, ethnic, cultural, social-class, and linguistic groups. It also promotes democracy and social justice.' This idea of multicultural education sees it as part of a wider reform movement whereby the education system and everything within it and outside it are expected to change in order to remove the barriers that students from diverse backgrounds might face.

 Activity 10.7   Achieving multicultural education

For Banks and other educationalists, at the heart of multicultural education is equality for ALL students. How can politicians, institutions and practitioners go about achieving this?

Therefore Gollnick and Chinn (2013, p. 24) listed six fundamental beliefs underlying multicultural education:

• Cultural differences have strength and value.

• Schools should be models for the expression of human rights and respect for cultural and group differences.

• Social justice and equality for all people should be of paramount importance in the design and delivery of curricula.

- Attitudes and values necessary for participation in a democratic society should be promoted in schools.

- Teachers are key to students learning the knowledge, skills and dispositions (values, attitudes and commitments) they need to be productive citizens.

- Educators working with families and communities can create an environment that is supportive of multiculturalism, equality and social justice.

Activity 10.8   UNESCO definition

UNESCO has proposed that 'Multicultural education uses learning about other cultures in order to produce acceptance, or at least tolerance, of these cultures' (UNESCO, 2006, p. 18). How does this definition compare to Banks' (2009) definition? Do you think this a superficial view?

Themes of equality, diversity, anti-racism and social justice are central to our understanding of multicultural education and, as such, multicultural education may be called slightly different things around the world (see Figure 10.1). There will, of course, be differences between them.

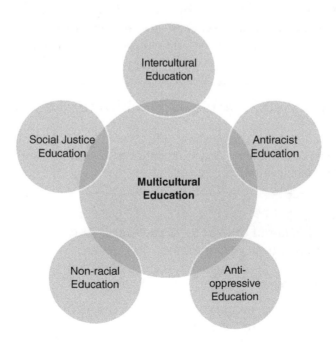

Figure 10.1   Multicultural education

Source: Adapted from Nieto, 2009

In Europe, the term 'intercultural education' is often used rather than 'multicultural education'. The term was introduced in Western Europe around 1975 and was being discussed particularly in Germany, Austria and a part of Switzerland by the late 1970s (Allemann-Ghionda, 2011). In fact, Coulby (2006) believes the terminological shift from multicultural to intercultural education occurred rapidly around 1980. At the time, the term was apparently accepted without question and hesitation. The shift occurred as a response to a backlash against multicultural education for two main reasons. First, for nationalists, schools should represent the state (and only the state) in terms of language, religion, culture and other values. Secondly, from a pluralistic perspective, issues of racism were not being adequately addressed by multicultural education, where it merely provided a token understanding of non-dominant knowledge and belittled cultural difference to the study of superficial topics such as food and music. Coulby believes that despite the fact that the terminological shift did not resolve the above concerns, the term 'intercultural education' seemed to offer a fresh start and one less influenced by the previously dominant and insular theory and practice of the USA and the UK.

What exactly does the term 'intercultural education' mean? 'Intercultural Education aims to go beyond passive coexistence, to achieve a developing and sustainable way of living together in multicultural societies through the creation of understanding of, respect for and dialogue between the different cultural groups' (UNESCO, 2006, p. 18). The key word here is dialogue. In other words, tolerance and mutual respect for one another happens as a result of communication between individuals or groups of individuals from diverse backgrounds. Portera (2011, p. 20) writes: 'Intercultural Education rejects immobility and cultural or human hierarchy, and is meant to encourage dialogue and relationship on equal terms, so that people do not feel constrained to sacrifice important aspects of their cultural identity.'

Activity 10.9   Intercultural or multicultural

What do you think the key differences are between intercultural education and multicultural education? Do these differences matter? Think back to Chapter 9 on global citizenship education and education for cosmopolitanism, and compare these to multicultural education. One places emphasis on the commonality of being human, while the other celebrates cultural difference and individual identity. As educators, are these two concepts at odds with one another?

After studying a number of documents from international conferences, UNESCO (2006, p. 32) believes that there are three main recurring principles that guide intercultural education:

- **Principle I** – Intercultural Education respects the cultural identity of the learner through the provision of culturally appropriate and responsive quality education for all.

- **Principle II** – Intercultural Education provides every learner with the cultural knowledge, attitudes and skills necessary to achieve active and full participation in society.

- **Principle III** – Intercultural Education provides all learners with cultural knowledge, attitudes and skills that enable them to contribute to respect, understanding and solidarity among individuals, ethnic, social, cultural and religious groups and nations.

 Activity 10.10   Three key principles of intercultural education

Reflect on the principles outlined above. How can these be achieved? You can access the full document at: http://unesdoc.unesco.org/images/0014/001478/147878e.pdf Compare your ideas with those offered by UNESCO. What do you think the potential limitations might be of either approach?

Acquiring the skills to communicate and cooperate beyond cultural barriers plays a central role in intercultural education. Intercultural communication occurs as a direct result of interaction between two individuals from culturally diverse backgrounds. It is a complex concept consisting of various components, including intercultural sensitivity and competence. Intercultural sensitivity is the ability to acknowledge and respect cultural differences as a result of positive emotional responses before, during, and after intercultural interaction, and is comprised of six elements: self-esteem, self-monitoring, open-mindedness, empathy, interaction involvement and non-judgement (Chen & Starosta, 1997). In other words, intercultural sensitivity involves the ability to interact with people from a different culture confidently and in a perceptive, respectful manner. In order to do this successfully, one must be aware of how cultural influences affect people's outlook, attitude, values and behaviour. Open and honest communication handled with intercultural sensitivity can ultimately lead to intercultural competence – a key goal of intercultural education. Olsen and Kroeger (2001, cited in Clifford & Joseph, 2005) believe that '[e]ssentially intercultural competence involves sensitivity to the perspective of others, a willingness to try and put oneself in the shoes of others and see how things might look from their perspective'.

Activity 10.11   Intercultural competence

How important is intercultural communication in a globalised world? Using Olsen and Kroger's definition of intercultural competence, imagine what the world might look like if everyone was able, at the very least, to try to put themselves in the shoes of others. Is this simply an ideal dreamt up by liberal academics? Can intercultural education achieve this?

Foreign language education

The teaching and learning of languages are also an important part of intercultural education. According to Coulby (2006, p. 252), '[u]nderstanding fully another culture is probably impossible for most people'. However, he believes that those who acquire additional languages have the best chance of doing so. The American Council on the Teaching and Learning of Foreign Languages (ACTFL) publishes national standards for foreign language learning in the USA to help practitioners in foreign language education on what students should know and be able to do in another language. They devised what is commonly known as the five Cs: Communication, Cultures, Connections, Comparisons and Communities. 'Through the study of other languages, students gain a knowledge and understanding of the cultures that use that language and, in fact, cannot truly master the language until they have also mastered the cultural contexts in which the language occurs' (ACTFL, 2006). The standards also set out the belief that through learning a foreign language, students are able to access other bodies of knowledge and may come to understand 'that there are multiple ways of viewing the world' and, when combined, it allows us 'to participate in multilingual communities at home and around the world in a variety of contexts and in culturally appropriate ways' (ACTFL, 2006).

If learning another language is an important part of understanding others, then what is the state of language learning around the world? In 2007, around 60% of students in upper secondary education (the final stage or equivalent to A-levels in the UK) studied two or more languages in the European Union (EU), while one-third studied only one language and 6% did not study any foreign language (Eurostat, 2009). More specifically, all students in upper secondary studied two or more foreign languages in the Czech Republic, Luxembourg, the Netherlands and Finland. Conversely, in the UK, more than half (51%) of students in upper secondary education did not study any foreign language in 2007.

In the UK, many have attributed the decline in the study of foreign languages as a result of the Labour government's decision in 2004 to make learning a language optional at GCSE level (lower secondary)

(Paton, 2011). There could also be others reasons for the decline, such as a lack of interest in other cultures, no perceived benefits in learning a language and limited opportunities to actually do so. However, the new National Curriculum, which is set to take effect in 2014, will make learning a language compulsory for pupils aged 7–11 (Key Stages 2 and 3, equivalent to upper primary and lower secondary). Would an increase in language learning in the UK enable students to become more interculturally competent and allow for a greater knowledge and understanding of others?

Bilingual education

All children should benefit from multicultural and intercultural education. However, the children of immigrants still face significant disadvantage. Despite an increase in our knowledge and our understanding of the issues they face, there is still a growing concern about the educational outcomes of the children of migrants in European OECD countries. According to PISA results, the children of immigrants in most European and OECD countries have lower educational outcomes than their native counterparts (OECD, 2009). Thomas and Collier (2000) similarly report that ethnolinguistic minorities of different language backgrounds are among the lowest achievers in American schools. How can the education system best support these students?

One of the biggest barriers these pupils face is language. Language can play a huge role in political and social exclusion. Over the years, various initiatives have been tried to help pupils with English as Additional Language (EAL) needs. These have included teaching them separately from native speakers in their own classes. Others include them in mainstream classes but with support. In the UK, very often those who support EAL learners are not English language specialists and have had little or no training.

Bilingual education is where any two languages are used in schools by both teachers and students for a variety of social and teaching or learning purposes (NABE, 2013). A number of bilingual programmes have existed in the USA, but in the UK they are not common unless you are referring to some fee-paying international schools or Welsh-medium schools where pupils are taught primarily in Welsh. The number of schools offering bilingual education in the UK is indeed very low (Kasprzak, 2012).

Bilingual programmes have been highly controversial and heavily criticised for a couple of reasons. The National Association for Bilingual Education (NABE), located in the USA, has summarised a number of these reasons which largely pertain to the idea that bilingual education defies the American melting-pot tradition. Some of the arguments listed by NABE (2013) are as follows:

- If non-English-speaking students are isolated in foreign-language classrooms, how are they ever going to learn English, the key to upward mobility?

- What was wrong with the old 'sink or swim' method that worked for generations of earlier immigrants?

- Isn't bilingual education just another example of 'political correctness' run amok – the inability to say no to a vociferous ethnic lobby?

There are also many Americans who argue for English-only because bilingualism threatens national identity and divides the country along ethnic lines. Moreover, they fear that by recognising minority languages, the government is sending the wrong message to immigrants, encouraging them not to assimilate into American society.

However, there is much evidence to suggest that bilingual programmes do in fact benefit learners (see Krashen, 1999; Thomas & Collier, 2000; Nieto, 2010; NABE, 2013). The problem for many immigrant children is not the fact that they do not speak English, but that they are not proficient in their own mother tongue. Bilingual education helps to promote literacy in knowledge in their native language as many programmes incorporate both content and language instruction. This in turns helps them to become more academically successful overall.

Conclusion

More than ever, the world needs multicultural and intercultural education for the benefit of all members of society. Increased migration, the existence of prejudice, human rights abuses (the list goes on) call for a heightened understanding of and respect for other people. Communities benefit when nobody is socially, politically or economically excluded from participating in society. Mutual understanding, respect for and tolerance of others are at the heart of multicultural/intercultural education. If we are to value diversity and champion equality, then multicultural/intercultural education must be given serious attention and be moved to the top of the educational agenda once again.

 Case Study 10   Intercultural and bilingual education in Mexico

Mexico, like most North and South American countries, is multicultural and its population consists of many ethnic groups. There are three main ethnic groups, the largest being the Mestizos, who are a mixture of European heritage (mainly Spanish) and indigenous (Amerindians). Others

(Continued)

(Continued)

include whites of European heritage (around 9% of the population) and indigenous groups such as the Mayans, Zapotecs, Mixtecs and Tarascans, who make up around 10% of the population (see Schmal, 2008).

The indigenous groups are the most affected by poverty in Mexico and have largely been left out of the mainstream Mexican economy (Gamboa & Linse, 2006). 'An indigenous person has a 57 per cent probability of being extremely poor, compared with a 13 per cent probability for a nonindigenous individual' (Ramirez, 2006, p. 162). The illiteracy rate among indigenous peoples is significantly higher at more than twice the national rate for the population as a whole. Indigenous people have fewer years of schooling and are also much more likely than non-indigenous children to be in a lower grade year than is appropriate for their age. Ramirez also reports that there is evidence that indigenous peoples suffer not only from fewer years of schooling, but also from lower-quality schooling. The evidence comes from lower reading and mathematics scores in indigenous schools than in other types of school.

Some indigenous children can attend an indigenous primary school that offers bilingual education for those who do not speak Spanish as their primary language. Bilingual education is offered in 44 indigenous languages, 33 of which are used in textbooks, and in 15 dialectical variations, but without specific textbooks (Ramirez, 2006). However, there are indigenous children in the remaining 18 small linguistic groups who do not have the option of being taught in their own language and have to attend a general primary school, an indigenous primary school that teaches in a different indigenous language, or a rural community school. Gamboa and Linse (2006) state that the main difficulty is finding trained teachers whose mother tongue is an indigenous language.

Bilingual education is underpinned by the Ministry of Education's policy document entitled *Policies and Foundations of Intercultural Bilingual Education* in Mexico (Ahuja et al., 2004), where intercultural education is combined with bilingual education. The reasons stem from the belief that learning Spanish and retaining and developing one's mother tongue integrates the country (Pineda & Landorf, 2011). Intercultural education, as defined by the Ministry of Education, aims to transform society by fighting structural and systematic exclusion and social injustice as well as respecting and benefiting from cultural diversity.

Key questions:

- What are the advantages of bilingual education in the context of Mexico?

- What could potentially be the disadvantages?

- What challenges does bilingual and intercultural education face in Mexico?

Suggested reading

There are many comprehensive books on multicultural education. I have selected a few from well-known scholars in the field.

Banks, J. (ed.) (2009) *The Routledge International Companion to Multicultural Education*. Abingdon: Routledge
This is the international edition so is comparative in its approach. It includes a wide range of topics, which makes it an excellent resource.

Banks, J. & Banks, C. (2013) *Multicultural Education: Issues and Perspectives* (8th edition). Hoboken, NJ: Wiley
A classic, comprehensive text covering all aspects of multicultural education.

Gollnick, D. & Chinn, P. (2013) *Multicultural Education in a Pluralistic Society* (9th edition). Boston, MA: Pearson
A very accessible text but with a focus on the USA.

Grant, C. & Portera, A. (eds) (2011) *Intercultural and Multicultural Education: Enhancing Global Interconnectedness*. Abingdon: Routledge
Includes many articles on both multicultural and intercultural education around the world (e.g. in Germany, Greece, Japan, Mexico, Spain and Taiwan) and links nicely to key themes in this book.

References

ACTFL (2006) *Standards for Foreign Language Learning: Preparing for the 21st Century.* Available online at: www.actfl.org/sites/default/files/StandardsforFLLexecsumm_rev.pdf

Ahuja, R. et al. (2004) *Políticas y Fundamentos de la Educacion Bilingue (Policies and Foundations of Intercultural Bilingual Education in Mexico)*. Mexico City: Secretaria de Educacion Publica (SEP)

Allemann-Ghionda, C. (2011) Comments on intercultural education in German guidelines and curricula, in C. Grant & A. Portera (eds), *Intercultural and Multicultural Education: Enhancing Global Interconnectedness*. Abingdon: Routledge

Banks, J. (ed.) (2009) *The Routledge International Companion to Multicultural Education*. Abingdon: Routledge

Banks, J. & Banks, C. (2013) *Multicultural Education: Issues and Perspectives* (8th edition). Hoboken, NJ: Wiley

BBC (2011) *Multiculturalism: What Does It Mean?* Available online at: www.bbc.co.uk/news/magazine-12381027

Castles, S. (2009) World population movements, diversity, and education, in J. Banks (ed.), *The Routledge International Companion to Multicultural Education*. Abingdon: Routledge

Chen, G.M. & Starosta, W.J. (1997) A review of the concept of intercultural sensitivity. *Human Communication*, 1, 1–16.

Clifford, V. & Joseph, C. (2005) *Report of the Internationalisation of the Curriculum Project*. Higher Education Development Unit, Monash University. Available online at: www.brookes.ac.uk/services/ocsld/ioc/definitions.html

Cole, M. (2012) Racism and education, in M. Cole (ed.), *Education, Equality and Human Rights: Issues of Gender, Race, Sexuality, Disability and Social Class* (3rd edition). Abingdon: Routledge

Coulby, D. (2006) Intercultural education: Theory and practice. *Intercultural Education*, 17(3), 245–257

Domnwachukwu, C.S. (2010) *An Introduction to Multicultural Education: From Theory to Practice*. Lanham, MD: Rowman & Littlefield

Eurostat (2009) *Eurostat Newsrelease: European Day of Languages*. Available online at: http://epp.eurostat.ec.europa.eu/cache/ITY_PUBLIC/3-2409 2009-AP/EN/3-24092009-AP-EN.PDF

Feinberg, W. (1996) The goals of multicultural education: A critical re-evaluation. *Philosophy of Education*. Available online at: http://culture intheclassroom.webs.com/EDEL%20103/Feinberg%201996.pdf

Gamboa, A. & Linse, C. (2006) Mexican education: A melding of history, cultural roots, and reforms, in K. Mazurek & M. Winzer (eds), *Schooling Around the World*. Boston, MA: Pearson

Gillard, D. (2008) *The Rampton Report (1981) West Indian Children in our Schools*. Available online at: www.educationengland.org.uk/documents/rampton/index.html

Gloor, L. (2006) From the melting pot to the tossed salad metaphor: Why coercive assimilation lacks the flavors Americans crave. *Hohonu*, 4(1). Available online at: http://hilo.hawaii.edu/academics/hohonu/writing.php?id=91

Gollnick, D. & Chinn, P. (2013) *Multicultural Education in a Pluralistic Society* (9th edition). Boston, MA: Pearson

Heckmann, F. (1993) Multiculturalism defined seven ways. *The Social Contract*, 3(4), 245–246

House of Commons Select Committee on Race Relations and Immigration (1977) *The West Indian Community*. HC 180–1–111, February

IOM (International Organisation for Migration) (2011) *Key Migration Terms*. Available online at: www.iom.int/cms/en/sites/iom/home/about-migration/key-migration-terms-1.html#Migrant

Kasprzak, E. (2012) *En Français: The Rise of England's Bilingual Schools*. Available online at: www.bbc.co.uk/news/uk-england-19355147

Koppelman, K. (2014) *Understanding Human Differences: Multicultural Education for a Diverse America* (4th edition). Upper Saddle River, NJ: Pearson

Krashen, S. (1999) *Condemned without a Trial: Bogus Arguments against Bilingual Education*. Portsmouth, NH: Heinemann

Modood, T. (2007) *Multiculuralism*. Cambridge: Polity Press

NABE (2013) *What is Bilingual Education?* Available online at: www.nabe.org/BilingualEducation

Nieto, S. (2009) Multicultural education in the United States: Historical realities, ongoing challenges, and transformative possibilities, in J. Banks (ed.), *The Routledge International Companion to Multicultural Education*. Abingdon: Routledge

Nieto, S. (2010) *Language, Culture and Teaching: Critical Perspectives*. Abingdon: Routledge

OECD (2009) *Children of Immigrants in the Labour Markets of EU and OECD Countries: An Overview*. Available online at: www.oecd.org/berlin/43880918.pdf

Ohmae, K. (1991, 1999) *The Borderless World: Power and Strategy in the Interlinked Economy*. New York: Harper Collins

Paton, G. (2011) UK pupils 'worst in Europe for learning foreign languages'. The Daily Telegraph. Available online at: www.telegraph.co.uk/education/educationnews/8729278/UK-pupils-worst-in-Europe-for-learning-foreign-languages.html

Pineda, F. & Landorf, H. (2011) Philosophical and historical foundations of intercultural education in Mexico, in C. Grant & A. Portera (eds), *Intercultural and Multicultural Education: Enhancing Global Interconnectedness*. Abingdon: Routledge

Portera, A. (2011) Intercultural and multicultural education: Epistemological and semantic aspects, in C. Grant & A. Portera (eds), *Intercultural and Multicultural Education: Enhancing Global Interconnectedness*. Abingdon: Routledge

Ramirez, A. (2006) Mexico, in G. Hall & H. Patrinos (eds), *Indigenous Peoples, Poverty and Human Development in Latin America*. Basingstoke: Palgrave Macmillan

Rampton, A. (1981) *West Indian Children in our Schools: Interim Report of the Committee of Inquiry into the Education of Children from Ethnic Minority Groups* (The Rampton Report). London: HMSO

Schmal, J. (2008) *Indigenous Mexico: An Overview*. Available online at: www.mexconnect.com/articles/372-indigenous-mexico-an-overview

Suárez-Orozco, M. & Suárez-Orozco, C. (2009) Globalization, immigration, and schooling, in J. Banks (ed.), *The Routledge International Companion to Multicultural Education*. Abingdon: Routledge

Swann Report (1985) *Education for All*. London: HMSO. Available online at: www.educationengland.org.uk/documents/swann/swann18.html

Thomas, W. & Collier, V. (2000) Accelerated schooling for all students: Research findings on education in multilingual communities, in S. Shaw (ed.), *Intercultural Education in European Classrooms*. Stoke on Trent: Trentham Books

UNESCO (2006) *UNESCO Guidelines on Intercultural Education*. Available online at: http://unesdoc.unesco.org/images/0014/001478/147878e.pdf

UNESCO (2014) *Migration and Inclusive Societies*. Available online at: www.unesco.org/new/en/social-and-human-sciences/themes/international-migration/

United Nations (2011) *International Migration Report 2009: A Global Assessment*. Available online at: www.un.org/esa/population/publications/migration/WorldMigrationReport2009.pdf

Walters, S. (2012) *Ethnicity, Race and Education: An Introduction*. London: Continuum

Woolfolk, A., Hughes, M. & Walkup, V. (2008) *Psychology in Education*. Harlow: Pearson

CHAPTER 11

INTERNATIONAL SCHOOLS

This chapter explores:

- What international schools are and why they exist;
- What curricula they offer;
- The concept of Third Culture Kids;
- The potential downsides to international schooling.

 Activity 11.1   The international schools

What do you think an international school is? Who might go there? What do they teach? Where are they located? Make a list of criteria.

There are around 3.3 million students studying in over 6,500 English medium international schools worldwide with the majority located in Asia (ISC, 2013). The number of international schools is growing every year and nearly 1,200 new British international schools opened world-wide in 2007 (Lynch, 2008). Why are international schools gaining in popularity? What makes them international and what kind of curriculum do they offer? What purpose do they serve and what are the benefits of attending such schools? This chapter will explore the answers to these questions and also invite you to think critically about internationally schooling by exploring their potential downsides.

What is an international school? There are many different types of international school located around the world and they offer a variety of programmes, so to precisely define them is quite difficult. The big question is what makes a school international? The location, curriculum and who the students are all contribute to how international a school is. However, these factors all vary from school to school and location to location. Hayden (2006, p. 11) believes that '[a]ttempts to define international schools are fraught with risk: almost any definition, other than the entirely vague and general, is likely to be contestable by someone familiar with an international school that does not fit the definition given'. However, in spite of the wide variety, she believes that they still share a number of common characteristics. First, they are usually private and charge fees. It is worth noting that some are for profit and others are not. Other characteristics international schools may have in common are:

- International schools serve the children of those international organisations and multinational companies whose parents are called upon to work in many different countries and to change their assignments at frequent intervals;

- The schools also educate the children of the diplomatic corps;

- They offer educational opportunities to children of host country nationals who want their children to learn English or who prefer the greater flexibility which an international school offers over the national system.

(Murphy, 1991, p. 1)

McKenzie (2012, p. 220) describes international schools as 'predominantly day schools in large cities, their students are often enrolled from a globally itinerant community, their teachers tend habitually to travel the international circuit, their boards and their heads change regularly, and their academic curriculum is frequently one or more of the programmes of the International Baccalaureate'.

 Activity 11.2   Potential downsides

Reflecting on McKenzie's description can you think any potential downsides to international schools?

Hill (2006) has proposed a typology (classification system) of international schools with types ranging on a continuum from national to international.

In this typology: 'A national school will have culturally homogeneous students and staff from the same country; it may be public or private and offers an education programme prescribed by the nation state' (Hill, 2006, p. 8). In other words, in a national school 'the majority of students are originally from the same country and are taught a national programme' (p. 8). However, Hill believes that this type 'rarely exists' as most national schools are comprised of staff and students from other countries. As we saw in Chapter 10, there has been a huge increase in the number of migrants settling in countries worldwide, and as a result the student population in national school systems has become much more diverse. There are also a number of national schools that teach international education programmes (e.g. the International Baccalaureate) or capture international perspectives in the curriculum of national programmes.

In Hill's (2006) typology, he proposes two types of international school. The first type revolves around the idea that '[i]nternational schools have a very culturally diverse student body, ideally with no one nationality significantly dominating the others. They are almost invariably private, independent institutions and they teach an international education programme. Many were created as a service to internationally mobile parents and the majority teach in English' (Hill, 2006, p. 8). Examples of this type include the United World Colleges (UWC), even though they were not created to serve internationally mobile parents. However, the reality at many international schools is that the majority of students come from one country.

The other type of international school that Hill describes is one which offers national programmes alongside international education. There are a number of schools that use the word 'international' in their name but really only offer one or more national education programme to accommodate students mainly from a particular nation. Moreover, '[a] number of schools include the word "international" in their title because it sounds prestigious, or because it legitimately reflects the international mindedness of the educational programme while the student body may be quite culturally homogeneous' (Hill, 2006, p. 9).

 Activity 11.3   Examples of international schools

Have a look at the websites of the following schools:

1. Lycée Français Charles de Gaulle London
2. British School Paris
3. The David Young Community Academy
4. Vienna International School
5. The International School in Birmingham

Do you consider these to be international schools? Justify your answer with evidence.

Because of the difficulties with defining international schools, at the 2009 International Association of School Librarianship (IASL) conference, a list of criteria was devised in order to set out clear guidelines as to what could be called an international school (Nagrath, 2011). As long as schools meet the majority of the criteria, they can be considered international. The IASL's criteria for international schools are:

1. The transferability of students' education across international schools.

2. A moving population (higher than in national public schools).

3. A multinational and multilingual student body.

4. An international curriculum.

5. An international accreditation.

6. A transient and multinational teacher population.

7. Non-selective student enrolment.

8. The language of instruction is usually English or bilingual.

> ### Activity 11.4   IASL's criteria
>
> Reflect on the IASL's criteria for international schools. How does this compare to Murphy's definition and Hall's typology? What type of school might the IASL's list exclude? Can you arrange the criteria in order of importance?

History of international schools

When and where the first international school began is the subject of much debate. However, as stated in Chapter 7, Sylvester (2002) thinks that the first attempts to establish international schools were during the period from the mid-1800s to the late 1920s. Many believe that the establishment of Spring Grove School (officially, its name was the London College of the International Education Society) in London in 1886 was the first international school. However, it was not until after the First World War (1914–1918) that a sizeable rise in international schooling began to happen worldwide (Hill, 2007). This was largely due to the perception 'that the school could be effectively used as a medium of international understanding' (Arora, Koehler & Reich, 1994, p. 11). In the twentieth century, the number of international schools slowly began to rise, with the opening of the Odenwald School in Germany and the International School of Peace in Boston in 1910, followed by schools in Geneva and Yokohama in 1924 (Sylvester, 2007). Some scholars consider

Table 11.1 International school organisations

Organisation	Year started	School membership
Council of International Schools (CIS)	1983	660
Council of British Schools (COBIS)	1973	250
English Schools Foundation	1967	15
European Council of International Schools (ECIS)	1965	366
European Schools	1953	14
International Schools Association (ISA)	1951	47
International Schools Europe (ISE)	1958	5
International Schools Group (ISG)	1962	8
Japan Council of International Schools (JCIS)	1972	27
Round Square	1951	100
United World Colleges (UWC)	1962	12

the International School in Geneva, which was created for the children of parents working at the International Labour Organisation and the League of Nations (later to become the United Nations), to be first and longest-surviving international school (Hill, 2012).

Though most international schools are independent, many are linked to the numerous international school organisations around the world, some of which are listed in Table 11.1. Generally speaking, these organisations assist their members with professional development, accreditation, consultancy services and other administrative tasks. One of the largest is the Council of International Schools (CIS).

The Council of International Schools is a non-profit association of schools and post-secondary institutions which provide services that support the continuous improvement of international education. Some of the services include helping 'schools access new international educational practices, gain recognition for accomplishments, attract qualified staff, facilitate student connections with leading universities around the world, and provide a quality international education experience to students and parents' (CIS, 2013). One of the oldest organisations is the International Schools Association (ISA), founded in 1951 in Switzerland. The ISA was involved in the creation of the International Baccalaureate (Diploma) in the 1960s and the 1980s helped to develop the Middle Years Programme (ISA, 2012). The ISA's stated mission is:

1. To further world peace and international understanding through education.

2. To encourage the creation of new international schools.

3. To encourage co-operation among international or internationally-minded schools through consultation on teaching and administrative questions.

4. To facilitate or undertake the study of educational problems of interest to such schools.

5. To nurture interest in national schools of international matters as a means of improving international understanding.

6. To publicize the aims and principles of international schools and promote international understanding among national schools.

(ISA, 2012)

 Activity 11.5   International schools and globalisation

How might the proliferation of international schools contribute to the globalisation of education and the convergence of a world culture? Do you think international schools are better equipped to produce global citizens?

Curriculum

According to Thompson (1998), international schools export, adapt, integrate or create curricula. The schools that export curricula are the ones that typically follow a national curriculum and take nationally-based exams, such as GCSEs or American Advanced Placement (AP), with very little modification to their context or 'host country'. In other words, the curriculum content is recognisable to parents, students and teachers from the 'home' country. An example of this type of school would perhaps be the American School in Japan (ASIJ). According to the ASIJ (2013) website, if offers an American-based college preparatory curriculum and Advanced Placement courses in high school.

 Activity 11.6   Advanced Placement (AP) exams

Find out more about AP courses and exams at: https://apstudent.collegeboard. org/home?navid=ap-ap

Do these compare to anything in the UK? How international are schools that solely follow a national-type curriculum in another country?

Some schools adapt national curricula for the international school context. Examples of this can be found in the Advanced Placement International Diploma (APID), the International GCSE (IGCSE), the

Advanced International Certificate of Education (AICE) and the French Baccalaureat Option Internationale (Thompson, 1998; Hayden, 2006).

Many schools deliver 'integrated' curricula. Thompson (1998, p. 279) writes: 'This occurs when "best practices" from a range of "successful" curricula are brought together to determine a curriculum that may be operated across a number of systems or countries'. Examples of this include the European Baccalaureate (EB) and the International Baccalaureate Diploma (IBDP). The EB, as described by Sayer (2012, p. 188), 'is accepted because it has just about everything which 27 national curricula require and so much more besides'.

The EB was established in 1958 as a qualification for students studying at European schools. European schools were originally founded to educate the children of employees of the European Coal and Steel Community (ECSC), an international organisation consisting of Belgium, France, Italy, Luxembourg, the Netherlands and West Germany (Christmann, 2012). The ECSC, a precursor to the European Union, was created after the Second World War in order to unify Europe and to help prevent any future European conflict. Now the schools provide education for the children of employees of EU institutions such as the European Commission, the European Patent Office and the European Central Bank. There are 14 European schools in seven countries: Belgium, the Netherlands, Germany, Italy, the UK, Spain and Luxembourg (Schola Europaea, 2009). The schools are administered by the European Schools' Board of Governors. Around 24,000 students are currently studying the EB and approximately 1,500 students take the final exam every year (DfE, 2013). The European schools cater for nursery, primary and secondary pupils and their stated objectives are:

- to give pupils confidence in their own cultural identity – the bedrock for their development as European citizens;

- to provide a broad education of high quality, from nursery level to university entrance;

- to develop high standards in the mother tongue and in foreign languages;

- to develop mathematical and scientific skills throughout the whole period of schooling;

- to encourage a European and global perspective overall and particularly in the study of the human sciences;

- to encourage creativity in music and the plastic arts and an appreciation of all that is best in a common European artistic heritage;

- to develop physical skills and instil in pupils an appreciation of the need for healthy living through participation in sporting and recreational activities;

- to offer pupils professional guidance on their choice of subjects and on career/university decisions in the later years of the secondary school;

- to foster tolerance, co-operation, communication and concern for others throughout the school community and beyond;

- to cultivate pupils' personal, social and academic development and to prepare them for the next stage of education;

- to provide Education for Sustainable Development with a cross-curriculum approach in line with European and international documents.

(Schola Europaea, 2009)

 Activity 11.7   Philosophy of education

Compare the stated objectives of European schools to that of your local primary or comprehensive school. Can you find both similarities and differences? How might these objectives (or aims) be manifested in the curriculum and overall ethos of a school?

European Schools were only open to the employees of European institutions or agencies until 2005. However, the European Parliament adopted resolutions in 2002 and 2005 which opened up their curricula and the EB to national schools so that the examination could be taken by students other than those attending European schools. These schools are called Accredited European Schools and have their accreditation renewed every three years (Christmann, 2012): 'Accredited European Schools are schools which offer a European education that meets the pedagogical requirements laid down for the European Schools but within the framework of the national school networks of the Member States and hence outside the legal, administrative and financial framework to which the European Schools are compulsorily subject' (Schola Europaea, 2009). In other words, these schools are administered and financed by the national education systems of the individual member states of the EU and not by the European Schools' Board of Governors. There are currently eight Accredited European Schools in Denmark, Estonia, France, Finland, Germany, Greece, Ireland, Italy and the Netherlands, and two other schools in Tallin and Copenhagen have plans to become Accredited European Schools in 2013.

The EB was created so that those children whose parents were involved in European projects would not be disadvantaged by their education and qualifications when they returned home (Sayer, 2012). As such, 'The EB is officially recognised by treaty as an entry qualification for higher education in all EU countries, as well as many others' (DfE, 2013).

The final type of curriculum that Thompson proposed is 'created' from the first principles in the development of an entirely new programme of study. A good example of this is the International Baccalaureate, which many international and some national schools follow. There are four International Baccalaureate programmes.

The *IB Diploma Programme* (IBDP) was the first and was established in the 1960s with the help of the International School of Geneva and the International Schools Association (ISA). Trial examinations were carried out at the following schools in 1968: the United World College of the Atlantic (Wales, UK); the International School of Geneva (Switzerland); the United Nations International School or UNIS (New York); the International College (Beirut, Lebanon); the Copenhagen International School (Denmark); the Iranzamin International School (Teheran, Iran); and the North Manchester High School for Girls (UK). The programme was created to prepare internationally mobile students aged 16–19 for university and also consisted of common set of external examinations (IBO, 2013).

The *IB Middle Years Programme* (IBMYP) is for pupils aged 11–16 and the curriculum centres on eight subject groups: language acquisition, language and literature, individuals and societies, sciences, mathematics, arts, physical and health education, and design. Students are required to study at least two languages as part of their multilingual profile. The IBMYP builds upon the *IB Primary Years Programme* (IBPYP) which is intended for pupils aged 3–12. 'It focuses on the development of the whole child as an inquirer, both in the classroom and in the world outside. It is defined by six transdisciplinary themes of global significance, [which are] explored using knowledge and skills derived from six subject areas, with a powerful emphasis on inquiry-based learning' (IBO, 2013). Recently, the *IB Career-related Certificate* (IBCC) was introduced for 16–19 year olds interested in career-related learning which combines both academic and practical areas of study.

Like the EB, schools that want to deliver one of the IB programmes have to become accredited or authorised to do so. These schools are called IB World Schools and although the first schools to deliver the IB were primarily private international schools, over half of the IB World Schools are now state schools forming part of national systems of education (IBO, 2013). For example, in 2007 the Dutch government introduced new education policy that allows for Dutch pre-university students to take part in the IBDP in government-sponsored schools (Prickarts, 2010). Some Dutch schools have also introduced the IBMYP and a number are preparing to do (Visser, 2010).

Third Culture Kids

As previously stated, international schools were created in part to serve the children of highly mobile parents, many of whom work abroad in large multinational corporations, the military, as diplomats or as religious missionaries (Heyward, 2002). Over the years, these children have been referred to as globally mobile children, military brats, corporate brats, Foreign Service kids, missionary or preacher kids and global nomads. Many of these children spend a significant proportion of their life living abroad in a country other than their place of birth. As a result, they often have difficulty identifying with any one particular culture. These young people are known as Third Culture Kids (TCKs).

According to Pollock and Van Reken (2009, p. 13): 'A Third Culture Kid (TCK) is a person who has spent a significant part of his or her developmental years outside the parents' culture. The TCK frequently builds relationships to all of the cultures, while not having full ownership in any. Although elements from each culture may be assimilated into the TCK's life experience, the sense of belonging is in relationships to others of similar background.' In other words, TCKs have more in common with other TCKs rather than their home/first culture or the host country/ second culture. TCKs often have great difficulty in answering the question 'where is home?'

 Activity 11.8   Advantages and disadvantages of TCKs

Put yourself in the shoes of a TCK. What do you think the advantages and disadvantages might be? Make a list.

One of the biggest disadvantages of being a TCK can be 'a confused sense of identity due to the fragmented nature of their personal histories' (Grimshaw & Sears, 2008, p. 259). Many TCKs frequently move not only between different parts of the world, but also between multiple cultures throughout their school years, which can lead to a self-questioning attitude towards their identity as a result of having very complex linguistic, cultural and academic backgrounds. TCKs also experience less emotional stability (Dewaele & van Oudenhoven, 2009), perhaps as a consequence of having to say frequent good-byes to family and friends.

However, there a number of advantages of being a TCK. In a study of both TCKs and non-TCKs, Dewaele and van Oudenhoven (2009) found that TCKs were more open-minded and marginally more cultural empathetic than their non-TCKs counterparts. Useem and Cottrell (1993/1999) found that 81% of adult TCKs (from a sample of nearly 700 TCKs) have earned at least a bachelor's degree (87% men and 76% women) and half of that number have gone on to earn Master's degrees and doctorates. Additionally, many TCKs have an expanded worldview, excellent cross-cultural skills and are adaptable in new situations (Pollock & Van Reken, 2009).

Meeting the educational needs of TCKs can be a particular challenge due to the options available to parents when posted overseas. The choices for formal education include home schooling or attending online schools, local national schools, local international schools and boarding schools. Each of these options poses its own challenges as well as benefits. Sending your children to the local school is a good way for them to become immersed in the culture of the host country. However, the biggest barrier to this is language. If the child does not speak the local language at all or even very little of it, then the chances of succeeding in the local educational context are much narrowed (Pollock & Van Reken, 2009).

English language and international schools

One of the main reasons why many internationally mobile parents choose to send their children to international schools is because of the English-medium education they can provide. Hayden (2006) cites several studies which surveyed parents on the reasons why they chose to send their children to international schools. The majority of these support the view that international schools are important for providing an English-medium education. For example, MacKenzie, Hayden and Thompson (2001) surveyed and interviewed parents whose children attended a European international school. They found that an English-language education was repeatedly named as the foremost reason for choosing the school.

Local parents may also choose to send their children to an international school because education is delivered in the medium of English. Some parents may find international education synonymous with English language education and it offers the chance for their children to become proficient in English (Hayden, 2006). However, international schools can be hugely expensive for local people, excluding those on lower incomes. Moreover, not all countries allow nationals to attend local international schools. Some countries, such as Singapore, have forbidden by law international schools from accepting host country nationals without the permission of the Ministry of Education. Others, such as Saudi Arabia, have recently begun to allow nationals to attend international schools (Parker, 2013).

Criticisms of international schools

One of the biggest questions is exactly how international are some schools. Many international schools are not engaged with the local community or the host country in which they find themselves. Heyward (2002, p. 26) argues that international schools have a unique advantage in terms of facilitating authentic cross-cultural exchange, but '[t]he irony is that international schools often work to shelter students from that engagement'. Furthermore, Heyward states that with the addition of optional studies, such as history and world religions, for example, 'the degree to which the curriculum either is genuinely international or remains Eurocentric and western-biased is a matter of ongoing debate within IB circles' (Heyward, 2002, p. 24). Lastly, Drake (2004) points out that the IB is derived from a Western humanist model of learning and that the IB has a tendency to promote cultural imperialism. Drake advises educators in the non-Eurocentric world to take caution when simply trying to 'clone' IB programmes as this could potentially lead to discord and cultural tension.

 Activity 11.9   Culture and the IB

Look back at Chapter 3 on culture. How might some of the values and beliefs in the IB learner profile clash with some cultures? The full learner profile can be found at: www.ibo.org/programmes/profile/documents/Learnerprofileguide.pdf

---

Many have criticised international schools for their privileged nature and for helping to create a new transnational ruling class. Heyward (2002, p. 27) writes:

> International schools in developing nations face further obstacles in this context. In being defined by distance, they are also defined by exclusivity, by economic and political advantage, by elitism. Genuine attempts to engage with local cultures may unwittingly reinforce attitudes of superiority and paternalism, of cultural chauvinism. Disparities in salary and conditions for host-nation teachers, coupled with the problems of cross-cultural teaching, also tend to devalue the study of local culture and language, further reinforcing distance and chauvinistic attitudes.

Brown and Lauder (2011, p. 39) believe there are issues that the international schools present. They ask: 'Are there groups who gain an unfair advantage in the competition for credentials by attending international schools, and do the latter act as a key route to positions of power within the global economy?' As we saw in Chapter 8, English has become the global language and many see English-medium international schools as the key to unlocking access to an elite world of English-speaking universities and the global marketplace, thus leading to potentially lucrative international careers. Furthermore, international schools exclude individuals who cannot afford to pay the often extortionate fees or those who are unable to learn in English.

Conclusion

While international schools might share some common characteristics, to precisely define what they are can be difficult due to the variety that exist worldwide. A truly international school will embed some of the principles of international education in their curriculum, philosophy or staff and student makeup. However, from a critical perspective, international schools can pose some challenges for society and questions remain as to what role they play in creating a new transnational ruling class where only the wealthy have access. Are international schools centred more on providing pupils with English-language training and Western models of education rather than fostering the principles of world peace and international understanding? Lastly, do we really fully understand how international schools shape identity in light of globalisation and what their lasting effects on TCKs are?

 Case Study 11 International School of Geneva

According to its website, the International School of Geneva is '[a] not-for-profit foundation established in 1924 ... [It] is, with its 4,300 students, the oldest and largest international school in the world' (Fondation de l'Ecole Internationale de Genève, 2011). The school consists of three campuses offering both primary and secondary bilingual education in French and English. The school has a varied curriculum offering qualifications from both international and different national systems. The qualifications include the International Baccalaureate Diploma (IBDP), The International Baccalaureate Career-related Certificate (IBCC), the Maturité Suisse, the International GCSE (IGCSE) and the Diplôme National du Brevet (DNB).

   The school was the first to offer the International Baccalaureate in the late 1960s, and so has a unique perspective on what international education is. The mission of the school is 'to provide a distinctive high quality international education through which all our students are helped to develop their abilities to the highest level of their potential. We respect students' individual and cultural identities, encouraging them to become independent learners eager to carry on learning throughout their lives.' As such, it has defined the main principles of international education as follows:

- Encouraging important international values
- Supporting the student's language development
- Ensuring an international dimension to the curriculum
- Recognising the importance of global issues
- Showing respect for, and integration with, the host country

(Fondation de l'Ecole Internationale de Genève, 2011)

Key questions:

Have a look at the curriculum guides of the schools which are available under the tab that says Learning at Ecolint, and then look at the programmes at: www.ecolint.ch/learning-ecolint/programme.

- What makes the curriculum international? How does the curriculum contribute to the schools' vision of what international education is?

- One of the principles of international education is to encourage important international values. What do you think those international values might be and how are they demonstrated in the curriculum and the numerous activities the school offers?

- What global issues are of utmost importance and can international schools contribute to the resolution of some of these issues? If so, in what ways?

- Have a look through the website pages of the school. Can you find evidence of its commitment to 'recognising the importance of global issues'?

- What global issues are of utmost importance and can international schools contribute to the resolution of some of these issues? If so, in what ways?

- Is it possible that international schools actually contribute in some way to the creation of global issues?

- Do you feel that the International School of Geneva is a good example of a truly International school? Give a rationale for your answer.

Suggested reading

Bates, R. (ed.) (2011) *Schooling Internationally: Globalisation, Internationalisation, and the Future for International Schools*. Abingdon: Routledge
Offers a range of chapters linked to international schooling and provides some really good critical discussions on teaching, learning, assessment and the curriculum.

Hayden, M. (2006) *Introduction to International Education*. London: Sage
Mary Haden is an authority on international education and schooling in particular. As a key book in this area, it provides the reader with a basic understanding of various aspects of international schooling – from who the parents are to the teachers who work there.

Pollock, D. & Van Reken, R.E. (2009) *Third Culture Kids: Growing Up among Worlds*. London: Nicholas Brealey
A really good book on understanding the life of Third Culture Kids or TCKs.

Sayer, J. & Erler, L. (eds) (2012) *Schools for the Future of Europe: Values and Change beyond Lisbon.* London: Continuum
This book provides a wide variety of topics on European education. There are also several chapters on European Schools and the European Baccalaureate.

References

Arora, G.L., Koehler, W. & Reich, B. (1994) International education – past and present, in B. Reich, B. & V. Pivovarov (eds), *International Practical Guide on the Implementation of the Recommendation concerning Education for International Understanding, Co-operation and Peace and Education relating to Human Rights and Fundamental Freedoms.* Paris: UNESCO

ASIJ (2013) *The American School in Japan: School Profile.* Available online at: www.asij.ac.jp/page.aspx?pid=2195

Brown, C. & Lauder, H. (2011) The political economy of international schools in social class formation, in R. Bates (ed.), *Schooling Internationally: Globalisation, Internationalisation, and the Future for International Schools.* Abingdon: Routledge

Christmann, R. (2012) The European schools and enlargement, in J. Sayer & L. Erler (eds), *Schools for the Future of Europe: Values and Change Beyond Lisbon.* London: Continuum

CIS (2013) *Membership Benefits.* Available online at: www.cois.org/page.cfm?p=1055

Dewaele, J.M. & van Oudenhoven, J.P. (2009) The effect of multilingualism/multiculturalism on personality: No gain without pain for Third Culture Kids? *International Journal of Multilingualism,* 6(4), 443–459

DfE (2013) *The European Baccalaureate: Information for Admissions Officers of Universities and Other Higher Education Institutions.* London: Department for Education. Available online at: www.gov.uk/government/uploads/system/uploads/attachment_data/file/225819/Information_on_the_European_Baccalaureate.pdf

Drake, B. (2004) International education and IB programmes: Worldwide expansion and potential cultural dissonance. *Journal of Research in International Education,* 3(2), 189–205

Fondation de l'Ecole Internationale de Genève (2011) *Welcome to the International School of Geneva.* Available online at: www.ecolint.ch/

Grimshaw, T. & Sears, C. (2008) 'Where am I from?' 'Where do I belong?' The negotiation and maintenance of identity by international school students. *Journal of Research in International Education,* 7(3), 259–278

Hayden, M. (2006) *Introduction to International Education.* London: Sage

Heyward, M. (2002) From international to intercultural: Redefining the international school for a globalized world. *Journal of Research in International Education,* 1(1), 9–32.

Hill, I. (2006) Student types, school types and their combined influence on the development of intercultural understanding. *Journal of Research in International Education,* 5(1), 5–33

Hill, I. (2007) International education as developed by the International Baccalaureate Organisation, in M. Hayden, J. Levy & J. Thompson (eds), *The Sage Handbook of Research in International Education.* London: Sage

Hill, I. (2012) *Editorial: How Schools Became Truly International.* Available online at: www.johncatt.com/pubinternational.html

IBO (International Baccalaureate Organisation) (2013) *About the International Baccalaureate.* Available online at: www.ibo.org/general/who.cfm

ISA (2012) *Mission Objectives.* Available online at: http://isaschools.org/services-view/consultancy-services-for-internationalism-in-schools-a-self-study-guide/

ISC (International School Consultancy Group) (2013) *Who We Are.* Available online at:_www.iscresearch.com/company/who-we-are.aspx

Lynch, S. (2008) From Egypt to Brunei, British schools are growing in popularity. *The Independent.* Available online at: www.independent.co.uk/news/education/schools/from-egypt-to-brunei-british-schools-are-growing-in-popularity-969209.html

MacKenzie, P., Hayden, M. & Thompson, J. (2001) The third constituency: Parents in international schools, *International Schools Journal,* 20(2), 57–64

McKenzie, M. (2012) Learning from the world and learning for the world: An essay on world schools. *Journal of Research in International Education,* 11(3), 218–229

Murphy, E. (ed.) (1991) *ESL: A Handbook for Teachers and Administrators in International Schools.* Clevedon: Multilingual Matters

Nagrath, C. (2011) *What Makes a School International?* Available online at: www.tieonline.com/view_article.cfm?ArticleID=87

Parker, A. (2013) International schools in the Kingdom: Quality education or costly learning? Saudi Gazette. Available online at: www.saudigazette.com.sa/index.cfm?contentid=20130311156297&method=home.regcon

Pollock, D. & Van Reken, R.E. (2009) Third Culture Kids: Growing Up among Worlds. London: Nicholas Brealey

Prickarts, B. (2010) Equality or equity, player or guardian? The Dutch government and its role in providing access opportunities for government-sponsored international secondary education, 1979–2009. Journal of Research in International Education, 9(3), 227–244

Sayer, J. (2012) The future of the European Baccalauareate: Recognition and reform, in J. Sayer & L. Erler (eds), Schools for the Future of Europe: Values and Change beyond Lisbon. London: Continuum

Schola Europaea (2009) *The Mission of European Schools.* Available online at: www.eursc.eu/index.php?l=2

Sylvester, R. (2002) The 'first' international school, in M. Hayden, J. Thompson & G. Walker (eds), *International Education in Practice.* Abingdon: Routledge, pp. 3–17

Sylvester, R. (2007) Historical resources for research in international education (1851–1950), in M. Hayden, J. Levy & J. Thompson (eds), *The Sage Handbook of Research in International Education.* London: Sage

Thompson, J. (1998) Towards a model for international education, in M. Hayden & J. Thompson (eds), *International Education: Principles and Practice.* Abingdon: Taylor & Francis

Useem, R.H. & Cottrell, A.B. (1993/1999) TCKs four times more likely to earn Bachelor's degrees. *NewsLinks* (the newspaper of the International Schools Service), 12(5). Published online in 1999. Available at: www.tckworld.com/useem/art2.html

Visser, A. (2010) International education in a national context: Introducing the International Baccalaureate Middle Years Programme in Dutch public schools. *Journal of Research in International Education,* 9(2), 141–152

CHAPTER 12

INTERNATIONALISATION OF HIGHER EDUCATION

This chapter explores:

- What internationalisation means;
- How it is reflected in policy both at a national and institutional level;
- How it shapes the curriculum and the student experience.

 Activity 12.1   Internationalisation and globalisation

What do you think internationalisation means? How is this different from globalisation?

Internationalisation has been the key driver of change in higher education in recent years (Sursock & Smidt, 2010). Yang (2002, p. 81) writes that 'internationalisation has become a catchword of the times in higher education'. Many would agree that it 'has become a mantra in higher education. The knowledge economy is a global network ... and universities across the world are encouraged to "plug in" in various ways in order to reap the benefits of global interconnectedness, as well as to avoid the perils of parochialism' (Tadaki, 2013). What is the economic, political, academic, social and cultural rationale for this trend? What has been the impact of this change? This chapter will explore internationalisation from a range of perspectives from a global level down to the student.

Jiang (2008, p. 347) declares that '[t]he internationalisation of higher education (HE) is not a recent phenomenon'. Knight and de Wit (1995) outlined key phases in the history of the internationalisation of higher education, dating back to the Middle Ages. And according to Enders and Fulton (2002, p. 3), '[t]he university in its medieval Western tradition has always been perceived as a highly international institution compared to other major institutions of society'. For example, in medieval Europe, around 10% of the student population consisted of foreign students compared with around 2% worldwide today (Gürüz, 2011). Furthermore, as Knight (2004, p. 8) states: 'Internationalization is not a new term. It has been used for centuries in political science and governmental relations but its popularity in the education sector has really only soared since the early 80s.' However, the concept of internationalisation only really began to be debated in higher education policy and research circles in the 1990s (Teichler, 1999).

So what does it mean and why is it important? 'Internationalisation has always meant different things to different people, institutions and countries' (Knight, 2011a). One of the most commonly cited and fairly accepted definitions has been offered by Knight (1994, p. 3), a key scholar in the field, which is as follows:

> Internationalisation of higher education is the process of integrating an international dimension into the teaching/learning, research and service functions of a university or college. An international dimension means a perspective, activity or service which introduces or integrates an international/intercultural/global outlook into the major functions of an institution of higher education.

Later, Knight (2004, p. 11) proposed a slightly different version, which she believes complements the earlier one, where '[i]nternationalization at the national/sector/institutional level is defined as the process of integrating an international, intercultural or global dimension into the purpose, functions or delivery of post-secondary education'.

There are some key considerations in the definitions above. First, internationalisation is understood as a process rather than a product. Knight (2004, p. 11) states: 'The term *process* is deliberately used to convey that internationalization is an ongoing and continuing effort. The term process denotes an evolutionary or developmental quality to the concept.' Secondly, linked to this is the notion of integration, which is important in seeing internationalisation not as a set of isolated activities but an integral part of an institution (Qiang, 2003). Thirdly, the earlier definition encompasses the core activities of a university: teaching and learning, research and the services it offers. These definitions combined means that internationalisation should be inclusive of a wide range of activities and is concerned with all students, both home and international students alike. Furthermore, Jiang (2008, p. 349) believes that, '[m]ost importantly, this definition draws attention to the fact that internationalisation is not only confined to relationships between and amongst countries, but also embraces the diverse cultural/ethnic groups within a country'. This suggests that internationalisation is about meeting the needs of a diverse student population.

The more recent definition uses generic terms (purpose, function and delivery) instead of teaching, research and service to reflect the diverse nature of education providers who have very different interests and approaches to the international/intercultural/global dimension (Knight, 2004). The newer definition also 'attempts to address the realities of today's context where the national/sector level is extremely important' (Knight, 2004, p. 12).

 Activity 12.2   Internationalisation definition

Reflect on both of Knight's definitions. What do you think is meant by an international/intercultural outlook? How can this be integrated into teaching and learning strategies? What does an international/intercultural dimension in terms of research look like? What services do institutions offer? How can these services incorporate an international/intercultural dimension?

Knight's earlier definition has been criticised for being an end in itself rather than using internationalisation as a means to try to achieve a wider goal, such as improving the quality of higher education (Qiang, 2003). However, this is something Knight (2011a) firmly denies: 'Internationalisation has been guided by the principles that it must be linked to local context and purpose, that there isn't "one way or a right way" to internationalise, and that it is a means to an end not an end unto itself.' Furthermore, Yang (2002) believes that in order to understand Knight's definition we have to be familiar with the socio-cultural context in which it was written. In other words, are definitions such as Knight's a Western concept? In a survey of administrators working in institutions of higher learning in Guangzhou, China, Yang (2002) found that around half of those surveyed did not know what 'international perspective' meant. In China, internationalisation is associated with the concept of *jiegui*, which aims to link Chinese educational practice to mainstream international trends. This is quite different from the ideas that are discussed in this chapter. As Knight reiterates throughout her numerous published works, internationalisation, no matter how we define it, will mean different things to different people. 'The challenge of strengthening and reinforcing the values of cooperation, exchange, partnership over the current emphasis on competitiveness and commercialisation is front and centre. Are we up to the challenge – can we focus on values and not only on definitions?' (Knight, 2011a).

Internationalisation and globalisation

It is really important here to note that while the terms 'internationalisation' and 'globalisation' are often used interchangeably and are considered to be closely linked, they are not the same thing. 'Globalization is the context of economic and academic trends that are part of the reality of the twenty-first century. Internationalization includes the policies and practices undertaken by academic systems and institutions – and even individuals – to cope with the global academic environment' (Altbach & Knight, 2007, p. 290). 'Internationalization of higher education is seen as one of the ways a country responds to the impact of globalization, yet at the same time respects the individuality of a nation' (Qiang, 2003, p. 249).

Let us consider the definition of globalisation discussed in Chapter 8: 'Globalization may be thought of initially as the widening, deepening and speeding up of worldwide interconnectedness in all aspects of contemporary social life, from the cultural to the criminal, the financial to the spiritual' (Held et al., 1999, p. 2). We also saw in Chapter 8 that the world has become 'borderless', making economic exchange and trade much easier. There has also been an increased movement in people and knowledge across borders.

One of the ten key components of the globalisation of education mentioned in Chapter 8 pertains to the global marketing of higher education. Spring (2009, p. 100) asserts that '[h]igher education has become a globalized enterprise'. Many universities are in fierce competition with one another to attract foreign students, the best and brightest academics and funding from various international organisations.

Globalisation has influenced the way we learn; advances in technology have made e-learning and studying online distance courses a reality. Nowadays, you can be sitting in your home in Kenya and studying for a degree at a university in Germany, the UK or Australia. Recently, massive open online courses (MOOCs), have enabled many students from around the world to participate in mainly free, non-credit-bearing courses from elite universities such as Harvard on topics ranging from creative writing to quantum physics. Therefore, there can be very little doubt that higher education in recent years has also been shaped by global forces.

Institutional approaches to internationalisation

How do the principles of internationalisation manifest themselves in practice? Institutions have different approaches to how they implement internationalisation strategies, based on their priorities, culture, history, politics and resources (Knight, 2004). Knight outlines several different approaches to internationalisation at an institutional level (see Table 12.1), but the most common approach centres around what is known as the activity approach. In this approach, internationalisation is described in terms of the various activities institutions carry out. These activities can include study abroad, staff mobility, internationalising the curriculum, opening up of branch campuses, development projects and institutional linkages and networks. The expansion of these activities has dramatically increased in the past two decades (Altbach & Knight, 2007).

Table 12.1 Approaches at the institutional level

Approaches at institutional level	Description
Activity	Internationalisation is described in terms of activities, such as study abroad, curriculum and academic programmes, institutional linkages and networks, development projects and branch campuses.
Outcomes	Internationalisation is presented in the form of desired outcomes, such as student competencies, increased profile, more international agreements, and partners or projects.
Rationales	Internationalisation is described with respect to the primary motivations or rationales driving it. This can include academic standards, income generation, cultural diversity, and student and staff development.
Process	Internationalisation is considered to be a process where an international dimension is integrated into teaching, learning and service functions of the institution.
At home	Internationalisation is interpreted to be the creation of a culture or climate on campus that promotes and supports international/intercultural understanding and focuses on campus-based activities.
Abroad (cross-border)	Internationalisation is seen as the cross-border delivery of education to other countries through a variety of delivery modes (face to face, distance, e-learning) and through different administrative arrangements (franchise, twinning, branch campuses, etc.).

Source: Knight, 2004

Activity 12.3   Institutional approaches

Have a look at your institution's internationalisation policy. If yours does not have one, look at the following:

1 The University of Ballarat in Australia at: http://policy.ballarat. edu.au/learning_and_teaching/academic_programs_and_courses/ internationalisation/ch01.php_

2 The University of Glasgow in Scotland at: www.gla.ac.uk/about/ internationalisation/ourpriorities/internationalisationstrategy/

3 Leeds Metropolitan University in England at: www.leedsmet.ac.uk/ world-widehorizons/index_Internationalisation_at%20_Leeds%20 Met.htm

Do they offer a definition of internationalisation? If so, how does it compare to Knight's definition?

Using Table 12.1, Knight's 'approaches to internationalisation at institutional level' (Knight, 2004) as a guide, what approach does your institution take? What might be the disadvantages of certain approaches?

The main aims of internationalisation according to Valiulis and Valiulis (2006, p. 221) are as follows (see also Figure 12.1):

• To promote multicultural and intercultural education;

• To contribute to the improvement of the learning experiences of exchange students at host institutions;

• To contribute to improving the teaching experiences of teachers who instruct exchange students in mixed groups with home students;

• To improve the level of intercultural competences of all those involved in university education;

• To raise awareness within universities regarding multiculturalism;

• To describe exchange students' specific needs in the classroom;

• To promote continuous staff training for multiculturalism and interculturalism.

International student recruitment

Many universities in the UK have seen the recruitment of international students as a key component of their internationalisation strategies. The number of international students in the higher education sector in the UK

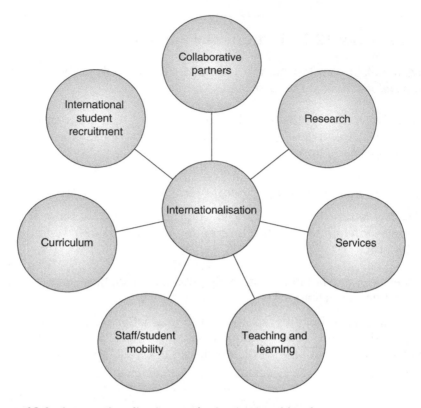

Figure 12.1   Internationalisation at the institutional level

has grown considerably from around 28,000 in 1955–1956 (Bolsmann & Miller, 2008) to 435,230 in 2011–2012 (132,550 from other EU member countries and 302,680 were from non-EU countries) (HESA, 2013a). The majority of non-EU domiciled students in 2011/2012 came from Asia, the number of Chinese students being the highest at 78,715, and expected to grow. The number of students from India and Pakistan fell for the first time, but remains in the top ten of non-EU countries that send students to UK higher education institutions (HEIs).

International students contribute greatly to the academic and social fabric of an institution, but many universities in the UK have been heavily criticised for their unethical recruitment and poor treatment of them once they have arrived. According to statistics from the Higher Education Statistics Agency (HESA, 2013b), around 12% of the total income of UK universities comes from overseas students' fees. 'To date, recruitment of international students has been seen by many primarily as a source of income generation, a "cash cow", and often diverse students, once recruited, were problematized by the academy and seen as needy of support in a kind of deficit model' (Brown & Jones, 2007, p. 2). This deficit model is evident in the media as well. Paton (2012) revealed that despite the requirement for a legal minimum standard of English, '[t]wo-thirds of universities are admitting foreign students with a poor grasp of English' and '[i]t also emerged that institutions spent more than £12m on language classes to bring foreigners up to scratch in English after they had been admitted, although the true figure could be twice as high'. Paton also believes that this recent disclosure 'will prompt renewed concerns over the recruitment of overseas students to British universities and fuel concerns that many institutions are using them a "cash cow" to plug holes in budgets. Students recruited from outside the EU are not subject to Government number controls and can be charged far higher tuition fees than European counterparts.'

 Activity 12.4   International students

What are the challenges that international students face while studying in a foreign country? What should institutions do to support them? Have a look at some university websites and find out what services they offer specifically to international students. Put yourself in their shoes. Why do you think so many international students study in the UK or abroad? Could you study at degree level in another country?

Rationale for internationalisation

There are four main reasons for the internationalisation of higher education: political, economic, academic and cultural/social (Knight & de Wit, 1995; Knight, 2004; Jiang, 2008; De Wit, 2010). A major political rationale for the internationalisation of higher education is that educational cooperation can be seen as an extension of foreign policy (Knight & de Wit, 1995). Central to this argument is the belief that international student exchange is a form of 'diplomatic investment in future political relations' (Knight & de Wit, 1995, p. 11). The idea is that foreign students will get to know the host country's culture, values and political system and therefore will be more congenial towards the host country in future economic or political negotiations. Collaborative partnerships can also serve to develop or strengthen political relations between countries. One of the main aims of the UK's policy on internationalisation (the Prime Minister's Initiative will be discussed below) was to increase the number of countries sending students to study in higher education institutions. In order for this to be achieved, political cooperation between the UK and the targeted countries is a necessary factor.

The political rationale was dominant after the Second World War and during the Cold War era as a means to provide national security, technical assistance, peace and mutual understanding, and national and regional identity (De Wit, 2010). After 11 September 2001, there has been a renewed sense of the importance of internationalisation in terms of national security.

International cooperation and internationalisation initiatives or agreements between countries are highly politicised. A good example of this is the Bologna Process, which began in 1999 with the Bologna Declaration. The Bologna Process consists of several reforms to European higher education and the three key objectives have been the introduction of the three cycle system (bachelor/master/doctorate), quality assurance and recognition of qualifications and periods of study (European Commission, 2013a). There are now 46 countries signed up to the Bologna Process and in 2010 the European Higher Education Area (EHEA) was launched at the Budapest–Vienna Ministerial Conference. As stated in the *Strategy for European Higher Education in a Global Setting* (London Ministerial Conference, 2007): 'The strength of the Bologna Process rests on the voluntary cooperation of 45 countries to create a European Higher Education Area by converging important structural features of their national systems of higher education.' There is very little doubt that European Higher Education Area (EHEA) serves the political interests (and economies) of European member states.

In the past several decades, the predominant rationale for internationalisation has been an economic one. The rise of the knowledge economy (see Chapter 8) has contributed significantly to the internationalisation of higher education. Jiang (2008, p. 350) suggests that 'the internationalisation of HE is envisaged as contributing significantly to the professional and skilled human resource necessary for maintaining and sharpening a country's competitive edge in the international marketplace'. Moreover, international students are seen to be a valuable economic resource for many HEIs. The income generated by international student fees has been increasingly important in the UK since the 1980s as a shift in government policy created shortfalls in funding for higher education (Bolsmann & Miller, 2008). International students also contribute significantly to a country's economy. For example, in Australia in 2011, international students alone spent $15,127 million, while their visiting friends and relatives spent an additional $317 million. This spending is attributed to sustaining approximately 130,000 full-time workers (ACPET, 2013). The UK's Department for Business, Innovation and Skills (DBIS, 2011) estimated that the value of UK education exports was around £14.1 billion in 2008/09. This figure includes tuition fees for higher education, further education, English Language Teaching, and independent schools. It also comprises income derived from education-related publishing, equipment, consulting and broadcasting.

A third rationale for internationalisation is academic. This rationale is closely linked to the historical development of universities. 'For centuries there has been international mobility of students and scholars and an international dimension to research' (Jiang, 2008, p. 350). Yang (2002, p. 81) points out that, '[f]or some, internationalisation is seen as an extension of the traditional commitment of universities to learning, and as an exchange of knowledge'. Universities, by their very nature, are committed to the advancement of knowledge, which requires them to be outward-looking and international in scope, particularly in terms of research. The UK Council for International Students Affairs (UKCISA, 2013) states: 'International students help sustain the UK's research base, especially in science, technology, engineering and mathematics: they account for over 40% of UK postgraduate students, 50% of those doing full-time research degrees.' This adds to the argument that internationalisation can raise the academic quality, standards and reputation of an institution.

Lastly, there is a cultural/social rationale for internationalising higher education institutions. This rationale 'focuses on the role and position of a nation's own culture and language, and on the significance of understanding foreign languages and culture' (Jiang, 2008, pp. 350–351). International students and staff can contribute greatly to fostering intercultural competencies through a heightened awareness of other cultures and improved communication. Perhaps it is the cultural rationale that is the most important but, as De Wit (2010, p. 9) notes, 'there is concern that the role of universities in social and cultural cohesion is under pressure these days'. The ever-increasing economic pressures that universities face have overshadowed the cultural benefits that international students can bring.

The internationalisation of the curriculum

Many see the internationalisation in terms of reforms to the curriculum. According to the Higher Education Academy (HEA, 2013), '[i]nternationalising the curriculum involves providing students with global perspectives of their discipline and giving them a broader knowledge base for their future careers'. This also involves providing them with a set of values and skills to operate in diverse cultural environments, skills often labelled 'intercultural competencies' or 'cross-cultural capabilities'. Cross-cultural capability comprises three key components: intercultural awareness and related communication skills; international and multicultural perspectives in the discipline; and application in practice (the ability to apply the above both personally and professionally) (Killick, 2007). It is thought that these values, skills and knowledge are linked with global citizenship and reflect the graduate attributes needed in order 'to communicate and compete in a rapidly changing, complex global workforce and world' (HEA, 2013).

Clifford (2013) believes that an 'internationalised curriculum may have several recognisable components: global perspectives; intercultural communication; and socially responsible citizenship'. University courses should enable students to develop these through various mechanisms: teaching and learning strategies, module content, and the assessment process.

Activity 12.5   Internationalised curriculum review

Think about the course you are currently participating in or have done or will do in the future. Carry out your own mini curriculum review according to Killick's cross-cultural capabilities (Killick, 2007). Killick asks some of the following key questions:

1 How does the course seek to incorporate the knowledge and understanding brought to it by students from diverse backgrounds?

2 What level of use does the course make of materials from outside the 'traditional' canon?

3 How does the course encourage students to be curious beyond their own cultural boundaries?

4 How is a student from this course prepared to interact with/benefit from/contribute to diversity in the world beyond the university?

Study abroad and student/staff mobility

Student and staff mobility has played a key role in internationalisation policy in Europe and elsewhere. There is very little doubt the exchange programmes and study abroad offer the chance to broaden one's horizons and increase one's cross-cultural capabilities. Today, there are around 2.75 million foreign students worldwide studying in one of the more than 17,000 institutions of higher education in 184 countries and territories in the world (Gürüz, 2011). Students often have the opportunity to study for all or part of their degree in other countries and exchange programmes such as Erasmus make this possible.

The Erasmus Exchange Programme was part of the EU Lifelong Learning Programme (2007–2013) and is currently being replaced by Erasmus Plus (2014–2020). A key goal of Erasmus Plus is mobility, where overall 4 million individuals will benefit from various schemes with over half that figure in higher education alone. In terms of staff mobility, around 800,000 lecturers, teachers, trainers, education staff and youth workers will also benefit (European Commission, 2013b).

UK government policy

In 1999, Tony Blair introduced the Prime Minister's Initiative (PMI) at the London School of Economics in the UK. The purpose of the Initiative was to increase the number of international students studying in the UK and to support cooperation between the Government and universities, colleges and other organisations involved in international education to promote UK education in other countries overseas. In order to achieve this, 'it set targets to increase the number of non-EU international students studying in the UK by 75,000 by the year 2005, 50,000 in Higher Education (HE) and 25,000 in Further Education (FE). The targets were exceeded ahead of schedule, with an extra 93,000 in HE and 23,300 in FE' (DIUS, 2009).

Building on the first phase, a second phase, known as the Prime Minister's Initiative 2 (PMI2), was introduced in April 2006 with the overall aim to '[s]ecure the UK's position as a leader in international education and sustain the managed growth of UK international education delivered both in the UK and overseas' (DIUS, 2009). The government's stated priority was to further increase the number of international students studying in the UK. As a result, it set targets to secure the UK as a leader in international education and also to diversify markets so as not to be dependent on a small number of countries sending the majority of students to study in the UK. Central to this plan was to develop more collaborative partnerships overseas. PMI2 also focused on the quality of the student experience in a bid to broaden the aims of PMI, which was mainly focused on student recruitment.

To pursue the aims of PMI2, the Government set a number of targets to achieve by 2011:

- An additional 70,000 international students in UK higher education and 30,000 in further education;

- Double the number of countries sending more than 10,000 students per annum to the UK;

- Demonstrable improvements to student satisfaction ratings in the UK;

- Achieve significant growth in the number of partnerships between the UK and other countries. (DIUS, 2009)

The Department for Innovation, Universities and Skills (DIUS), now called the Department for Business, Innovation and Skills (DBIS), appointed DTZ to carry out an independent review of PMI2 in 2009. The published review (DTZ, 2011) stated that PMI2 had met some of its targets. For example, there had been an increase in the number of partnerships (in both HE and FE) and student satisfaction ratings had risen over the five-year period. According to i-Graduate (2011), international student satisfaction at UK universities has increased on average, by 9 percentage points (pp), from 72% to 81% since 2006. They further report that across the lifetime of PMI2 (from 2006 to 2011) there have been measurable improvements in the international student experience, the largest being in the area of language support which was up by 12 pp to 89%. Other areas that saw in increase in satisfaction scores were worship facilities, visa advice, careers advice and work experience.

Criticisms of internationalisation

Knight (2011b) cautions that internationalisation has become a much more confused and misunderstood concept. She identified five myths of internationalisation:

- Myth one – foreign students act as internationalisation agents (the belief that the more international students there are on campus the more internationalised the curriculum and culture);

- Myth two – international reputation as a proxy for quality (the belief that the more international a university is – in terms of students, faculty, curriculum, research, agreements, network memberships – the better its reputation is);

- Myth three – international institutional agreements (the belief that the greater number of international agreements or network memberships a university has the more prestigious and attractive it is to other institutions and students);

- Myth four – international accreditations (the belief that the more international accreditation stars an institution has the more internationalised and better it is);

- Myth five – global branding (the belief that the purpose of a university's internationalisation efforts is to improve global brand or standing, which confuses an international marketing campaign with an internationalisation plan).

According to Knight (2011b), many 'international students feel marginalised socially and academically and often experience ethnic or racial tensions'. They can feel isolated and lonely and it is often the case that it is very difficult for them to mix with home students. Knight also suggest that there is very little evidence that internationalisation improves the quality and standards of a university. In fact, '[t]he increased numbers of international students in Western universities bring challenges for lecturers and international students alike' (Ryan & Carroll, 2005, p. 5).

Many international students face 'culture shock' and find the transition of being in a foreign country very stressful because they have to learn a new culture and way of living. Academically, students may also struggle with the language of the host country, even though they may have studied it for years in schools and appear to be proficient. They will experience different ways of teaching and learning and have to learn new academic conventions (e.g. referencing). There is much literature pertaining to internationalisation and how institutions can and should deal with an increasingly diverse student population (see Carroll & Ryan, 2005; Jones & Brown, 2007).

Conclusion

Globalisation has led to the internationalisation of higher education around the world. A global/international/intercultural dimension has become a necessary component in higher education institutions in order to succeed in a twenty-first-century knowledge economy. While the future direction of internationalisation may be less certain, there is no doubt that international cooperation will continue to play an important role in the mobility of individuals, the rise of transnational education (TNE) and high-quality research. With more and more students studying abroad and the proliferation of collaborative research and academic partnerships, there are greater chances for peace, understanding and tolerance among individuals and nations. The internationalisation of higher education, its policy and practices have such an immense role to play in helping to achieve this.

 Activity 12.6   Transnational education

Before you read the case study below, consider the following question. What do you think transnational education might be and what role does it play in internationalising higher education?

 Case Study 12   Transnational education: Successes and failures

Transnational education (TNE) has played a key role in internationalising higher education around the world. TNE can be defined as 'higher education activities in which the learners are located in a host country different from the one where the awarding institution is based' (Van der Wende, 2001, p. 440). In other words, TNE is where students study in their home country for a degree or other qualification from an institution abroad. According to Higher Education Statistics Agency (HESA, 2013a), there were 570,665 students studying UK HE-level qualifications abroad in 2011/2012.

   According to the Department for Business, Innovation and Skills (DBIS, 2013), approximately 75% of UK higher education institutions (HEIs) now engage in transnational education, in more than 200 countries. TNE is delivered in a number of different ways, which include distance learning (with or without face-to-face teaching support) and in-country delivery,

(Continued)

(Continued)

such as branch campuses, twinning programmes, and franchising arrangement. Oxford Brookes University is the largest single UK institution operating in the TNE market, with over 250,000 students. However, this statistic mainly comprises students studying on the BSc in Applied Accounting, and has a very low completion rate of around 10%.

The British Council have identified growth opportunities in TNE to 2020 (British Council, 2013). Currently, the countries offering a conducive climate for TNE are Hong Kong, Malaysia, Singapore and the United Arab Emirates (UAE). Other countries with future potential are Bahrain, Botswana, China, India, Mauritius, Oman, Qatar, Spain, South Korea, Thailand and Vietnam (DBIS, 2013).

Since the United Arab Emirates became a country in 1971, the government has invested heavily in higher education: 'Over the past five years many universities have opened their doors in the UAE, with some succeeding while others failing to deliver results either academically or economically' (Mahani & Molki, 2011, p. 3). Successful institutions include the University of Wollongong (Australia), Heriot-Watt University (Scotland) and New York University, Abu Dhabi (USA), while the failures include George Mason University (USA), Michigan State University (USA) and the University of Pune (India).

Key questions:

- What are the pros and cons of TNE?

- Why do you think established universities want to open up branch campuses in the UAE? What makes the UAE so attractive?

- What are the key factors in the success or failure of branch campuses in the UAE? Make a list.

Suggested reading

Carroll, J. & Ryan, J. (eds) (2005) *Teaching International Students*. Abingdon: Routledge
This book is divided into three parts: Cultural migration and learning; Methodologies and pedagogies; and a third part on internationalising the curriculum. It is an excellent source for those who work with international students.

Jones, E. & Brown, S. (eds) (2007) *Internationalising Higher Education*. Abingdon: Routledge
This book provides a good range of perspectives on internationalisation and is divided into five parts: Perspectives on policy and institutional cultures; Perspectives on assessment, learning, teaching and student support; Perspectives on curriculum enhancement; European perspectives; and Conclusions.

References

ACPET (Australian Council for Private Education and Training) (2013) *The Economic Contribution of International Students*. Available online at: www.acpet.edu.au/uploads/files/Reports_Submissions/2013/Economic-Contribution-Executive-Summary.pdf

Altbach, P. & Knight, J. (2007) The internationalization of higher education: Motivations and realities. *Journal of Studies in International Education*, 3(4/4), 290–305

Bolsmann, C. & Miller, H. (2008) International student recruitment to universities in England: Discourse, rationales and globalisation. *Globalisation, Societies and Education*, 6(1), 75–88

British Council (2013) *New Research: Transnational Education Continuing to Expand*. Available online at: www.britishcouncil.org/organisation/press/transnational-education

Brown, S. & Jones, E. (2007) Introduction: Values, valuing and value in the internationalised Higher Education context, in E. Jones & S. Brown (eds), *Internationalising Higher Education*. Abingdon: Routledge

Carroll, J. & Ryan, J. (eds) (2005) *Teaching International Students*. Abingdon: Routledge

Clifford, V. (2013) *The Elusive Concept of Internationalisation of the Curriculum*. Available online at: www.brookes.ac.uk/services/cci/definitions.html

DBIS (2011) *Estimating the Value to the UK of Education Exports*. BIS Research Paper No. 46. London: Department for Business, Innovation and Skills. Available online at: www.bis.gov.uk/assets/biscore/higher-education/docs/e/11-980-estimating-value-of-education-exports.pdf

DBIS (2013) *International Education – Global Growth and Prosperity: An Accompanying Analytical Narrative*. London: Department for Business, Innovation and Skills. Available online at: www.gov.uk/government/uploads/system/uploads/attachment_data/file/229845/bis-13-1082-international-education-accompanying-analytical-narrative.pdf

De Wit, H. (2010) *Internationalisation of Higher Education in Europe and its Assessment, Trends and Issues*. Available online at: www.nvao.net/page/downloads/Internationalisation_of_Higher_Education_in_Europe_DEF_december_2010.pdf

DIUS (2009) *Prime Minister's Initiative*. London: Department for Innovation, Universities and Skills. Available online at: http://webarchive.national archives.gov.uk/+/http://www.dius.gov.uk/international/pmi/index.html

DTZ (2011) *Prime Minister's Initiative for International Education Phase 2 (PMI2): Final Evaluation Report*. Available online at: www.britishcouncil.org/pmi2_final_evaluation_report.pdf

Enders, J. & Fulton, O. (2002) Blurring boundaries and blistering institutions: An introduction, in J. Enders & O. Fulton (eds), *Higher Education in a Globalising World: International Trends & Mutual Observations*. Dordrecht: Kluwer

European Commission (2013a) *The Bologna Process: Towards the European Higher Education Area*. Available online at: http://ec.europa.eu/education/higher-education/bologna_en.htm

European Commission (2013b) *Erasmus Plus*. Available online at: http://ec.europa.eu/education/erasmus-plus/index_en.htm

Gürüz, K. (2011) *Higher Education and International Student Mobility in the Global Knowledge Economy* (2nd edition). Albany, NY: State University of New York Press

HEA (Higher Education Academy) (2013) *Internationalising the Curriculum.* Available online at: www.heacademy.ac.uk/resources/detail/internation alisation/ISL_internationalising_the_curriculum

Held, D., McGrew, A., Goldblatt, D. & Perraton, J. (1999) *Global Transformations.* Cambridge: Polity Press

HESA (2013a) *Non-UK Domicile Students.* Available online at: www.hesa.ac.uk/index.php?option=com_content&task=view&id=2663&Itemid=161

HESA (2013b) *Finances of UK HE Institutions 2011/12.* Available online at: www.hesa.ac.uk/index.php?option=com_content&task=view&id=2712&Itemid=161 #non-EU_fees

i-graduate (2011) *Measuring the Effect of the Prime Minister's Initiative on the International Student Experience in the UK 2011: Final Report.* Available online at: www.britishcouncil.org/pmi-isb_2011_final_report.pdf

Jiang, X. (2008) Towards the internationalisation of higher education from a critical perspective. *Journal of Further and Higher Education,* 32(4), 347–358

Jones, E. & Brown, S. (eds) (2007) *Internationalising Higher Education.* Abingdon: Routledge

Killick, D. (2007) World-wide horizons: Cross-cultural capability and global perspectives – guidelines for curriculum review, in E. Jones & S. Brown (eds), *Internationalising Higher Education.* Abingdon: Routledge

Knight, J. (1994) *Internationalization: Elements and Checkpoints.* Research Monograph No. 7. Ottawa: Canadian Bureau for International Education

Knight, J. (2004) Internationalization remodeled: Definition, approaches, and rationales. *Journal of Studies in International Education,* 8(1), 5–31

Knight, J. (2011a) *Is Internationalisation Having an Identity Crisis?* Available online at: www.oecd.org/edu/imhe/48506334.pdf

Knight, J. (2011b) *Five Myths about Internationalisation.* Available online at: www.international.ac.uk/media/1417436/International_Focus_67.pdf

Knight, J. & de Wit, H. (1995) Strategies for internationalisation of higher education: Historical and conceptual perspectives, in H. de Wit (1997), *Strategies for Internationalisation of Higher Education: A Comparative Study of Australia, Canada, Europe and the United States of America.* Amsterdam: European Association for International Education (EAIE)

London Ministerial Conference (2007) *European Higher Education in a Global Setting: A Strategy for the External Dimension of the Bologna Process.* Available online at: www.ond.vlaanderen.be/hogeronderwijs/bologna/documents/ WGR2007/Strategy-for-EHEA-in-global-setting.pdf

Mahani, S. & Molki, A. (2011) Internationalization of higher education: A reflection on success and failures among foreign universities in the United Arab Emirates. *Journal of International Education Research,* 7(3), 1–8

Paton, G. (2012) Universities 'admitting foreign students with poor English'. *The Daily Telegraph.* Available online at: www.telegraph.co.uk/education/ universityeducation/9497191/Universities-admitting-foreign-students-with-poor-English.html

Qiang, Z. (2003) Internationalization of higher education: Towards a conceptual framework. *Policy Futures in Education,* 1(2), 248–270

Ryan, J. & Carroll, J. (2005) Canaries in the coalmine: International students in Western universities, in J. Carroll & J. Ryan (eds), *Teaching International Students: Improving Learning for All*. Abingdon: Routledge

Spring, J. (2009) *Globalization of Education: An Introduction*. New York: Routledge

Sursock, A. & Smidt, H. (2010) *Trends 2010: A Decade of Change in European Higher Education*. Brussels: European University Association

Tadaki, M. (2013) How are we doing higher education internationalisation? *University World News*, 274. Available online at: www.universityworldnews.com/article.php?story=2013052818005080

Teichler, U. (1999) Internationalisation as a challenge for higher education in Europe. *Tertiary Education and Management*, 5(1), 5–23

UKCISA (UK Council for International Student Affairs) (2013) *Impact of International Students*. Available online at: www.ukcisa.org.uk/Info-for-universities-colleges--schools/Policy-research--statistics/Policy-and-lobbying/Impact-of-international-students/

Valiulis, A. & Valiulis, D. (2006) The internationalisation of higher education: A challenge for universities. *Global Journal of Engineering Education*, 10(2), 221–228

Van der Wende, M. (2001) The international dimension in national higher education policies: What has changed in Europe in the last five years? *European Journal of Education*, 36(4), 431–442

Yang, R. (2002) University internationalisation: Its meanings, rationales and implications. *Intercultural Education*, 13(1), 81–95

INDEX